AN
URDU MANUAL

AN
URDU MANUAL

OF THE PHONETIC, INDUCTIVE OR DIRECT METHOD
BASED ON THE GOSPEL OF JOHN

WITH A PROGRESSIVE INTRODUCTION TO THE
CONSTRUCTIONS OF THE URDU LANGUAGE

THOMAS F. CUMMINGS, D.D.,

Bible Teachers' Training School, New York, formerly of the
United Presbyterian Punjab Mission

The Ear is the Medium of Language

Second and Revised Edition

GYAN

Published by

GYAN

Gyan Publishing House
5, Ansari Road
Daryaganj, New Delhi-110002
Phone: 011-47034999, 9811692060
E-mail: books@gyanbooks.com

Distribution Network
gyanbooks.com
India, USA, Canada, UK, Australia, France

ISBN : 978-81-212-3087-2 (PB)
First Published, 1916

2nd Impression 2020

Printed at: Gyan Press, Delhi.

An Urdu Manual
Author: Thomas F. Cummings

AN

URDU MANUAL

OF THE PHONETIC, INDUCTIVE OR DIRECT METHOD

BASED ON THE GOSPEL OF JOHN

WITH A PROGRESSIVE INTRODUCTION TO THE CONSTRUCTIONS OF THE URDU LANGUAGE.

THOMAS F. CUMMINGS, D.D.,

Bible Teachers' Training School, New York, formerly of the United Presbyterian Punjab Mission.

The Ear is the Medium of Language.

Second and Revised Edition.

PUBLISHED BY THE SIALKOT MISSION OF THE UNITED PRESBYTERIAN CHURCH OF NORTH AMERICA.

1916.

DEDICATED

TO MY FELLOW-SERVANTS

WHOSE AIM IT IS TO ESTABLISH

HIS KINGDOM.

PREFACE.

THE sale of the First Edition, and the consequent demand for a second, permits the realisation of the hope expressed in the Preface of the First, the publication of a Manual worked out on the basis of the Gospel of John, and the necessary terms in daily use. This Manual is the product, as it ought to be, of class-room work, but it has not been tested with successive classes. Under the circumstances, it is the best that could be done. Special thanks are due to Rev. Henry Forman for reviewing the book, and seeing it through the press.

The Manual is the result of fifty odd years of language study, but it is particularly the outgrowth of experience in learning, and helping others to learn, Urdu and Panjabi. It owes most to a severe lesson from Providence that ears and not eyes were given us to learn languages, as well as to further sick-leave leisure to prosecute these studies.

From books, Prendergast's idea of a definite speed standard of attainment has been most helpful. Sweet's Primer of Phonetics gave the clue to analysis of sounds. Many, many methods have been examined, and the student may find nothing that seems to him new, for it is possible to parallel many of these ideas with those from other sources. Indeed, it was a surprise and satisfaction to find, after its publication, that the First Edition closely paralleled the "Reform" Method of Germany, which is called the "Direct" Method in England and America. In France, it goes by the name of "Phonetic" or "Inductive." The Berlitz Method is a direct method, but has no adequate provision for securing a good pronunciation.

In this book, the use of the "five-syllable per second" standard, and the homoinymic sentences for training in pronunciation, is, so far as is known, unique. So also is the methodical development, in progressive order of the constructions, by using this Gospel. Some may object to this use of the Gospel, but it has many things in its favour. It is simple, yet complex. In reading its very familiarity supplies the idea, of which the new word gives us the expression. It abounds in common words, incidents, and discourse, and has almost all the ordinary constructions of the Urdu. If it is objected to as a translation, so is our Bible a translation, and yet for all that it is a classic. It is probable that few objectors will ever use better Urdu.

Some who used the First Edition got little or nothing out of it. Doubtless they never read the warning in the Preface. Others will likely do the same with this. As a book, no claim is made for it, for a book cannot and never has taught a language. That can be done only by a living teacher through a living ear, not through the eye. He who makes the eye his medium is bound to fail, and this book cannot help him. As a method every possible claim may be made for this. It produces results. It gives the ability to talk. It compels success. No doubt some will stop when they should know that they have only begun, but the book, if mastered, will lay a good foundation, and a wise master-builder may erect on it a spacious dwelling,—and the indolent may make out to get on fairly well in the basement. Although the Gospel has been made the basis of the work, yet the aim has not been to develop a technical vocabulary, but rather to give drill in those ordinary constructions which must be the foundation of all future successful work.

THOMAS F. CUMMINGS.

NEW YORK.
July 31, 1915.

CONTENTS.

	Pages
Preface	v
Errata	x
Introduction. How to Learn a Language	xi
Phonetics	xx
Romanisation	xxxviii
Pronunciation Charts	xlii–xlvi
Pronunciation Exercises	xlvii
Résumé of Method	lv
Learning to Read	lvi
Lessons I–LXXXVI	1–156
Appendix. Urdu Grammar.	
Gender	1
Declension of nouns	1, 2
Verb	3
Order of words in sentence	4, 5
Interrogatives	5–20
Drill tables	20–22
Exercises in Declensions	22, 23
,, Gender	23, 24
,, Adjectives, Possessives	24
Verb Synopses	24–26
Special idiomatic verb forms	26, 27
Exercises in Prepositions	27–29
,, Relatives	29, 30
,, Conjunctions	30–33
Index	1

ERRATA.

Page 7,	4th line from bottom,	*for* (first) thá	*read*	ṭhá
,, 12, 13,		,, Y'isú'	,,	Yisú'
,, 13,	7th ,, from bottom,	,, piyása	,,	piyásá
,, 17,	10th ,,	,, *with*	,,	with
,, 21,	4th ,,	,, Garíb	,,	Ġaríb
,, 30,	1st ,,	,, ek hí	,,	usí
,, 32,	7th ,, from bottom,	,, sachchã	,,	sachchá
,, 38,	11th ,,	,, Garíb	,,	Ġaríb
,, 41,	4th ,,	,, dekkhe	,,	dekhke
,, ,,	,, ,,	,, garíbo	,,	ġaríb
,, 43,	last ,,	,, ṭoṛná	,,	toṛná
,, 58,	5th ,,	,, khush	,,	k<u>h</u>ush
,, 59,	10th ,,	,, chirág	,,	chiráġ
,, 63,	6th ,,	,, Yahúdío<u>n</u> ne	,,	Yahúdí
,, 32,	and repeatedly	,, Ginti	,,	Gintí
,, 68,	7th line from bottom,	,, ke par	,,	ke pár
,, 69,	12th ,,	,, chakí	,,	chakhí
,, 70,	2nd ,,	,, chori	,,	chorí
,, ,,	2nd ,, from bottom,	,, uthá,	,,	uṭhá
,, 72,	1st ,,	,, mausami	,,	mausam-i-
,, 73,	20th ,,	,, maujudagí	,,	maujúdgí
,, 74,	last ,,	,, unho<u>n</u> ne . . . samjhí	,,	we. . .samjhe
,, 78,	3rd ,,	,, jaṭámasí	,,	jaṭámásí
,, 79,	2nd line, *for* charged with *read* guilty or convicted of			
,, 81,	9th line	*for* ká	*read*	ke
	14th ,,	,, Dhulái	,,	Dhuláí
	3rd ,, from bottom	,, maskin	,,	maskan

INTRODUCTION.

HOW TO LEARN A LANGUAGE.

LANGUAGE is a method of conveying thought by means of symbols, whether audible or visible. Audible symbols, words, are the material of ordinary speech. Visible symbols include all sign language as well as writing and printing. Spoken language is primary and fundamental, while writing is artificial and secondary. In really learning a language we must begin with speech, and permit the artificial, reading, to await the mastery of the natural, speaking. To learn a language is to acquire the ability to express and understand thought in the symbols used by any particular people. While we shall aim to include both the natural and artificial symbols, yet primarily our purpose is to learn to speak so as to be understood, and to hear so as to understand.

The method which we shall follow is not that of the schools. There nature is violated. The eye is put in place of the ear, and reading and writing have usurped the place of the living voice. The ideal of the school is to read and understand the book. Yet to this, because their method is faulty, they seldom attain. THE EAR IS THE MEDIUM OF LANGUAGE is our motto, and the eye must be used merely as an assistant to the ear.

The natural method whereby infants learn to speak is, 1. To hear; 2. To remember the sound; 3. To associate the sound and the idea. This is the passive side and engrosses the child's attention for the first year or two of life. Along with this comes the active side; 4. Thinking; 5. Recollecting the sounds that stand for the ideas; 6.

Uttering these sounds, that is, speaking the language. In all normal cases this is the process. Shall we follow it, or shall we improve on nature?

The infant must learn to hear, to remember, to associate, to think, to recollect, to speak. The adult learner has already a command of these processes, and needs but to give them a new direction. It takes the child a decade or two to master his mother tongue, but if we take the child of eight to a foreign country, we shall find him in a few months able to talk about almost everything. Hence we may fairly conclude that three to six months should enable one to gain a good working knowledge of a foreign tongue. Accordingly we find schools in Germany advertising to teach pupils the German language in three months, if they will put aside all use of the mother tongue, and immerse themselves in the vernacular. Double the time, and it would seem that six months should give one a fair command of Urdu.

Certainly the adult has some very great advantages over the child. 1. He has learned to think. 2. He knows that repetition is the secret of memorising. 3. He is able to apply himself much better than is the child, so that although the child has a more retentive memory, yet the adult from his greater application is able to outdistance the child. In one point the adult is handicapped, his hearing has become dulled—or at least he has grown careless. He does not discriminate. He hears, not the exact sounds of the foreign tongue, but the similar sounds of his mother tongue, and he speaks with his own native accent. This is where the adult is in need of special help. Phonetics, the science of pronunciation, stands ready to solve his difficulties. The difficulties of remembering and associating sounds and ideas are to be overcome by repetition.

Here is where the true method will point out the psychological laws involved, and lead the adult, through his increased capacity for repetition, to attainment beyond the ability of the child.

We observe that every language has three difficulties—those of pronunciation, vocabulary, and construction. The mastery of individual sounds, of words, and of the peculiar rhythm of the language as present in its sentences, these all are a part of the difficult pronunciation problem. Various ideas, possibly old and familiar, are expressed in combinations of sounds that may be new and strange. To fix these in the memory is the problem of vocabulary. Then come those matters of word-order, case endings, signs of mood, tense, whereby the logical and grammatical interrelationship of ideas is clearly indicated—these make up that great problem of idiomatic construction, the most difficult of the three. A mastery of the simples and principal words, a ready use of all those methods whereby the language reveals the logical union of its parts of speech, a pronunciation that is clear and accurate and an ear that readily apprehends these things when heard, is the very least that we can demand. Beyond this, elegance and eloquence, the ability to read and compose, are much to be desired, but the former are absolutely essential, and when we have them we may be said to know the language.

By what method, however, shall we insure that steady progress, week by week, and month by month, which in due time shall bring us to the desired end. The secret of this is found in setting *automaticity* as the standard of our attainment. If our mental response is instant and accurate, we know the thing. Every art has its basic principles, and he who would be master of that art must be master of these principles to the degree that they have become automatic, as for example the response to the query, What is the product of nine times seven? He who hesitates for the reply is no master of arithmetic.

Apply this criterion to language-speaking and we find a ready and accurate standard to test language proficiency. If your command of foreign expressions is as ready, fluent, and accurate as is your knowledge of the multiplication tables, then you know the language. But if you halt at vocabulary, stumble over pronunciations, and err in construction, that is bungling, not mastery.

It may be easily ascertained, by taking a bit of prose, say the Lord's Prayer, counting the syllables in it, and then reciting it at normal speed, that an ordinary rate of speech is five syllables per second. If day by day, week by week, and month by month we bring our work up to this rate and keep it there, we shall soon have the satisfaction of finding that it has become automatic, and is a ready tool to do our bidding.

The aim of this Manual is to give the student material enough for three to six months' study, during which he may learn a vocabulary of a thousand to fifteen hundred words, master all the pronunciation difficulties, get an insight into the rhythm, and become acquainted with the fundamental constructions of the Urdu language. The Manual does not contemplate an exhaustive scientific study of the science of Urdu grammar, but rather aims to lead the student to the practical use of the language as a means of expression. Toward the end of the year one may profitably take up the study of the grammar, but it must be remembered that correct expression is not mastered by learning grammatical rules, but by memorising and imitating correct model sentences.

The problem of getting a language is largely a problem

of memory. It is not, however, the intellectual, recollective memory that is involved, but the motor-memory, which is sometimes called the mechanical, sometimes the rote memory. It is the same memory that is involved in the learning to knit or play the piano; but, instead of the fingers, it means the training of the vocal organs to make the movements that are required to produce the proper sounds.

Speech, from one point of view, is a habit, and a habit is a product of many conscious acts until, at last, it passes over into the realm of the unconscious or automatic. Learning a new language is the acquiring of a new habit of expressing our thoughts. Instead of saying "What is this?" we must say, "*Yih kyá hai?*" and so on. The problem here is the problem of habit formation. In considering the subject from this standpoint, then, we note that the habit of speaking English is, so far as Urdu is concerned, a bad habit. The tendency to indifference whether our consonants are aspirated or not, which is quite immaterial indeed in English, is perfectly subversive of good Urdu. Our English method of forming *t* and *d* must be changed into two other methods. Our disregard of genders in our verb and adjective forms, our refusal to hold the verb to the end of the sentence—this all must be changed, and the changing of it is as difficult as is the relinquishment of any old habit and the substitution of another. If we could absolutely give over speaking English, it would probably simplify the learning of Urdu, since our holding on to English, and making it our daily medium of speech complicates the problem still further, in that the old habit is kept up, as we try to develop the new alongside. They who can make the plunge and stop the use of their mother tongue for some months will find their problem made considerably easier. It is this that has evolved the dictum of the Reform Method, *Each language must be the medium of its own impartation.* Never speak English when teaching Urdu. Speak Urdu to teach Urdu.

The question as to what constructions we must learn can be best answered by considering how language should be classified. The unit of language is the sentence. Sentences are assertive, imperative, assumptive, and these may be thrown into interrogative forms. Hence we may say that it will be necessary for the pupil to learn to use the indicative, the imperative or optative, the conditional or subjunctive, and these in their ordinary, negative, emphatic and interrogative forms. One of each of these forms, when firmly fixed in the memory, will form the basis from which all its ordinary variations may be worked out, and when thus fixed, it will be a thought-mould into which all similar expressions of the language naturally fall.

The laws that govern language learning may be stated thus:—

1. The sentence, not the single word,* is the Unit of Speech.
2. This sentence must be repeated 10 to 100 times before the pupil can give it alone, and many, many times daily for many weeks before it has become automatic.
3. Sentences have a tempo and a tune, a rate and rhythm. The rate is 5 syllables per second, and the rhythm varies. The teacher should speak the sentences

---

* "Our children still learn the languages they speak by first acquiring the knowledge of certain phrases and sentences and then gradually analysing them into words, and the adult who wishes to gain a successful acquaintance with another tongue, must pursue the same plan."—Sayce, *Nature and Science of Language.*

naturally, as if saying them, and the pupil should imitate him.

4. Repetition is the cure of bad memory, but it must be with attention, and interest. Repeat until the pupil can hear the rapidly spoken sentences, and also give them with the required rapidity. It is intense effort that educates.

5. Changing *familiar* sentences into new forms of gender, person, number, mood, and tense, will teach grammar in a concrete and practical manner. So also will telling stories, and re-telling them in different genders and persons, relating incidents, taking make-believe journeys and shopping excursions.

6. The laws for training the motor-memory, which is the memory of speech, are:—

   (*a*) Start with a decided purpose to succeed.

   (*b*) Do the thing as nearly right as possible from the very first.

   (*c*) Set a definite standard to which you must attain (here it is 5 syllables per second).

   (*d*) Keep a record of your daily attainments, and rouse your interest to-day by trying to beat the record of yesterday.

   (*e*) Work hard for 15 or 20 minutes at repeating new matter, and then turn to old and familiar material, reading or writing, for rest.

   (*f*) Make actual use of your old and new sentences as often as possible in talking.

   (*g*) Better have a number of short periods of study than one long one, since there is no value in tired, uninterested study.

   (*h*) Have your teacher note your mistakes at times of speaking or reading, classify them, and then give special attention to these at the time of pronunciation drill.

(i) When your speaking has become automatically correct, your motor-memory is trained.

Some may be inclined to use this book as they would any other. If they do, they are sure to fail. This book can only be used through the medium of a teacher's voice, who as living mouthpiece shall teach his pupil to hear it all. Those who wish to study by themselves, along classical lines, had better get some other book. If any one will give this method one month's thorough trial, holding himself fast to rules and directions, and then allow some one who knows the failure of the old method to advise him, he is sure to continue this.

It is possible some would like to use this who yet feel that the course which their Committee has laid out for examination is so heavy that they dare not experiment on an untried thing. To such it would be well to say, put three months on this and learn the language so that your future work will be done rapidly and well, and if you do fail in extent, do not fail to get the language. The extended course of reading that many committees mistakenly saddle on the beginner is only a hindrance to intensive and good work.

In taking up this course, expect something new and suspend judgment for a few weeks, until the method of repetition has had a chance to crystallise into habit.

Dangers to be avoided by the Pupil.

1. Trying to study alone.
2. Thinking you can learn Urdu by reading, whether in the Roman or Persian character.

3. Permitting your teacher to use English when he addresses you.
4. Fearing to make mistakes before other foreigners.
5. Translating English phrases and using them without your teacher's approval.
6. Thinking your teacher's compliments mean attainment, instead of encouragement.
7. Supposing your Urdu sounds better than the English of the raw school-boy.
8. Resenting by word or manner criticism of your abuse of the Urdu in sound or idiom, when you should express your thanks for such interest in your progress.
9. Thinking it does not matter whether you learn the character or not.
10. Thinking it immaterial whether you can read and write letters.
11. Thinking you ever get to the point where you know the language "better than the native."
12. Working too long at a time, and when you are tired. Better many and shorter times, than one long time.

Dangers to be avoided by the Teacher.

1. Using English.
2. Thinking your pupil can never acquire a good pronunciation.
3. Thinking that your pronunciation of English is much superior to the way your pupil pronounces Urdu, and
4. Forgetting that Urdu pronunciation is no easier for him than English is for you, and that probably according to the degree that he misses Urdu, by that same degree do you miss the English.

[3 and 4 for the Indian teacher.]

5. Forgetting that he cannot hear the differences between Urdu *t*, *th*, *ṭ* and *ṭh*, and all the other sounds in the Charts, and that it is your work to teach him to *hear* these differences, before he can speak them.
6. Forgetting that it will take hundreds of repetitions before he learns to say things correctly, and that these must be kept at patiently for many months.
7. Forgetting that the pupil is more anxious to learn than the teacher.
8. Forgetting that as children speak the way their parents do, so pupils copy their teacher, hence you must be careful to see that they learn to use correct sentences, for this will be your certificate of good work.
9. Forgetting that when you correct him without pointing out the error, it does no good, but only irritates him. You may tell him "It is not *khá*, but *ká*," but he hears no difference, although it is perfectly plain to you.
10. Permitting yourself to grow careless about mistakes of the pupil.
11. Failing to review the same thing over and over again till he has it.

Phonetics.

Phonetics is the science of pronunciation. Technically it may be defined as the science of the positions, tensions and actions of the vocal organs in the production of speech-sounds, and is sometimes called phonics.

Speech-sounds are formed from the breath as it is being expelled. One may say a few words on an inspiration, but this is the exception not the rule. By a steady contraction of the diaphragm, or walls of the chest, the breath in the lungs is forced up through the windpipe. At the top of the windpipe, in the larynx, or Adam's apple, are two lips, the vocal chords, between which the breath current is forced by this pressure. This changes it into a vocal current. If the chords are slightly approximated, it gives a current that makes *s*, *f*, *sh*, *t*, etc., but if they are held tightly together, as are the lips of the mouth in blowing a trumpet, then the current becomes voiced, and out of it are formed such letters as *z*, *v*, *d*, *b*, etc. and also all vowels. The old nomenclature was vocals, sub-vocals and aspirates, which we shall call vowels, voice and breath consonants.

A VOWEL is a voiced speech-sound made by passing a voiced vocal current through the oral passage, while it is held in an open and fixed position. In contrast with the sixteen or eighteen vowels of English, Urdu has eight, and two diphthongs to our four.

Organic Basis.—Urdu vowels differ from the similar English vowels because of the different organic basis. Urdu speakers draw back the corners of their mouth, flatten their tongue and lower it at the back, and tense all the soft parts of the mouth, so that the voice seems to be projected on the upper front teeth, and this gives it a distinct metallic quality. This position of the vocal organs colours all the sounds of the language. With the English normal position it is impossible to speak good Urdu, and with the Urdu position it is impossible to speak good English.

A mirror is indispensable for learning a foreign language. The best is one where the faces of teacher and pupil are reflected side by side. Failing that a hand mirror must be used. The pupil should observe carefully his teacher's mouth, nostrils, jaw and larynx, and imitate their actions in his own speech

Level vowels are characteristic of the Urdu, but not of English. If one will contrast in the mirror English *o*, and

Positional Names	Names by Formation									
	Stops		Fricatives		Nasals		Aspirates		Trills	
	breath	voice	breath	voice	breath	voice	breath	voice	breath	voice
Labial	p	b	*			m	ph	bh		
			f†	v						
Dental	t	d	s	z		n	th	dh		r
Palatal	ch	j	sh*	zh, y		ñ	chh	jh		l
Cerebral	ṭ	ḍ				ṇ	ṭh	ḍh		ṛ
Guttural	k, q	g	ḳh*	ain, ġ		*n*, ng	kh	gh		

* h is a breath fricative, with friction now in one part, now in another part of the mouth.
† f and v may be called labio-dentals.

1, A lips.
   E lower front teeth
2 lower edge of upper front teeth.
3 back of upper front teeth.
4 gums above upper front teeth.
5 arch of palate.
6 roof of mouth, hard palate.
7 division of soft and hard palates.
8 soft palate, or velum.
9 Uvula.
10 back wall of pharynx.
11 nasal passage.
12 Epiglottis.
13, 14 vocal cords.
15 larynx, "Adam's apple."
16 gullet.
17 stream of breath.
18 where its direction is determined by the uvula.
I tongue tip.
O tongue blade.
U tongue back.
Y extreme back.

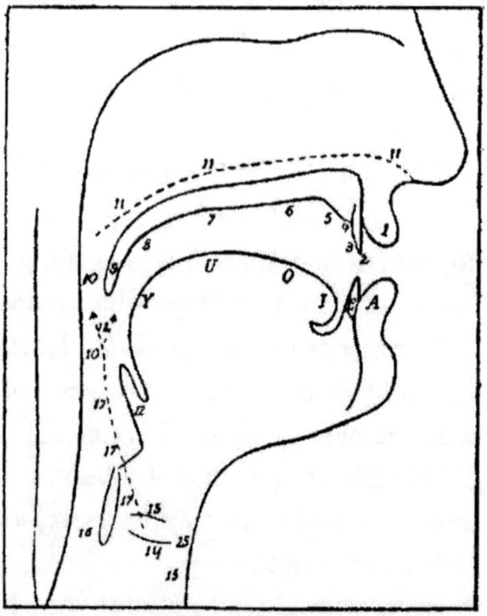

Let B represent the aspirate stream of breath
2 B represent the aspirate stream of breath divided
V represent the voiced stream of breath
2 V represent the voiced stream of breath divided
N represent the nasal passage open.

Breath and a closed nasal passage are assumed in all unless otherwise expressed.

Then of the Stops	Aspirates	Continuants or Fricatives	Nasals
$A + 1$ = p	$(A + 1)^{B}$ = ph	[2] $\frac{A + 2}{2B}$ [3] = f	$(A + 1)^{VN}$ = m
$(A + 1)^{V}$ = b	$(A + 1)^{VB}$ = bh	$\frac{A + 2}{2V}$ = v	$(I + 3)^{VN}$ = n[5]
$I + 3$ = t[1]	$(I + 3)^{B}$ = th	[4] $\frac{I + 3}{B}$ = s	$(U + 7)^{VN}$ = ng or ṅ
$(I + 3)^{V}$ = d	$(I + 3)^{VB}$ = dh	$\frac{I + 3}{V}$ = z	Trill[6] $I \pm 3$ = r
$O + 4$ = ch	$(O + 4)^{B}$ = chh	[3] $\frac{I + 3}{2V}$ = l	
$(O + 4)^{V}$ = j	$(O + 4)^{VB}$ = jh	$\frac{O + 4}{B}$ = sh	Flap from $\frac{I + 6}{V}$ to $I + E$ = ṛ
$I + 6$ = ṭ	$(I + 6)^{B}$ = ṭh	$\frac{O + 4}{V}$ = zh	
$(I + 6)^{V}$ = ḍ	$(I + 6)^{VB}$ = ḍh	$\frac{O + 5}{V}$ = y	
$U + 7$ = k	$(U + 7)^{B}$ = kh	$\frac{U + 7}{H}$ = ḳh	
$(U + 7)^{V}$ = g	$(U + 7)^{VB}$ = gh	$\frac{U + 7}{V}$ = ġ	
$Y + 8$ = q			

[1] English t is $I + 5$ Italian t is $I + 3$ Turkish t is $I + 5, 6$

[2] This means the lower lip placed against the upper teeth, that the stream of breath is divided, which also keeps lips and teeth apart.

[3] $\frac{I + 3}{2B}$ = Eng. th in thin. $\frac{I + 3}{2V}$ = Eng. *th* in thee, but it differs from *l* in being front divided, while l is back divided.

[4] That is, the tip of the tongue is kept from touching the teeth by the breath.

[5] $(O + 4)^{NV}$ = ñ, Punjabi, Spanish $(I + 6)^{NV}$ = ṇ, Punjabi, cerebral ṇ.

[6] That is, a touching and then an opening of that position.

Urdu *o*, he will at once see the difference. All English long vowels have a glide or vanish at the end, when final, and the student must eliminate this from the Urdu vowels, giving them with immobile and tensed organs. Daily Chart practice will secure this. Where English *o* and *u* have protruded and rounded lips, Urdu *o* and *ú* are made with lips spread wide, i.e. drawn back at the corners.

The diphthongs *ai* and *au* are really compounded of *a*+*e* = *ai*, *a*+*o* = *au*, all short sounds.

A Consonant is a speech-sound made by the vocal current, when it is stopped or squeezed by a complete or partial closure of the oral passage at one or more given points. This gives us consonants of several classes, stops and continuants; nasals and trills, and a combination of both.

Voice and Breath.—If you will lay your fingers on your larynx, or stick them in your ears, hiss ssss, and buzz zzzz, you will feel a vibration for the latter. That shows a voiced sound. Compare *s z*, *f v*, *sh zh*, eat aid, up ebb, etch edge, oak egg, and see which has the vibration. Compare with the table.

Articulation.—This means the bringing of the organs into the position necessary to make the given sound. It should be quick and definite in assuming the position, and also in releasing it. Every consonant has a normal position, to which there is an on- and off-glide. This off-glide is also called recoil.

The organs of articulation are the lips, teeth, tongue, palate and velum or nasal veil, also called the soft-palate, and, occasionally, the glottis and epiglottis.

Stops and Aspirates.—Stop consonants are of two kinds, simple and explosive or aspirate. A certain amount of free breath, over and above that which is used to form the letter, rushes out along with the recoil, and gives it this aspirated character. Most persons aspirate their initial stop consonants in English. Hold a bit of thread, paper, candle-flame, or hand, a half inch from the mouth as you say paper, and note the puff of breath with the first *p*, but not, or not so much with the second *p*. Compare the *p* in peach, with that in speech, tone with stone, initial and final *ch* in church, Kate and skate, and notice the differences. Some do not aspirate either, but they must learn. All must learn to give it both ways. If you will say *b d j g*, you will not feel the breath. Now if you will make *a p* with the same muscular sensation about the mouth that goes with the *b*, you will get the non-aspirate *p*; and if you will reverse and make a *bh* with the same feeling that accompanies the explosive *p*, really *ph*, you will get the *bh*. So for the *dh*, *jh*, *ḍh* and *gh* sounds.

Points of Articulation.—The cardinal articulation points in Urdu are five:—Lip to lip, tongue tip and sides to inside of upper teeth, tongue blade to front of hard palate, tongue tip to palatal arch, and tongue back to velum. Besides this, *h* has its friction in the glottis. So we call these labial, dental, blade-palatal, tip-palatal or cacuminal, often called cerebral, and velar, and *h* glottal. Besides these we have in *f* a labio-dental, where the upper teeth touch the inner edge of the lower lip.

(1) *p* and *b* are formed by closing the lips on the breath or voice vocal current. So with *ph* and *bh*, only the pressure is stronger so that the cavity behind the lips (or other point of stoppage in the case of *th*, *chh*, *ṭh*, *kh*, etc.) is overfull of air, and this rushes out the moment the organs part. Urdu *w* is a bilabial, but differing from our *w* in that the lips are spread at the corners and not rounded, as with us, neither is it rounded at the back of the tongue.

Cut I.

Formulae.

$A + 1 = p$,

$(A + 1)^{V} = b$,

$(A + 1)^{H} = ph$,

$(A + 1)^{VH} = bh$.

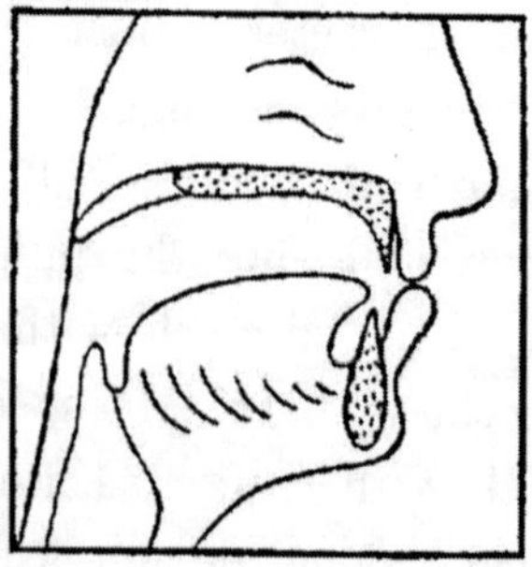

(2) *t* and *d* are pure dentals in Urdu but are not in English. With many English they are pre-palatal, and with others alveolar, that is, on the gums, but in Urdu they are pure dentals, being made by stopping the passage as you press the tongue tip against the back of the upper front teeth. Urdu *th* and *dh* are formed in the same place, only with the explosive action as for *ph* and *bh*. If the tongue draws back enough from the *t* position to leave a central channel, its sides still remaining against the side gums and teeth, we shall get *s*, and, with voice, *z*. If we put the tip forward as for *d*, we get *l* and *n*. Urdu *n* is as when we say *n* in *month*, our *n* is made on the back of the teeth, though in *moon* the *n* is higher up.

Cut II.

Formulae.

$I + 3 = t$,

$(I + 3)^{V} = d$,

$(I + 3)^{H} = th$,

$(I + 3)^{HV} = dh$.

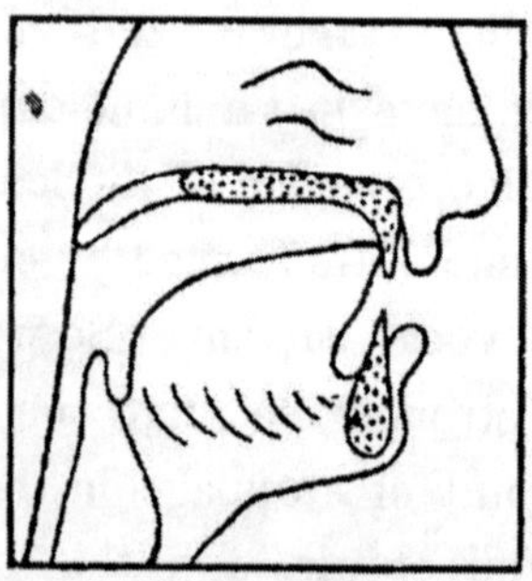

(3) Urdu *f* is not indigenous, but brought in with Persian, and is made by putting the upper teeth against the inner side of the lower lip, and expelling a breath vocal current. So English *v* is made with the same articulation

by a voiced current. There is a sound which passes current as *f* made by blowing through the nearly closed and spread lips.

Cut III.

$$\frac{A+2}{2H}=f,$$

$$\frac{A+2}{2V}=v.$$

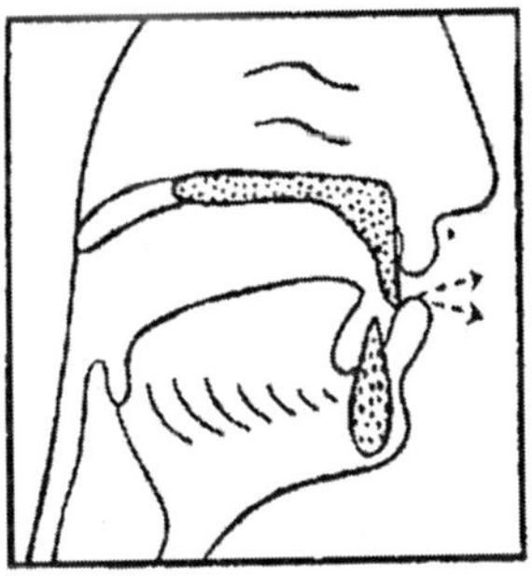

(4) *ch** and *j* are simple stops made by pressing the blade (front top) of the tongue against the hard palate, while the tip of the tongue is, incidentally, at the upper teeth. Put on the pressure and you get *chh* and *jh*.

Cut IV.

$O+4=$ ch,

$(O+4)^{V}=$ j,

$(O+4)^{H}=$ chh,

$(O+4)^{VH}=$ jh.

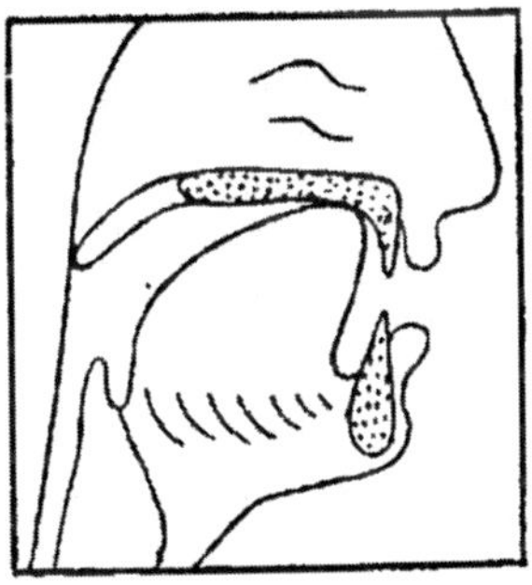

* Many phoneticians claim that *ch* and *j* are compound sounds. They were probably led into this error because the sounds are not heard in French and German, and they were led to analyse them as compounds of *tsh* and *dzh* in order to explain them. All nations that have them have heard them as simple sounds. The position is a cardinal one, because it has its complement of a nasal, *ñ*, and two continuants *sh zh*, and also a lateral *ĩ*. The difficulty has been in the inability to hear the difference between a closed *ch* and a *t*, a closed *j* and a *d*, so that *kachcha* is usually Anglicized katcha. The vital characteristic of *ch* and *j*, *sh* and *zh* is that the friction of the passing current is over the side gums, as well as in the centre. As compared with *s*, *sh* is made by a wide flat current, while that of *s* is round and deep.

Release the tongue slightly from the *ch* position and pass your vocal current and you get *sh* and *zh*. If you will now bend the tip of your tongue still further downward, you will get the sound of *y*. It is unfortunate that we do not use *c* for this sound rather than *ch*.

Cut V.

$$\frac{O+4}{H} = \text{sh},$$

$$\frac{O+4}{V} = \text{zh}.$$

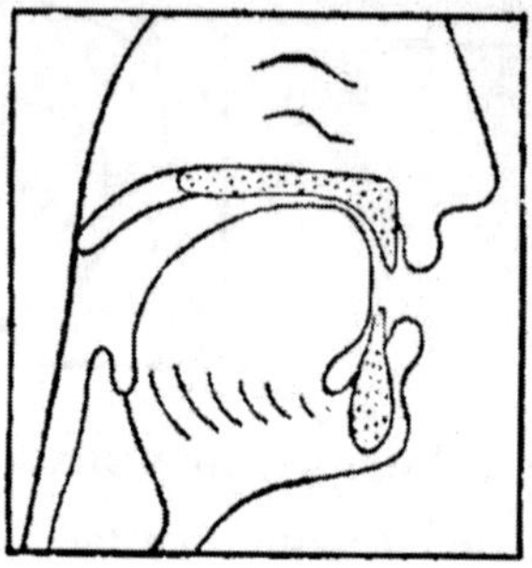

Sh.

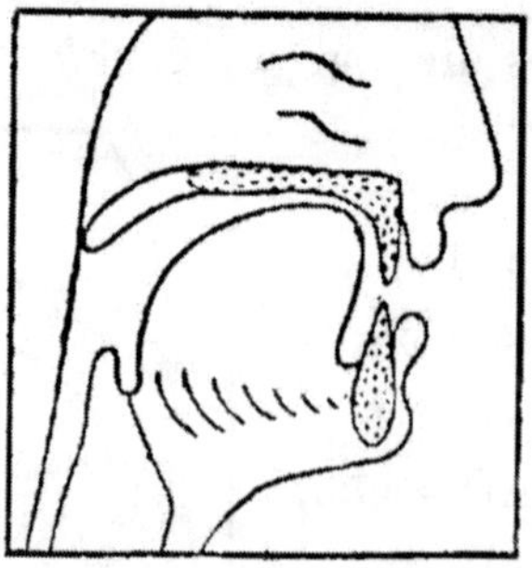

s

Cut VI.

$$\frac{O+5}{V} = \text{y}.$$

(5) *ṭ* and *ḍ* are cacuminals, high palatal, stop consonants. As a preliminary to their formation it is necessary to drop the tongue very low at the back, and then it can be easily put in the right position. Hindi uses an *ḷ*, *ṇ* and *ṣ*, formed in this position, as well as the *ṛ* which we have in Urdu. To form this draw the lips back at the corners, put the tip of the tongue almost to the roof of the mouth, widen out the sides of the tongue till they press hard against the sides of the palate and teeth, from about the second bi-cuspid, let the vocal current flow over the retracted tip and then flap it down quickly so that the tip comes down

below the lower gums. It may be called an "inverted flap consonant," but the tongue is nearer perpendicular at the front than inverted.

Cut VII.

$I + 6 =$ ṭ,

$(I + 6)^{H} =$ ṭh,

$(I + 6)^{V} =$ ḍ,

$(I + 6)^{VH} =$ ḍh.

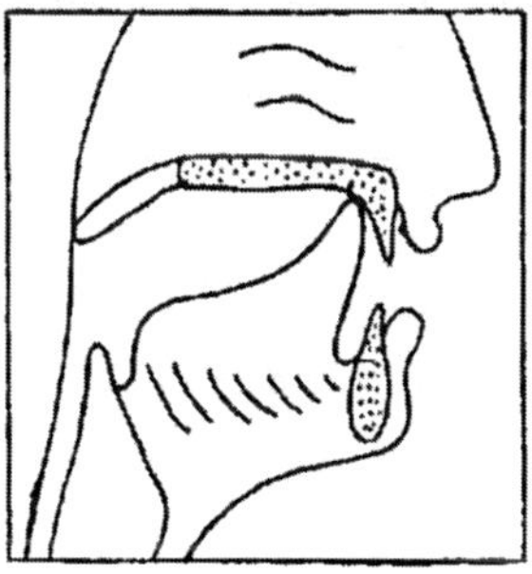

(6) *k* and *g* are simple velar stops. More air pressure gives us *kh* and *gh*. If you permit your tongue to open slightly from the *k* position and then pass a breath vocal current through, you will get *k͟h*. Voice this and you have the *g͟h* "ghain," *ġ*, sometimes written *g̲*.

Cut VIII.

$U + 7 =$ k,

$(U + 7)^{V} =$ g,

$(U + 7)^{H} =$ kh,

$(U + 7)^{VH} =$ gh.

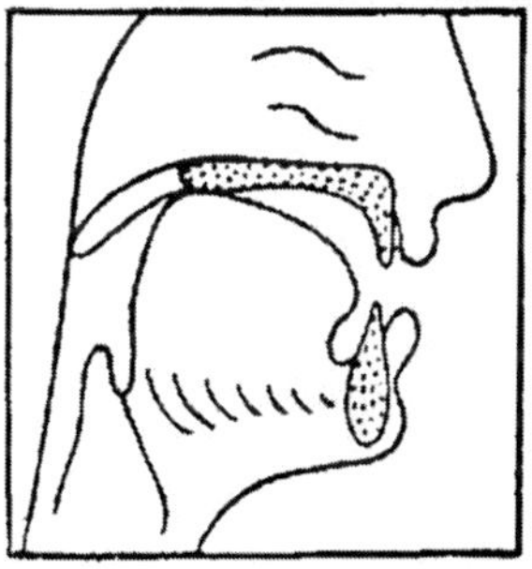

Cut IX.

$\frac{U + 7}{H} =$ ḳh,

$\frac{U + 7}{V} =$ ġ.

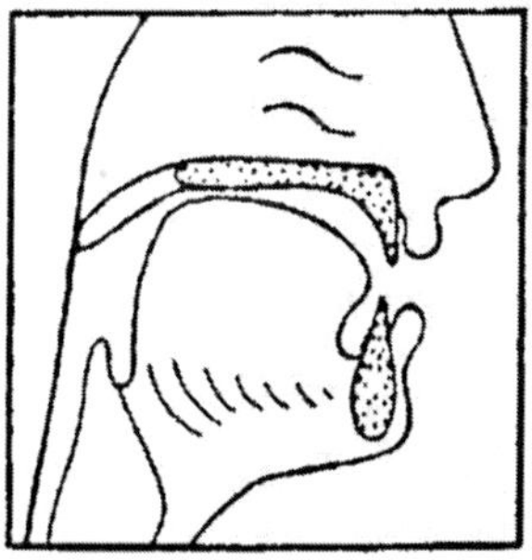

(7) *r* is a tip dental trill, and often has but one flap, rather than many as the real trill has. Some have great difficulty in making this. It would seem that it is caused by a current of voice, or breath, passing over a point that is so relaxed that it is blown forward and back by the current. The tongue must be tensed up to with a half inch of the tip, but that must be wholly relaxed. To do this bite the tongue on the sides just behind the tip, fix the attention on those points, as they press against the side teeth and then force the current over the tip. If this does not accomplish it, practising with a mirror, the words thrree, thrrough, thirrty, dirrt, and compelling the tongue to touch the teeth for the *t*'s and *d*'s, without any thought of the *r*, will eventually result in a trill.

Cut X.

$$\frac{I+3}{H} = s,$$

$$\frac{I+3}{V} = z,$$

$$\frac{I+3}{V} = r.$$

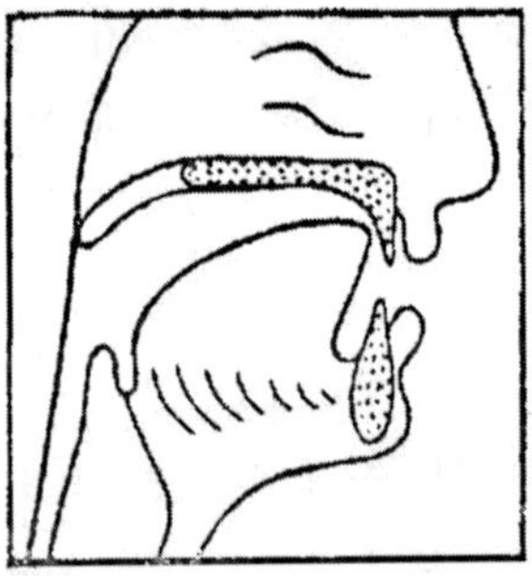

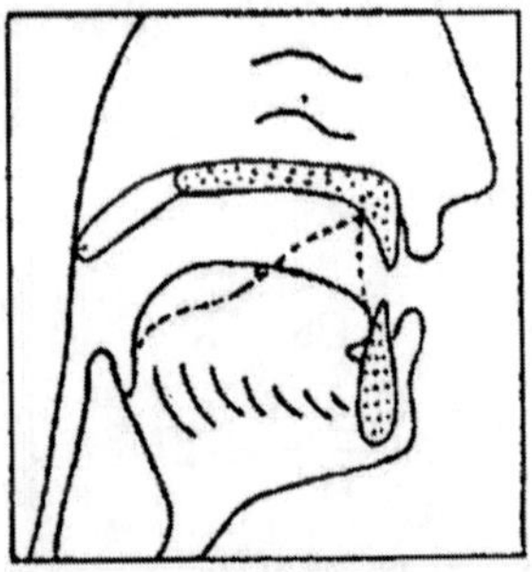

Cut XI.

$$\frac{(I+6)}{V}(E+I)^{V} = \underset{\cdot}{r}.$$

(8) *'Ain* and *Hha* are two letters that have come from the Arabic, but their sounds along with those of the *toe*,

zoe, *swad*, *zwad*, have fortunately been lost. The 'ain (') often modifies the succeeding vowel. It is probably an epiglottal fricative, like the contented blat of the water-buffalo, and *Hha* is its breath twin. *Hha* has a vowel value in words like *subh*, *sulh*, *fath* but is usually like *h*.

(9) *h* is a glottal breath continuant, though frequently modified by the succeeding vowel. As a final it is rather puzzling. Hold your hand close to the mouth, and say *hit*. Note how the breath strikes the hand for *h* in *hit*. Reverse it and make it give the same result when you say *tih*. Frequently its value in Urdu print is to indicate a higher pitch for the syllable which it closes, as in *ráh*, way, *rahná*, to stay.

(10) *m*, *n*, *ng* are nasals corresponding to the positions for *b*, *d*, *g*. The nasals of the stop positions *ḍ* and *j* (*ṇ* and *ñ*) are not used in Urdu. These are formed by holding the stop position indicated, and at the same time opening the nasal passage, when the sound passes out that way. Holding the nose soon brings a nasal to an end.

(11) *l* is called a lateral, or divided, consonant, because the vocal current flows off at either side of the tongue. The tongue should be in the position for *d*, tip and sides

Cut XII.

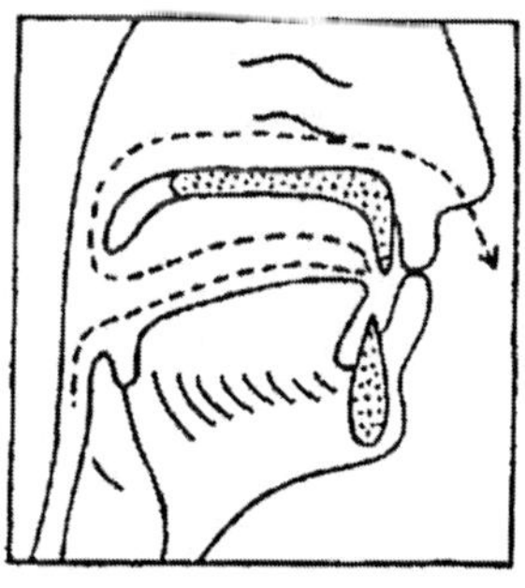

$(A + 1)^{VN} = m.$

Cut XIII.

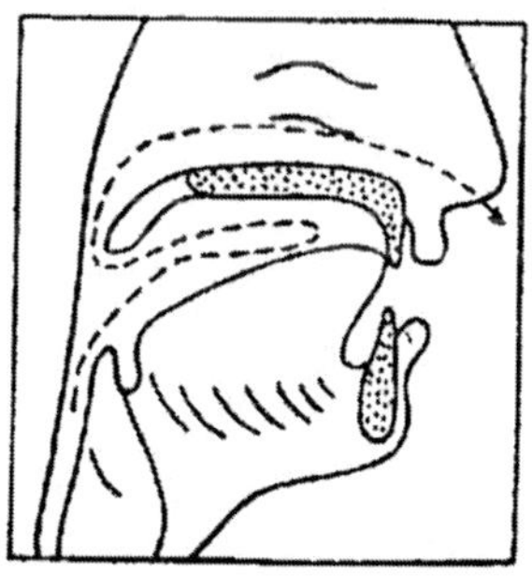

$(I + 3)^{VN} = n.$

Cut XIV.
$(U + 2)^{VN} = ng.$

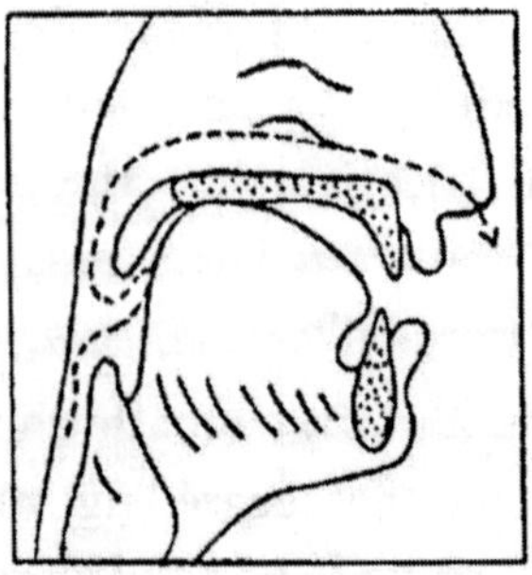

against the teeth, but openings at the sides farther back. In English, final *l*, *m*, *n*, *ng* and *r*, for those who sound it at all, have a peculiar downward glide at the end of a sentence, and many bring this glide, along with all their other English peculiarities, into Urdu. They are as a result frequently misunderstood.

(12) *n*, or *nun ġunna*, is the equivalent of the "French *n*," which is sometimes called "a nasal *n*." As all *n*'s are nasal, however, the designation is not permissible, particularly as it is often not really an "*n*" at all. It is a modification of the vowel sound, caused by having the nasal passage open. One must learn to distinguish carefully between *hai* and *hain̲*, *á* and *án̲*, *o* and *on̲*, etc. It would be more correct to print it *haĩ*, *ã′*, *õ*, than, *hain̲ án̲*, *on̲*, but the latter is the commoner way. Before consonants, *nun ġunna* takes a consonantal value according to the following consonant. *Sáṇp* is, and should be spelled, *sámp*; in *phen̲knā* it has the force of *ng*, as in English finger, as distinguished from *ng* in singer.

(13) *Table of English Consonants.*

	Stop.	Nasal.	Continuant or Fricative.		
			Central.	Lateral.	Trill or Flap.
Lip to lip ..	p b	m	wh w	..	..
Lip to teeth ..	..	..	..	f v	..
Tip tongue to teeth..	..	..	..	th[1] dh[2]	..
Tip to prepalate ..	t d	n	s z	l	r
Blade tongue to palate	ch j	ñ[3]	sh zh[4]		
				..	r[5]
Back tongue to velum	k g	ng	..	..	r[6]
Glottal	..	..	h	..	..

Table of Urdu Consonants.

	Stop.	Explosive or Aspirate.	Nasal.	Continuant or Fricative.		
				Central.	Lateral.	Trill.
Labial ..	..	..	..	..	..	..
Lip to lip ..	p b	ph bh	m	w	..	..
Labio-dental ..	..	..	..	..	..	..
Lip to teeth ..	..	..	..	..	f	..
Dental ..	..	..	..	..	..	..
Tip to teeth ..	t d	th dh	n	s z	..	r
Palatal ..	..	..	..	..	..	..
Blade to palate..	ch j	chh jh	(ñ)[7]	sh zh	l	..
Cacuminal ..	..	..	..	..	..	..
Tip to roof ..	ṭ ḍ	ṭh ḍh	(ṇ)[7]	..	(ḷ)[7]	ṛ
Velar ..	..	..	..	..	..	..
Back to velum..	k g	kh gh	ng	k͟h gh	..	..
Glottal ..	..	..	..	h	..	..

[1] Thin. [2] The. [3] Cañon. [4] Vision, rouge. [5] Raw. [6] Are.

[7] Not recognised in Urdu but in other dialects.

Transliterations of English words are interesting as showing how our sounds are heard. *Ṭikaṭ* shows our *t* is more like the high *ṭ*. So *ḍákṭár, búṭ Iskúl* shows their inability to start with a double consonant. Syce, gharry, godown, and charpoy seem to indicate lack of ability, on the other side, to hear well.

Cut XV.
X + 8 = q.

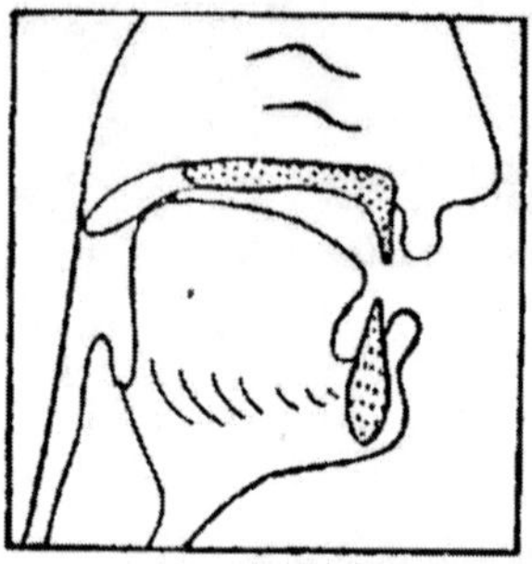

Cut XVI = á.

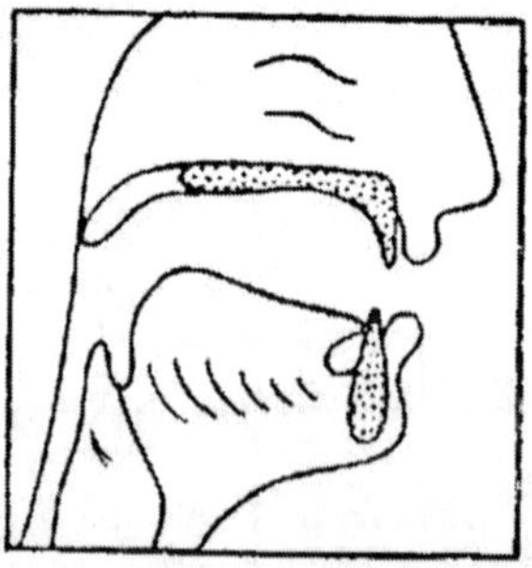

Cut XVII = $á^{N}$ = á*n*.

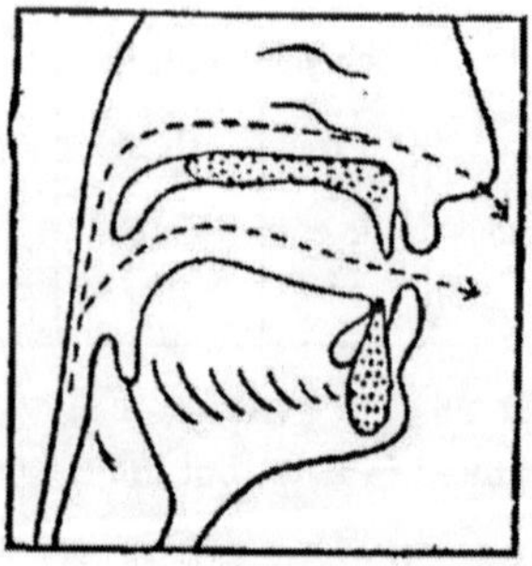

Doubling Consonants.—While we have many consonants doubled in English spelling, they are seldom if ever both pronounced, unless the word be a compound one. In *hitting* the *tt* indicates the preceding vowel is short. In *wholly* as distinguished from *holy*, the *ll* should be sounded as in mill-lock. When we say hillock comparing it with mill-lock, we note the difference So in re-case and book-case. A little attention will make the matter clear. In Urdu doubled stop consonants, the first is formed by the on-glide, and the second by a new impulse as the off-glide takes place. In continuants as in *billí*, cat, a new impulse interjected right into the first *l*, gives the second *l*, and the beginning of the second syllable. In *achchhá*, the closing of the tongue for *ch* gives the untrained ear the effect of a *t*, but it is not, and it follows the preceding description of a doubled stop formation.

Syllables.—A syllable is the least measure of speech, and is made by a single impulse of the voice. The Urdu grammarians, following Arabic rules, teach that every syllable begins with a consonant, but it is not so in Urdu. The real syllabication is *baṛ-á*, *likh-á*, *lí-á*, which last though usually spelled *liyá*, never sounds the *y*. Every Urdu syllable has a vowel, even though, as in *subh*, the vowel is indicated by *h*, as it never recognises syllabic consonants such as our *l*, *m*, *n*, in words like hidden (hidn), prism (two syllables), evil (evl), neither does it have the obscure sounds that occur in our final syllables, but it brings out clearly the distinction between short *a*, *i* and *u*. However, Arabic spelled words *fasl*, *ism*, *qabr*, have two syllables since the Indian cannot pronounce them in one, as does the Arab.

Accent.—Many insist that Urdu has no accent, but this is quite untrue. Its accents are not so obvious to us as those of English, but they are none the less evident. It is rather that the range of pitch in Urdu is much less than in English, but it is a mistake to deny it. All words that end with a long vowel followed by a consonant take the accent, or stress, on this last syllable,* or if it has a short vowel followed by two consonants it takes the accent, pas*and*, dú*kán*, though some say *pa*sand. If it is not on the ultima, it reverts till it finds a long syllable. The stressed syllable of an infinitive retains the stress through all its derivatives, as *utarná* and *utarnewálián*, with only secondary accent on the *wá*. Foreign words do not always conform to these rules, as we have *Khudá* with accent on now the first and now the last syllable. So other words, as *judá, sazá*.

Rhythm.—The rhythm of Urdu is vastly different from that of the English. Rhythm is that peculiar rise and fall of pitch which characterises the sentences of every language. It might be called the sentence tune, or melody. It is the speaking of Urdu in the English rhythm, and vice versa, that makes our best efforts seem ridiculous.

Speak the sentence "He was seated" and compare its rhythm with "He seated was," - _ ‾ - and - ‾ ‾ - and further note that its Urdu equivalent has nearly the rhythm of the latter, *wuh baiṭhá thá*, - ‾ ‾ -. Practice in humming out English rhythms will be the best aid to catching Urdu rhythm. Begin with short sentences, and when they are well in hand, go to longer ones.

---

* *Hawá*, wind; *dawá*, medicine; *balá*, calamity; *daryá*, river; are accented also on the final syllable.

INTONATION.—The tonal system of the Chinese is an adaptation of their language to the necessity of the case. They can make only 400 or 500 syllables, so they have to give each syllable many meanings, and they make themselves intelligible by putting these in different pitches. In English we have two "tones," the literal and the metaphorical. The second has the higher pitch. We call a man a bear, or a sheep, but we put it in a higher pitch than when we speak of the quadruped. If we call a woman a cat, it is not in the level tone, but the higher, the metaphorical. So when we put "a glass on the table," as compared with putting "a motion on the table," the latter is higher. Does this run through the whole language? Urdu has a trace of tones in those syllables that have their higher pitch indicated by *h*, *rahná*, *sahná*, *kahná*, as compared with *kaisá*. So we find the higher pitch in *tumhen*, *unhen*. We have both spellings in *ṭhahr-ná*, and *ṭhairná*, to stop. Further than this some one else should investigate.

PERSONAL AND NATIONAL DIFFICULTIES.—Occasionally a person goes to India who is tongue-tied, and must find the *ṭ* and *ḍ* class of sounds impossible. A simple operation will solve the difficulty, but it must be done by a skilled surgeon.

National difficulties arise from a tendency that some have to slur a final *r*. This must be carefully avoided, and such words as *dúr* be given as they ought to be, not like English doer. Some have the tendency to nasalise all vowels, making no difference between *hai* and *haiṇ*. This must be carefully corrected. All our tendency to import our own sounds into Urdu must be studiously overcome.

A GOOD EAR.—Few adults have this by nature, but it can be acquired by a painstaking following of the Charts.

GESTURES.—A study of these should be made so as to be able to understand and to use them.

CLICKS.—The sound that we use for calling a dog or starting a horse, is used in India to stop a horse. They have other clicks for driving animals and some for expressing emotion. Learn them.

ROMANISATION.

The representation of Hindustani sounds with English, or Roman letters, is a rather simple process. The Roman alphabet with simple diacriticals is much more suitable for Hindustani, than it is for English. The consonants have but single values, and there are vowels enough to cover all the vowel sounds of the Urdu language, and we are not compelled, as in English, to make five vowel signs do duty for sixteen sounds. The long vowels, *á*, *e*, *í*, *o*, *ú*, have the same value, almost, as in Italian, while the short, *a*, *i*, *u*, are really the short sounds of *á*, *í*, *ú*. The diphthongs *ai* and *au* are slightly different, but not hard to get.

The consonants offer more difficulty. Those sounds which do not occur in English should be carefully heard before they are committed to writing, or the pupil is permitted to read them. It must be noted that none of the sounds is exactly the equivalent of that sound which the same letter represents in English. Consequently one must be alert to discover exactly what they do stand for. The distinction between the single consonants and the doubled ones, between those alone and with the *h*, as *p* and *ph*, must be carefully appreciated, but particular attention must be given to the mastery of the two sets of "*t*'s," as they are very distinct from each other and from the English sounds. Those that are unmarked are almost the same as the Italian letters, but those with the dot under, *ṭ*, *ḍ*, *ṭh*, *ḍh*, *ṛ*, are quite different from our sounds, though our *t* is heard by the Indians as "*ṭ*."

The spelling *ba'd* shows Arabic ain thus (').

In the prevailing method of romanising, as shown in the New Testament, a few forms occur, without sufficient justification, and are to be explained from a misapprehension of the Urdu spelling, as taught by native grammarians, or a too slavish adherence to transliteration of Urdu, Persian or Arabic spelling, rather than a representation of sound. The most glaring of these errors is in the introduction of *y* in such words as *áyá, diyá, liyá, liye, diye roṭiyán̲, choriyán̲*, although the *y* is not sounded, save by newly arrived foreigners, and the words are pronounced *áiá, dĭá, lĭá, líe, díe, roṭĭán̲, chorĭán̲*. But, because the munshis teach, following Arabic rule, that a syllable cannot begin with a vowel, they say the *y* here found in the Urdu character is a consonant, though it never has its consonantal value in their pronunciation. We have ruled it out at first and largely in the book, though afterward permitted, as a concession to custom.

In Mat. 15: 19 we find two ways of spelling, *choriyán̲* and *gawáhián̲*, the final syllables *ián̲*, of which the latter is preferable.

The numerals *bárah, terah*, etc., are ended with "*h*," although it is not sounded, but it persists in the declined form, *bárahon̲*, so *jagahon̲*, and so it seems better to retain it. Certain Arabic spellings, pedantically imported into Urdu, are retained in the Urdu N. T. as, instead of *bil* and *fil* we have *bilkull, fi'l haqiqat*, where the (') indicates an anomalous and unpronounced *aleph*. *Dark͟hwást*, for a word properly pronounced *dark͟hást*, is justified by its Persian spelling, although no one proposes "*khwud*" or "*k͟hwushí*." So we find a word pronounced "*sámp*" transliterated, not spelled, *sán̲p*.

Possibly "*pán̲w*" and *gán̲w* are pronounced as printed, but it seems as if *páon̲* and *gáon̲* would be better.

In the case of the N. T. proper names, it may be that it was intended to accent them on their last syllable, but no rule is apparent, as they conform neither to Greek nor to English accent.

This transliteration of foreign words instead of conforming them to Urdu standards will, in due time, bring roman Urdu into the same miserable case as that in which we find English spelling.

There is a strong prejudice in the minds of many against the use of roman by beginners. It is well said that they who begin to read roman never get a good pronunciation. This is often true, but it need not be so, although it is likely to be. That there is danger in the use of roman is easily seen, but that there are advantages is quite as manifest. The advantage is that the pupil is enabled to remember more easily and to recall by the use of roman. The danger lies in the fact that he is sure at first to give old values to these letters and so mispronounce the Urdu words. We see what we are used to seeing, and when we see *thá*, for example, we wish to pronounce it as *th* in *thin* or in *thine*, we are not sure which, but after hearing the teacher say it is not *t*, it is *th*, we pronounce it as *th* in *thin*, or perhaps we make no difference between *tá* and *thí*, just as in English we pay no attention to it in *Thames*. When a pupil begins reading the character, he is held up by its strangeness, so that the teacher usually has to pronounce it for him before he can utter it himself. Thus he gets the sound in his ear before he speaks it, but if he begins by reading roman, he recognises the letters at once and, strong in this consciousness, he calls them by their English values, and all unknown to himself makes an appalling mess of it.

Then when he talks, he is astonished that "the people do not understand their own language."

The remedy is obvious. Let him read nothing that he has not previously memorised by ear and let him continue to study to differentiate such words as *átá* and *áṭá*, *pata*, *patta*, *paṭṭha*, and *phaṭá*, both by ear and tongue, and in a six months he will have mastered pronunciation, regardless of whether it be in roman or in character. No, the trouble is not in reading roman, it is in failure to train the ear to hear.

CHART FOR PRONUNCIATION EXERCISES No. 1.

(The teacher should point to each sound before he utters it.)

á e í o ú a i u ai au

آ ے ی و ُو َ ِ ُ اَے اَو

á ã́ e ẽ í ĩ́ o õ ú ṹ ai aĩ au aũ

آ آں ے یں ی یں و وں ُو ُوں اَے اَیں اَو اَوں

átá átí áte átĩ́ á áo áyá áí áe áĩ́ áná átá hai haĩ

آتا آتی آتے آتیں آ آؤ آیا آئی آئے آئیں آنا آتا ہے ہیں

dená detá dete detí detĩ́ de do de dí de dẽ do dho ḍho

دینا دیتا دیتے دیتی دیتیں دے دو دے دِی دے دیں دو دھو ڈھو

jáná játá játí játe játĩ́ já jáo jáe jáẽ jáyá

جانا جاتا جاتی جاتے جاتیں جا جاؤ جائے جائیں جایا

gayá gayí gaye gayĩ́ gáe gáẽ áti thí áti thĩ́

گیا گئی گئے گئیں گائے گائیں آتی تھی آتی تھیں

PRONUNCIATION CHART No. 2.

(The first two or three months let the teacher first point to, then utter the sounds.)

tú	to	dú	do	dono	bas	kis	kaun	ká	kã́	kán	káná	kháná
تُو	تو	دُو	دو	دونو	بس	کس	کون	کا	کاں	کان	کانا	کھانا
thou	then		two	both	stop!	whose	who	of	caw	ear	one-eye	food

ká	ke	ki	ko	gás	g̀hás	paká	pakká	patá	pattá	paṭṭha	phaṭá	phaṭṭá
کا	کے	کی	کو	گاس	گھاس	پکا	پکّا	پتا	پتّا	پٹھا	پھٹا	پھٹّا
of	of	of	to	gas	grass	cooked	strong	trace	leaf	youngster	torn	tearing

tatti	taṭṭi	ṭhaṭṭi	ṭhaṭṭhá	bari	baṛi	bhari	baṛhí	der	ḍher	ḍeṛh
تتّی	ٹٹّی	ٹھٹّی	ٹھٹّھا	بری	بڑی	بھری	بڑھی	دیر	ڈھیر	ڈیڑھ
warm	screen	ward	joke	full	big	filled	grown	late	pile	1½

khaṛá	khará	kaṛá	kará	burá	bhúrá	búṛhá	búrá	káhin	kahí	kahiṉ	kahiṉ
کھڑا	کھرا	کڑا	کرا	بُرا	بھُورا	بُوڑھا	بُورا	کاہن	کہی	کہیں	کہیں
standing	genuine	bracelet	bran	evil	blanket	old	sawdust	priest	said	said	somewbere

deke	dekhke	dekhe	galla	galá	ġalla	dabi	ḍibbi	mihnat	minnat	minaṭ
دیکے	دیکھکے	دیکھے	گلّہ	گلا	غلّہ	دبی	ڈبی	محنت	منّت	منٹ
having given	having seen	seen	flock	neck	grain	buried	box	labour	entreaty	minute

miṭṭí	míṭhi	miṭi	sát	sáth	sáṭh	bache	bachche	bág	bhág	bágh	báġ
مٹّی	میٹھی	مٹی	سات	ساتھ	ساٹھ	بچے	بچّے	باگ	بھاگ	باگھ	باغ
earth	sweet	shut (eyes)	seven	with	sixty	escaped	children	bridle	flec	lion	garden

bahs	bahtá	kaisá	kahtá	kahná	re	ráh	rahná	má	máh	já	jáh	bahut	pahunchná
بحث	بہتا	کیسا	کہتا	کہنا	ر	راہ	رہنا	ما	ماہ	جا	جاہ	بہت	پہنچنا
dispute	flowing	what sort?	speaking	to speak	r	way	to stay	ma	month	go	rank	much	to arrive

PRONUNCIATION CHART No. 3.

Ḳhudá	ḳhud	ḳháliq	Aġá Ḳhán	báġ	báġi	baġair	waġaira
God	self	Creator		garden,	rebel	except	etc.
خدا	خود	خالق	آغاخان	باغ	باغی	بغیر	وغیرہ
Ġází Ḳhán	ġol	ġusse	ġáib	ḳhidmat	ḳhána	ḳháss	ġam
	crowd	angry	hid	service	room	special	grief
غازی خان	غول	غصے	غائب	خدمت	خانہ	خاص	غم
ġamgín	ġaríb	ġurba	ġalat	ġulám	ġauġa	qaul	faqír
sorrowful	poor	poor (pl.)	mistake	slave	noise	promise	ʻmendicant
غمگین	غریب	غربہ	غلط	غلام	غوغہ	قول	فقیر
qism	qasam		qaraz	Qurán	qalam		qaid-ḳhána
kind, sort	oath		debt		pen		jail
قسم	قسم		قرض	قران	قلم		قیدخانہ

use	us se	hameṇ	ham meṇ	tumheṇ	tum meṇ	kise	qisse
tó him	from him;	to us,	in us;	to you,	in you;	to any one,	stories
اُسے	اُس سے	ہمین	ہم مین	تمھین	تم مین	کسے	قصے

meṇ	meṇh	muṇh	ghoṛe	gore	bái	bhái	Jaṭ	jhat	jál	jhál
in	rain,	mouth	horses,	whites,	lady,	brother,	Jat,	quickly;	net,	hot, burning.
مین	مینھ	مُنھ	گھوڑے	گورے	بائی	بھائی	جٹ	جھٹ	جال	جھال

Homoinymic Sentences for Pronunciation Exercises.

1. Wuh átá hai.
   He is coming.
   Wuh áṭá hai.
   That is meal (of wheat).
2. Yih rotí hai.
   She (this one) is crying.
   Yih roṭí hai.
   This is bread.
3. Wuh árí hai.
   That is a saw.
   Wuh áṛí hai.
   He is obstinate.
   Wuh á rahí hai.
   She is coming.
4. Yih dál hai.
   This is pulse.
   Yih ḍál hai.
   This is a branch.
   Yih ḍhál hai.
   This is a shield.
5. Wuh ghoṛe á rahe hain̲.
   Those horses are coming.
   Wuh gore á rahe hain.
   Those whites (soldiers) are coming.
6. Wuh kháná hai.
   That is dinner.
   Wuh káná hai.
   He is one-eyed.
   Wuh k̲hána hai.
   That is the compartment.
7. Wuh barí hai.
   He (She) is free.
   Wuh baṛí hai.
   She is big.
   Wuh bharí hai.
   She (It) is full.
   Wuh baṛhí hai.
   She has grown, increased.
8. Yih khá lí hai.
   (He, or, She) has eaten this.
   Yih k̲hálí hai.
   This is empty.
   Yih kálí hai.
   This (feminine) *is black.*
9. Wuh gol hai.
   He (or, That) is round.
   Wuh ġol hai.
   That is a crowd.
10. Ġul kyún̲ kiyá ?
    Why did you put it out (lamp) ?
    Ġul kyún̲ kiyá ?
    Why did you make a noise ?

11. Note the difference between the sounds of the contrasted English and Urdu words.

Málí, gardener	.. Molly.	Hai, is	.. High.
Billí, cat	.. Billy.	Ek, one	.. Ache.
Kar, do	.. Cur.	Sach, truth	.. Such.
Par, on	.. Purr.	Milí, got	.. Milly.
Dúr, far	.. Doer.	Mez, table	.. Maize.
Ḍák, post, mail	.. Dock.	Sáís, groom	.. Syce.
Peṭ, belly	.. Pate.	Fáram, corruption of form.	
Pit, bile	.. Pit.	Púr, as Núrpúr	.. Poor.
Ho, be	.. Hoe.	Lo, take	.. Low.
Pul, a bridge	.. Pull.	Do, give	.. Dough.

Doubled Letters.

12. Yih merá galla hai.
This is my flock.
Yih merá galá hai.
This is my neck.
Yih merá ġalla hai.
This is my grain.

13. Laṛká letá hai.
The boy takes (it) or is taking it.
Laṛká leṭá hai.
The boy is laid down.

14. Is ko do dená.
Give him two.
Is ko dho dená.
Wash this.
Is ko duh dená.
Milk this (cow).
Iṣ ko ḍho dená.
Carry this away.

15. Mere pás khará hai
I have the genuine.
Mere pás khaṛá hai.
He is standing by me.
Mere pás kaṛá hai.
I have a bracelet.
Mere pás kará (Punjabí) hai.
I have the bran (of gram).

16. Yih 'aurat khátí hai.
This woman eats.
Yih 'aurat kátti hai.
This woman spins.
Yih 'aurat káṭṭí hai.
This woman bites.

17. Laṛke deke gaye.
The boys gave and went.
Laṛke dekhke gaye.
The boys saw and went.

Laṛke dekhe gaye.
The boys were seen.

18. Pata mujh ko do.
Give me the information.
Pattá mujh ko do.
Give me the leaf.
Paṭṭá mujh ko do.
Give me the lease.
Paṭṭhá mujh ko do.
Give me the young one.
Merá kapṛá phaṭá hai.
My garment is torn.
Merá kapṛá phaṭṭá hai.
My garment is tearing.

19. Yih bakrá merá bak̲h̲rá hai.
This he-goat is my portion.
K̲h̲udá k̲h̲áliq hokár k̲h̲ud hamárí k̲h̲idmat kartá hai.
God although (lit. being) Creator does himself serve us.

20. 'Auraten̲ sáth hain̲.
The women are along.
'Auraten̲ sát hain̲.
There are seven women.
'Auraten̲ sáṭh hain̲.
There are sixty women.

21. Wuh "gol" kahtá hai.
He says "gol" (round).
Wuh "ġol" kahtá hai.
He says "ġol" (crowd).
Wuh "ghol" kahtá hai.
He says "ghol" (dissolve).

22. Wuh chízen̲ gharon̲ men̲ paṛí rahín̲.
Those things were lying in the houses.
Wuh chízen̲ ghaṛon̲ men̲ paṛí rahín̲.
Those things were lying in the water jars.
Wuh chízen̲ gaṛhon̲ men̲ paṛí rahín̲.
Those things were lying in the forts.

23. Ismit Sáhib daure gaye hain̲.
Mr. Smith has gone to camp (itinerating).
Ismit Sáhib dauṛe gaye hain̲.
Mr. Smith has gone running.

24. Ádmí chhappar men̲ baiṭhá thá.
A man was sitting (lit. seated) in the hut.
Ádmí chhappaṛ men̲ baiṭhá thá. (P)
A man was sitting in the pond.
Ádmí chhappar men̲ baiṭhtá thá.

A man was sitting in the hut (yesterday).

Note that it is "*baiṭhá thá*," not "*baiṭhá tá*," nor *baiṭhta tá* but *thá*.

25. Us ne baṛí minnat kí thí.

He pleaded very hard.

Us ne baṛí mihnat kí thí.

He worked very hard.

26. Wuh gayí hai.

She has gone.

Wuh gayí hain̲.

They (women) have gone.

Wuh gaye hain̲.

They (men) have gone.

Wuh gáe hai.

That is a cow.

Wuh gáe hain̲.

Those are cows.

27. Wuh kahán̲ paṛá hai?

Where is it (or, he) lying?

Wuh kahán̲ paṛhá hai?

Where did (you) read it?

28. Wuh ṭhaṭṭí hai.

That is the "thatti"—*outcaste quarter* (Punjab).

Wuh ṭaṭṭí hai.

That is a screen (privy, latrine).

Wuh tattí hai (P).

That is warm.

29. Us ne dhaṛí darí par dharí.

He put the 10-lb. *weigh on the carpet.*

Káf aur Qáf men̲ kyá farq hai?

What is the difference be̤tween k and q?

Ham K̲h̲udá ke hamk̲h̲idmat hain̲.

We are God's co-workers.

Us kí qabr kí k̲h̲abar dení cháhiye.

One ought to give news of his grave.

30. (*a*) Bát Thing, matter, *res*.

Bhát Rice, boiled.

Báṭ* Path, way.

Bháṭ* A bard.

(*b*) Bág .. Rein.

Bhág .. Fortune; (verb), Run.

Báġ .. Garden.

Bágh .. Tiger.

(*c*) Tárík .. Dark, night.

Tahrík .. Instigation.

Tárík̲h̲ .. Date (as of month).

---

* Not in frequent use.

(*d*)	Toṛí	Torn.
	Thoṛí	A little.
	Torí	Turnip like plant.
(*e*)	Battí	Wick, lamp.
	Baṭí	Twisted.
	Bhaṭí	Furance.
	Baṭṭí	Small weight.
(*f*)	Koṛí	Score, twenty.
	Korí	New, unused.
	Koṛhí	A leper.
	*Korhí	An alley.
(*g*)	Sáre	All.
	Sáṛe	Let him burn (P).
	Sáṛhe	1/2 more than.
(*h*)	Kíṛá	Worm, insect.
	Khírá	Cucumber.
	Kíṛhá*	Wormy.
(*i*)	Parí	A fairy.
	Paṛhí	Read (past part.).
	Paṛí	Lying, recumbent (fem. part.).
	Pharí*	Buckler.
(*j*)	Der	Lateness.
	Ḍeṛh	One and one half.
	Ḍher.	Pile, heap.

(*k*)	Dáná	Wise.
	Dána	Grain.
(*l*).	Síná	To sew.
	Sína	Breast.
(*m*)	Us se lá do.	Bring it from him.
	Use lá do	Bring and give it.
(*n*)	Ham meṉ	In us.
	Hameṉ	To us.
	Tumheṉ	To you.
	Tum meṉ	In you.
(*o*)	Bachcha	Child.
	Bachá	Escaped.
	Kám	Work.
	Ḵhám*	Immature.
(*p*)	Banná	To be made.
	Baná	Is made.
	Kam	Little.
	Ḵham	Curved.
(*q*)	Burá	Evil.
	Bhúrá	Brown, earth colour.
	Búṛhá	Old.
	Búrá	Sawdust.
(*r*)	Bheṛí	Ewe, sheep.
	Beṛí	Boat, hand-cuff.
	Berí	Punjab plums.
	Beṛhí* (Teṛhí).	Crooked.

---

* Not in frequent use.

Merí búṛhí bheṛí bhúrí beṛí meṉ beṛhí berí ke baṛe bure patte khá rahí thí. My old ewe was eating the very bad leaves of the crooked "*ber*" in a brown boat.

(*s*) Ká	.. Of.	(*t*) Rá	.. Name of r.
Káh	.. Grass.	Ráh	.. Way, path.
Já	.. Go.	Má	.. Mother.
Jáh*	.. Grandeur.	Máh	.. Month.

It will be well if the munshi puts these single words (the last thirty or so) into simple sentences.

A few most necessary imperatives, objects and adverbs, verb always last.

bring	.. láo	enough / stop it	.. bas; bas karo
give	.. do	look out!	.. k͟habardár!
take hold	.. pakaṛo	come	.. áo
take	.. le lo	go	.. jáo
look at / see	.. dekho	speak	.. bolo
lift up / pick up	.. uṭháo	eat	.. kháo
make	.. banáo	drink	.. pío
send	.. bhejo	hurry up / make haste	jaldí karo
put / place	.. rakkho	pass, *i.e.* serve	.. dikháo
fetch	.. le áo	make ready	.. taiyár karo
having given come	de áo	dinner	.. kháná
wait / stop	.. ṭhahr jáo	breakfast	.. házrí
close / shut	.. band karo	early breakfast. "little breakfast"	chhoṭí házrí
sit down	.. baiṭho	tiffin	.. ṭiffin

* Not in frequent use.

English	Hindustani
tea	chá
water	pání
milk	dúdh
meat	gosht
box, trunk	sandúq
luggage	asbáb
bedding	bistar
coat	koṭ
hat	ṭopí
clothes	kapṛe
shoes	júte
money	rúpae
carriage	gáṛí
chair	kursí
table	mez
book	kitáb
vegetables	sabzí
bread	roṭí
butter	makkhan
sugar	misrí, chíní
house	koṭhí, ghar
city	shahr
post office	ḍák-khána
bath	ġusl
letter	chiṭṭhí
here	yahán
there	wahán
to-day	áj
yesterday	kal
at once, just now	abhí
quickly	jald
to-morrow	kal
in the room	kamare men
in the house	koṭhí men
in the store room	godám men
in this room	is kamare men
in that room	us kamare men
from that room	us kamare se
on the table	mez par
slowly	áhista
carefully	khabardárí se
this direction	is taraf
that direction	us taraf
in the verandah	barámda men
in the cupboard	almárí men
from the house	koṭhí se
from the station	sṭeshan se
from the shop	dúkán se
to the city	shahr ko
from the city	shahr se
in the city	shahr men
in the cantonment	chháoní men
in this way	is tarah se
in that manner	us tarah se

*Directions to be used by and with the teacher.**

Speak slowly ..	Áhista† bolo.
Say it again ..	Phir kahiye.
Came the thing into understanding?	Bát samajh meṉ áí?
It came not into understanding.	Samajh meṉ nahíṉ áí.
Is it right? Yes, it's correct	Ṭhík hai? Háṉ, sahíh hai.
Say that word again ..	Wuh lafz phir kahiye.
Do you understand me? ..	Áp merí bát samajhte hain?
I do not understand ..	Nahíṉ, maiṉ nahíṉ samajhtá (samajhtí *fem.*) húṉ.
Sir, I will explain it to you.	Sáhib, maiṉ áp ko samjhá detá húṉ.
I can't pronounce this ..	Is ká talaffuz mujh se ṭhík nahíṉ átá.

Grammatical Questions.‡

Is this a verb? or a noun? adjective, pronoun, or "harf"?	Yih fi'l hai? yá ism? ism-i-sifat, zamír, yá harf?
Is it singular or plural? ..	Yih wáhid hai yá jama'?
Is it masculine or feminine?	Yih muzakkar hai, ya muannis?
Is this verb present or future?	Yih fi'l hál hai yá mustaqbil?
It is neither present nor future, it is past.	Na hál na mustaqbil, mází hai?
Is it simple past, or remote, or near?	Mází mutlaq, mází qaríb, yá mází ba'íd?

* These should be learned in the first week or two.

† Accent on the antepenult.

‡ These may be learned after the second month.

It is not imperative, it is infinitive.	Yih 'amr nahín hai, yih masdar hai.
"Aya hoga" is "doubtful past," isn't it?	"Áyá hogá" mází shakká hai, na?
Is "agar kartá" present tense?	Kyá "agar kartá" hál hai?
No, it is conditional. ..	Nahín, wuh mází shartiyá hai.
Is "hai" a verb? ..	Kyá "hai" fi'l hai?
No it is a "particle" ..	Nahin wuh "harf" hai.

Résumé of Method.

A.

I. Write the sentence to be learned on a slip.

II. Memorise it by repeating alternately with the teacher. (1) In short phrases of three to five syllables. (2) In longer phrases. (3) As a whole.

III. Repeat it, till it can be given at the rate of five syllables per second.

IV. Break it up and recombine into simple short sentences.

V. While learning it, hum out the rhythm—after the teacher—and note the difference between your English rhythm and that of the Urdu.

VI. Learn other new sentences in the same way.

VII. Always interweave the new and old till all como fluently, in any order.

VIII. Keep the slips under daily review for a month.

IX. Lay a bunch of slips aside for a week, then review them, and keep them under review, until they are again brought up to speed. Then try after two weeks, and after a month.

X. Review them from month to month. Never allow anything to be forgotten.

XI. After the first two months use your Drill Tables one or two hours daily, to gain a practical mastery of the parts of speech.

XII. Practise the Interrogatives until you can ask and answer every kind of a question.

XIII. Practise the pronunciation exercises, or Charts, twice daily for twenty minutes, for six months, until ear and tongue are quick and fluent.

XIV. After a few months, daily dictation to and by the student will be the best drill for accuracy.

Learning to Read.

B.

I. Above the English nouns, or principal words, write on your slips in character the Urdu words.

II. On the back you may write the Roman Urdu, with character above.

III. After a few days write another and then another word on the first slip until all are on, and can be recognised.

IV. Now write the characters in regular order, right to left, on another slip.

V. Write all the slips in character, both majors and minors, and practise reading them till you are as fluent in reading slips as you are in reciting.

VI. Now take up the book and begin to read matter that is absolutely familiar. Aim at the same readiness in reading the book as in reciting slips.

VII. Never begin with unfamillar material. Read what you know, thus passing from the known to the unknown.

VIII. In beginning to write, start with familar easy material, and copy under the teacher's direction, being careful to make the strokes in the right order. No "takhties".

Time Table.

(*Suggested*).

Min.	
15	Charts and Pronunciation Exercises.
15	Review old slips.
15	Learning new slip.
15 – 60	Practise on old slips, and interrogations.
15 – 30	Writing.
15 – 30	Reading.
	Drill work.
	Conversation.

Repeat this in the afternoon. After two months read Roman a half hour, and after three months read character an hour twice daily.

Five hours' study daily with the teacher is enough for most people.

Lessons I – IX have been well done in thirty hours. No work outside of class room Certainly not more than two weeks should be spent on them.

Lessons I – LXV, covering all of John's Gospel, will be covered by some pupils in three months. Others will take four to six months. The remaining lessons abounding in common constructions and idioms should be used in conjunction with the studies of the remainder of the year. Particular attention should be given to grammatical drill as brought out by the exercises in connection with the Drill Tables.

LESSON I.

The first sentence to be learned is "What is this?" It is to be taught directly by the teacher, as he indicates one of these articles after the other. He points to the table and says, **Yih mez hai, Yih mez hai, Yih mez hai.** Then he asks the class saying, **Yih kyá hai?** and it is probable that some one will say, **Yih mez hai,** when the teacher nods his head and says, **Ṭhík hai.** But if no one responds, then he must go through the repetition of **Yih mez hai,** until they do respond. When they respond readily, he lifts up a book, and says, **Yih kitáb hai,** repeating the sentence several times, never less than three, and then says, as he lifts the book, **Yih kyá hai?** until he gets the response, **Yih kitáb hai.**

Now he again points to the table and says, **Yih kyá hai?** and gets the response, **Yih mez hai.**

Now he lifts up a pen and says **Yih qalam hai,** several times, as before, till on his asking, **Yih kyá hai?** the class responds. Now he indicates the table, book and pen and requires a ready response to each repetition of the question, **Yih kyá hai?**

Now he does the same with a chair and a pencil, saying respectively, **Yih kursí hai, Yih pinsil hai,** and **Yih kyá hai?** until the class answers readily for all five objects.

In a second lesson he should introduce, in this same manner, several more words, never exceeding ten new words daily, until the words in the list, under Interrogations I, are thoroughly familiar. The aim in this exercise should be to accustom the pupil to the use of the Urdu names, so that they will occur to him as readily as do the

English names. Speed as well as accuracy in this and subsequent exercises is to be required.

Now let the teacher write in English on the board, so all the class may see* :—

I. A WOMAN CAME FROM THE CITY TO DRAW WATER. (11)

Above each noun he may write the Urdu character for the same, and then he may repeat the whole sentence, in Urdu, three times, before he asks any one to repeat it after him. If no one is able so to give it, let him break it up into breath-groups of three to six syllables, as **Ek 'aurat, shahr se, páni bharne áí** and repeat each group until the pupils can repeat it after him. He must now unite the groups and continue this alternate repetition until they can give the whole seven words of eleven syllables twice in five or six seconds. If they cannot do this in a short time, say 15 or 20 minutes, let him give on the board the sentences :—

1. A woman came. 2. A woman came from the city. 3. A woman came to draw water. And repeat their Urdu equivalents—**Ek 'aurat áí, ek 'aurat shahr se áí, ek 'aurat pání bharne áí**, until the pupils give 1, 2, 3 at will. Now let him take up I. again, and it is probable that the pupils will soon master it. When they can repeat these at the normal rate of speed, five syllables per second, i.e. six or seven seconds for I. 1, 2 and 3, the teacher may pass on to II. It is probable, however, that this will be at another hour.

LESSON II (a).

Begin the lesson with a rapid review of **mez, kitáb, qalam, kursí, pinsil,** and I. 1, 2, 3, watching for any egregious

* For the individual studying alone write on a 2 x 5 inch slip of cardboard, or paper stiff enough to shuffle.

blunders and calling attention to them. Too great accuracy of pronunciation should not be insisted on at this stage of learning. It is sufficient to call attention to the fact that **kitáb** has a dental **t,** as has **'aurat,** that the **r** is trilled, and that the vowels are level in intonation and, so, different from English vowels; but do not insist that the pupil must always so give them. Fluency first, then accuracy.

The teacher may now take up II, which is a continuation of I.

II. AND JESUS WHO WAS SEATED ON THE WELL—HE SAID TO HER, PLEASE GIVE ME A DRINK. (26)

Since this is too long to learn readily, let us begin with the last clause first, as that gives complete sense. The teacher will write on the board :—

Please give me a drink—Me water give-drink-please, and write the Urdu script above, over the words they represent, *Mujhe pání pilá díjiye.* He will repeat this in two sections of four and five syllables, alternately with the class, until they can give the nine syllables without hesitation. Now let him repeat the six syllables. He said to her, **Us ne us se kahá,** previously writing its English equivalent on the board, until this too can be given with fluency, and that in conjunction with **mujhe pání pilá díjiye,** in three seconds. If it worries the pupil to attain to such speed, drop it and go back to I. Draw a picture of a city, a well, a woman, a man seated on the well, another man on the path, also a boy near the man and a girl near the woman. Now ask, as you point to the city, the woman, *Yih kyá hai?* Point to the man and say, **Yih ádmí hai.** Then ask **Yih kyá hai?** Then point to the boy and the girl, and say, **Yih laṛká hai, yih laṛkí hai,** and review the question *Yih kyá hai?* until the class answers without hesitation.

2. Now introduce the sentences 4, 5, 6, 7, 8, writing only the English on the board :—

4. **Ek ádmí áyá.** 5. **Ek larká shahr se áyá.** 6. **Ek ádmí pání bharne áyá.** 7. **Ek laṛkí áí.** 8. **Ek laṛkí pání bharne áí.** 4. A man came. 5. A boy came from the city. 6. A man came to draw water. 7. A girl came. 8. A girl came to draw water.

The teacher may inquire as to any observations they have made of resulting verb changes. He should insist on no undue prominence being given to the last syllable, to indicate the genders.

A brief review of the various objects in the room that have already been taught should be given by way of rest.

There should each day be introduced another new word in the Urdu script into the sentences. For example the second day the sentence " A woman came " should have " *áí* " in character, written above " came." Then these words should be written off at one side in character and the pupils should be asked to recognize them as units. This should be continued until they recognize all the words of I, and 1-8, at sight.

It will then be time to introduce the slip method for character study, though it is not yet safe to permit the student to study alone.

LESSON II (b).

Review with ' *Yih kyá hai ?* ' the pictures, woman, man, boy, girl, city, and the classroom objects.

Review also the majors (Roman) and minors (Arabic numerals).

Now take up the additional relative clause, " who was seated on the well," and write it on the board and let the pupils memorise it at the teacher's mouth, as before, to speed, or nearly so, and then add the antecedent 'And Jesus,' combining it with the relative clause, and when these are mastered, further uniting with the preceding lesson II, till the class can give the whole without hesitation—*aur Yesú' ne, jo kúẽ par baiṭhá thá—us ne us se kahá mujhe páni pilá díjiye.*

It may be that during this process, it will become advisable, on account of the weariness of the class, to intermit the repetition and take up the minors under II.

II.

1. That man said to that woman, Please give me two chairs.	1. Us ádmí ne us 'aurat se kahá, Mujhe do kursíã' díjiye (or, de díjiye).
2. The boy said to the man, Drink.	2. Laṛke ne ádmí se kahá, Pío.
3. Give me drinking water.	3. Mujhe píne ká pání de do.
4. That woman said to that man, Please give me three books.	4. Us 'aurat ne us ádmí se kahá, Mujhe tín kitábẽ de díjiye.
5. That boy said to that man, Please give me four pencils.	5. Us laṛke ne us ádmí se kahá, Mujhe chár pinsil de díjiye.
6. That girl said to that boy, Please give me five watches.	6. Us laṛkí ne us laṛke se kahá, Mujhe pánch ghaṛíã' de díjiye.
7. The men said to her, Give us a drink.	7. Ádmiõ ne us se kahá, Ham ko pání piláo.
8. A man was sitting on the well.	8. Ek ádmı kúẽ par baiṭhá thá.
9. A boy was sitting on the chair.	9. Ek laṛká kursí par baiṭhá thá.

10. A girl was sitting on the well.	10. Ek laṛkí kúẽ par baiṭhí thí.
11. The girls were sitting on chairs.	11. Laṛkíã' kursíõ par baiṭhí thĩ'.
12. The boys were sitting on tables.	12. Laṛke mezõ par baiṭhe the.

There may now be introduced with the objects the additional question, WHERE ?

Where is the book ? chair ?. table ? pen ? pencil ? etc. The teacher should always require a full answer, as, *The book is on the table*, not merely "*On the table.*" It perhaps may be said that all necessary words should first be introduced, as *floor*, *carpet*, *mantel*, *hand*, before questions involving them are asked.

The question '*Yih kyá hai ?*' may now be required of the pupils from each other, or from the teacher, who will give the full answer. This should be varied until pupils can readily ask and answer all questions. They should also be encouraged to ask for the name of any object not yet introduced, which should, then, go to make up the daily total of ten new words for the day's lesson.

LESSON III.

Review all the objects and pictures, the major and minor sentences.

Now differentiate between *this* and *that*, yih and **wuh**, and get the pupils to answer accordingly. The teacher holding in his hand a book says, **Yih kyá hai ?** and the pupils answer **Wuh kitáb hai.** The teacher points to a note-book on the pupil's chair and says, **Wuh kyá hai ?** and the pupil answers, **Yih kápí hai.** He points to the door and says, **Wuh kyá hai ?** and the pupils answer, **Wuh**

darwáza hai. This exercise should now be carried forward continuously, differentiating between **yih** and **wuh.** The plurals should also be introduced. What are these ? What are those ?

Now let the question *where* ? be reviewed. **Kitáb kahã' hai ?** with the answers, **Kitáb mez par hai. Kitáb háth mẽ hai,** etc.

No. III may now be introduced.

III. For his disciples were gone to the city to buy food. Write the Urdu character above, then repeat as below.

(*a*) *kyũ'ki,* (*b*) *uske shágird shahr mẽ,* (*c*) *khání mol lene ko gaye the.* (17)

When they have learned (*c*), then let them learn (*b*), then (*a*) and (*b*), then (*a, b, c*); and when they can repeat III, let them repeat I and III, II and III, till they can give the tour thus at the required speed, in twelve seconds. The teacher must insist on this, for compliance with the speed test is the only way to secure the mental readiness and the lingual fluency which will, later, issue in accuracy of pronunciation and idiom. "It is intense effort that educates."

The teacher should also call the attention of the pupils, lesson by lesson, to vowel values, particularly to final vowels, as well as to wherein the consonants differ from the corresponding English consonants, as *t, d, s, l,* and the *k* in **ko** and the *bh* in **bharne.** The sentence rhythm should be carefully noted, as it is much more level than that of English, yet it is not so level as many beginners give it, a dead monotone, as, for example. in **baiṭhá thá,** where **bai** is rather high and **thá** intermediate to **thá,** which is somewhat lower in pitch; whereas in *was seated* the pitch runs –¯_, in contrast with the ¯–_ of the Urdu, which has rather the rhythm of the inverted "seated was."

Let the pupils count around, adding a few additional numbers occasionally. Now they are able to count 1-5, *ek, do, tin, chár, pánch,* so add 6, 7, *chha, sát.*

Numbers of books might now be introduced and the questions asked. How many books are on the table, on the chair, etc., requiring the replies.

Two-seven books are on the table: or, Only one book is on the chair.

The slip-method may now be introduced for use in class, or with the teacher. Up to this point no study should be carried on by the pupil when alone, as study without some one to check mistakes may result in more harm than good. Directions:—Write on a slip of paper 2×5 inches, and stiff enough to shuffle, the English of I, II, III, and of the minors of I and II. At the right-hand upper corner note the number of syllables of the Urdu equivalent, and on the reverse have the teacher write in character the Urdu, under which you may write, both interlinearly and in regular order, the roman Urdu. Later on, slips on which Urdu alone is written in the character on one side should be prepared, the Urdu of the previously memorized majors and minors, and these should be reviewed until they can be read with the same ease and facility as the English slips.

We may also write a list of the familiar objects on the board, in English, and request the pupils to substitute the nouns, first in singular, and then with 2, 3, 4, etc. *Mujhe kursí díjiye. Kitáb, mez, pinsal, ghaṛi, koṭ, jútá, kágaz,* etc.

Give me a chair, please; *mujhe do* (2-7) *kursíán dedíjiye.* then book, table, pencil, watch, coat, shoes, paper, etc. Then 2-7 books, tables, etc.

Also, Please take a book, etc., *Kitáb le líjiye,* etc., etc.

LESSON IV.

Ques.—Where had his disciples gone? Uske shágrid kahã′ gaye the?

Ans.—Uske shágird shahr mẽ, etc.

Ques.—What did Jesus say to the woman? Yisú' ne 'aurat se kyá kahá?

Ans. Yisú' ne 'aurat se kahá ki mujhe pání, etc.

Ques.—Where did the woman come from? 'Aurat kahã′ se ái?

Ans.—'Aurat shahr se ái.

Ques.—Why did she come? Shahr se kyũ′ ái?

Ans.—Pání bharne ko ái.

Ques.—Why did the disciples go to the city? Shágird shahr mẽ kyũ′ gaye?

Ans.—Khánά mol lene ko gae.

Ques.—Where was Jesus sitting? Yisú' kahã′ baiṭhá thá?

Ans.—Yisú' kúẽ par baiṭhá thá.

Review all majors and minors.

Uske shágird shahr mẽ pání bharne gaye the.	His disciples had gone into the city to draw water.
Ek 'aurat shahr mẽ khánά mol lene ái.	A woman came into the city to buy food.
Sát ádmí shahr mẽ kursíã′ mol lene áe.	Seven men came into the city to buy chairs.
Pánch laṛkíã′ shahr se pání bharne gai thĩ′.	Five girls went from the city to draw water.
Áṭh laṛke ṭopíã′ lene gae the.	Eight boys went to get (take) hats.
Nau 'auratẽ kitáben̲ mol lene áĩ′.	Nine women came to buy (take) books.
Das ádmí ghaṛíã′ mol lene gaye the.	Ten men went to buy watches.

Now have the pupils count in turn from one to ten, until they can do it with facility.

A beginning may be made on the next major.

IV. WHEN THEY CAME BACK, NO ONE SAID TO HIM. WHO IS THIS? OR, WHAT DO YOU WANT? OR, WHY ARE YOU TALKING TO HER? (34)

Write the Urdu character above and then it will be best to begin with the subordinate interrogative clauses first. Who is this? **Yih kaun hai?** Then **yá, Áp kyá cháhte haĩ?** Then *yā Áp us se kis líe bátẽ karte haĩ?* When the pupils can repeat these, write one question on each of three slips and repeat at random till the three can be given without hesitation.

When this result is reached, then give the principal clause, When they came back, no one said to him—**Jab wuh wápas áe, to kisí ne us se na kahá,** and repeat till the whole can be given in seven seconds. Then repeat I. IV, II. IV, III. IV, in 31 seconds. Then give I, II, III, IV in 18 seconds.

LESSON V.

Review all previous material.

Shahr se kaun áí? Kyũ′ áí?	Who came from the city? Why did she come?
Jab wuh shahr se áí, tab kaun kúẽ par baiṭhá thá?	When she came from the city, then who was seated on the well?
Jab shágird wápas áe, tab Yisú' kyá kartá thá?	When the disciples came back, what was Jesus doing?
Kisí ne koí bát kahí? Koí nahĩ′.	Did anyone say anything? Not a thing.

Yih kaun hai? Khudáwand Yisú'. Ek shágird.	Who is this? The Lord Jesus. A disciple.
Áp kyá cháhte haĩ? Maĩ ek, do, wag̃aira, kursí, kitáb, mez, koṭ, pinsil, cháhtá hũ'.	What do you want? I want one, two, etc., chair, book, table, coat, pencil, etc.
Áp kyá karte haĩ?	What are you doing?

Take your objects and illustrate the use of **ke níche, ke pás, ke úpar,** under, beside, over, holding the objects now under, now beside, now over other familiar objects. These exercises, like the others, must be repeated again and again, and day by day, and week after week till the words function directly, as readily as do the English. See Interrogatives II. (2)

Further exercises may be carried on in **Áp kis par baiṭhe haĩ? kis ke pás? Kitáb kis ke níche, kis ke úpar, kis ke pás hai?** Also **kitábẽ, kursíã',** wag̃aira. Also, **Wuh kyá cháhtá hai? Wuh kyá cháhtí hai? Áp kyá cháhte haĩ?** What are you sitting on? By whom (or, what) are you seated? What is the book under? over? beside? Also ask regarding books, chairs, etc. Also, what does he wish? What does she wish? What do you wish?

All answers should be in complete sentences. Several half hours at various sessions may be thus profitably employed.

Introduce the first part of V.

V. (*a*) WHOSO SHALL DRINK OF THIS WATER SHALL THIRST AGAIN. (18)

Jo koí is pání meṉ se píegá wuh phir piyásá hogá.

By way of recreation, one might teach:—

Chhoṭá Jack Horner kone mẽ baiṭhá,
Khátá hai kishmish ká pai:
Unglí ko ḍálá, kishmish nikálá,
Kahtá, kaisá "good boy" ham haĩ.

Then the following questions: *Kone mẽ kaun baiṭhá? Kyá khátá hai? Usne kháne meṉ kyá ḍálá? Usne kyá nikálá? Wuh kyá kahtá hai?*

Then teach V (*b*): but whoso shall drink of that water which I shall give him shall never thirst (29); V (*c*): rather that water in him shall become a fountain, which shall remain flowing until life everlasting (28); **magar jo koí us pání mẽ se píegá jo maĩ us ko dúngá, wuh abad tak piyásá na hogá.** Then V (*c*) **balki wuh pání us mẽ ek chashma ban jáegá, jo hamesha kí zindagí tak járí rahegá.** When these 75 syllables can be repeated in 15 seconds, then repeat the majors I. V, II. V, III. V, IV. V, until they can be given with readiness in 80 seconds. Now repeat them in regular order in 33 seconds, and then give them in any order at the same rate of speed.

Us kúẽ mẽ kyá thá? Pání us kúẽ mẽ thá.	What was in that well? Water.
Us kúẽ ke pání kí bábat Y'isú' ne kyá kahá?	What did Jesus say about the water of that well?
Dúsre pání kí bábat kyá kahá?	What did he say about another water?
Wuh dúsrá pání kyá banegá?	What will that other water become?
Wuh chashma kab tak rahegá?	Till when will that spring remain?
Wuh dúsrá pání kaun degá?	Who will give the other water?

Pupils should learn to *ask* and *answer* these questions.

The teacher should procure a number of books, thin and thick, large and small, red, black, green and brown, and then should exercise the pupils in distinguishing them. *Yih kitáb moṭí hai. Wuh patlí hai. Kyá lál kitáb moṭí hai yá khákí kitáb moṭí hai? Baṛí kitáb kahã' hai? Kaunsí kitáb chhoṭí hai? Kálí kitáb chhoṭí hai. Sabz kitáb kahã' hai? Sabz kitáb khákí kitáb ke níche hai: wagaira, wagaira.*

Let no lesson pass without exercising the pupils on asking and answering all sorts of questions with *kyá, kaun, kahã' kaunsá, kitne, kitná, kyũ'*, what, who, which, how many, how much, and why?

Wuh chhoṭá thá.
Wuh baiṭhá thá.
Wuh ḍálá thá.

Is kamare mẽ chár parde haĩ.
Kágaz par "Khudáwand" likho.

Note the difference between *hai*, and the English high.

Note the higher pitch of the first syllable in *rahegá* and *cháhte haĩ*.

LESSON VI.

Review and ask further:—

Kaun phir piyásá hogá? Jo koí us kúẽ ká pání píegá, wuh phir piyásá hogá. Kaun abad tak piyásá na hogá? Jo koí us pání mẽ se píegá, jo Masíh usko degá, wuh piyása na hogá. Wuh dúsrá pání kis mẽ ek chashma banegá? Wuh dúsrá páni us pínewále mẽ ek chashma ban jaegá. Áp pání kyũ' píte haĩ? Maĩ piyásá hũ'. Kyá áp pání cháhte haĩ? Hã', maĩ pání cháhtá hũ'. Y'isú' ne kis líe kahá, Mujhe pání pilá? Kyũ'ki wuh piyása thá.

Now take up major VI and teach it. Sir, give me this water, that I thirst not neither come hither to draw. (30)

VI. Ai Khudáwand wuh pání mujh ko de táki maĩ na piyásí hoũ' na pání bharne ko yahã' tak áũ'.

Teach it in three clauses of ten, nine and eleven syllables, and when able to repeat all to speed, interweave it with the previous majors thus: I. VI, II. VI, III. VI, IV. VI, V. VI, until the whole can be given in about 65 seconds. Then repeat in numerical order in 40 seconds, then in any order in 40 seconds.

During the process of attaining to this speed let the teacher ask and have answered, or have asked and answered, the following:—

Jab Masíh ne kahá, Dúsrá pání hamesha kí zindagí tak járí rahegá, to 'aurat ne kyá kahá? Jab . . . . . to . . . kahá, Ai Khudáwand, wağaira.

Wuh dúsrá pání kis líe cháhtí thí? Wuh . . . . ki wuh piyásí na howe, na pání bharne ko wahã' tak áe. Shágird shahr mẽ kis líe gaye the? Shágird shahr mẽ is líe gaye the táki wuh kháná mol lẽn. Jab ádmí piyásá hai, to wuh kyá kartá hai? Jab . . . . . wuh pání pítá hai. Jab yih 'aurat piyásí húí to us ne kyá kiyá? Jab wuh 'aurat piyásí húí to wuh pání bharne áí.

Maĩ kursí par baiṭhtá hũ'—suiting the action to the word. And so on, *Maĩ kursí par se uṭhtá hũ'. Maĩ darwáze ko játá hũ'. Maĩ darwáze ko band kartá hũ'. Maĩ darwáze ko kholtá hũ'. Maĩ darwáze se átá hũ' aur baiṭh játá hũ'.* The pupils will also do this, and the others may say. *Wuh kursí par baiṭhtá hai. Wuh darwáze ko játí hai*, according to circumstances.

Count up to 12. *Bárah tak gino.*

Note the difference in sound between *áũ'* and in how.

Wuh rotí hai. She is crying.	Ágá Khán ne kágaz bakhshá. Ágá Khán gave the paper.
Wuh roṭí hai. That is bread.	Káná kháná khátá hai. One-eye is eating dinner.

LESSON VII.

VII. If thou knewest the gift of God and knew this too, who is this speaker, then thou wouldst have asked of him and he would have given thee the water of life. (42)

Agar tú Khudá kí bakhshish ko jántí aur yih bhí jántí ki yih kahnewálá kaun hai to tú us se mángtí, aur wuh tujhe zindagí ká pání detá.

Learn, then repeat alternately with all preceding majors in 90 secs. Then in regular and in shuffled order, repeat the seven majors in 48 secs.

During and after this process teach the pupils to ask and answer thus :—

Kyá wuh 'aurat Yisú' ko jántí thí ? Nahĩ', wuh 'aurat Yisú' ko nahĩ' jántí thí.

Wuh usko kyá jántí thí ? Wuh use Yahúdí jántí thí.

Agar wuh use jántí, to kyá kartí ? Agar wuh use jántí, to us se mángtí.

Agar mángti, to wuh kyá detá ? Agar mángtí, to wuh zindagí ká pání detá.

Zindagí ká pání kyá hai ? Zindagí ká pání Khudá kí bakhshish hai.

Khudá kí bakhshish kaun detá hai ? Khudáwand Masíh Khudá kí bakhshish detá hai.

Yih kahnewálá kaun thá ? Yih kahnewálá Khudáwand Masíh thá.

Wuh kis ko detá hai ? Jo koí mánge, wuh usko detá hai.

Agar ádmí Khudá se mánge, to Khudá kyá degá ? Agar ádmí mánge, to Khudá usko zindagí ká pání degá.

Kúẽ par baiṭhnewálá kaun hai ? Kuẽ par baiṭhnewálá Masíh hai.

Yih shahr se ánewálí kaun hai ? Yih shahr se ánewálí Sámarí 'aurat hai.

Let the teacher exhibit some strange article and say, *Yih kyá hai?* The pupil shakes his head, and the teacher says, *Maĩ nahĩ jántá.*

Let the actions suit the word and teach :—

Maĩ darwáze ko játá hũ′, Maĩ darwáze se átí hũ′.	Ham darwáze se áte haĩ . . . átí haĩ.
Áp darwáze ko játe haĩ, Áp darwáze se átí haĩ.	Tum darwáze se áte ho . . . átí ho.
Wuh darwáze ko játá hai. Wuh darwáze se átí hai.	Wuh darwáze se áte haĩ . . . átí haĩ.

Note the difference in the final vowel of Urdu *málí*, gardener, *billí*, cat, and English molly and billy. Practise á, e, í, ó, ú. Also, *Khudá apní bakhshish ham ko detá hai.*

LESSON VIII.

VIII. Sir, the well is deep, thou hast nothing to draw with, and whence, then, hast thou (has come to thee) that living water ?

Janáb, tere pás to pání bharne ko kuchh hai nahín, aur kúã′ gahrá hai, phir wuh zindagí ká pání tere pás kahã′ se áyá ? (37)

After repeating these 37 syllables in seven or eight seconds, weave VIII in with the preceding seven majors in 100 seconds: then in regular and shuffled order in 56 seconds.

Questions for drill.

1. Wuh kúã′ kaisá thá ? Wuh kúã′ gahrá thá. Yisú' ke pás pání bharne ke liye kyá thá ? Kuchh bhí nahĩ′ thá. Kyá wuh zindagí ká pání kúẽ mẽ se áyá ? Nahĩ′, wuh Khudá ke pás se áyá. 'Aurat ke pás pání bharne ke liye kuchh thá ? Hã′, 'aurat ke pas ek ghaṛá thá, aur ek rassí bhí hogí. Yisú' ke pás koí ghaṛá thá ? Koí nahĩ′. Yisú'

ke pás koí shágird thá ? Us waqt koí nahī' thá. Wuh 'aurat kahã' rahtí thí ? Wuh shahr mẽ rahtí thí. Sámarí 'aurat kis se bátẽ kartí thí ? Wuh Yisú' se bátẽ kartí thí. Kaun pání bhartí thí ? Wuh Sámarí 'aurat pání bhartí thí. Sámarí 'aurat shahr se kab áí ? Jab Yisú' kúẽ par baiṭhá thá, wuh shahr se áí.

Get a number of books of various sizes and colors and ask, *Yih kaisí kitáb hai,* and *kaunsí kitáb mez par hai ? Chár kitábõ mẽ se kaunsí úpar hai ? wagaira.*

Introduce *my, your, his, our, their, with, hat, book, table, shoe, pen, notebook, chair,* etc.

Also *this is the man's. the boy's, the girl's, the woman's hat,* etc.

Have each pupil act and say in turn: **Maĩ kursí se uṭhkar darwáze ko játá hũ'. Darwáze ko band karke, maĩ kursí pás átá aur baíṭh játá hũ',** and the others may say, **Wuh uṭhkar,** *wagaira.*

A. Note the higher pitch of the first syllable in **gahrá, rahtá, cháhtá.**

Note the difference between the final syllables of **kahá** and kahã' in pitch as well as in nasalisation.

Review Chart I.

LESSON IX.

IX. Art thou greater than our father Jacob, who gave us this well, and drank thereof himself, his sons, and his cattle ?

Kyá tú hamáre báp Ya'qúb se baṛá hai, jis ne yih kúã' ham ko diyá, aur k͟hud us ne, aur uske beṭõ ne aur uske maweshí ne us mẽ se piyá ? (43)

Repeat in nine seconds, then interweave with I–VIII in 128 seconds, and in shuffled or regular order in 65 seconds.

Drill Questions.

Kyá Ya'qúb baṛá ádmí thá ? Hã', wuh bahut baṛá ádmí thá. Ya'qúb kaun thá ? Wuh Yahúdíõ ká báp thá. Sámarí usko kyá jánte the ? Sámarí bhí usko báp jánte the. Kis ne yih kúã' Sámaríõ ko diyá ? Ya'qúb ne diyá. Kis kis ne us kúẽ mẽ se piyá ? Ya'qúb ne aur uske beṭõ ne us mẽ se piyá. Ya'qúb ke kitne beṭe the ? Ya'qúb ke bárah beṭe the. Ya'qúb ke pás aur kyá thá ? Ya'qúb ke pás bahut maweshí the. Kyá Yisú' Ya'qúb se baṛá thá ? Hã', Yisú' Ya'qúb se bahut baṛá thá. Kyá Ya'qúb zindagí ká páni detá thá ? Nahĩ', Khudáwand Yisú' zindagí ká pání detá hai. Kis ko detá hai ? Jo koí mánge, wuh us ko detá hai.

Count to 15. Teach the class to say :—*Maĩ baṛá hũ' ; tú baṛá hai ; wuh baṛá hai ; ham baṛe haĩ, tum baṛe ho, áp baṛe haĩ, wuh baṛe haĩ*, discriminating genders when necessary. Also, *Yih kitáb us kitáb se baṛí hai. Yih ádmí us laṛke se baṛá hai. Yih laṛkí achchhí hai. Yih chhoṭí laṛkí us baṛí laṛkí se achchhí hai. Yih 'aurat sab se achchhí hai.*

Have the pupils write on slips, learning one slip at a time, the following, according to method, until all are in automatic control.

The man said, 'I will give you two books.'	Us ádmí ne kahá, ki Maĩ tum ko do kitábẽ dúngá. (14)
The woman said, 'I will give you a drink.'	Us 'aurat ne kahá, Maĩ ápko pání piláúngí. (14)
The boy said, 'He will give us the well.'	Laṛke ne kahá, Wuh ham ko wuh kúã' degá. (12)
The girl said, 'She will give you 5 chairs.'	Laṛkí ne kahá, Wuh tumko pánch kursíã' degí. (14)

The boys said, 'We will give them 6 eggs.'	Un laṛkõ ne kahá, kí ham unko chha anḍe denge. (13)
The girls said, 'We will give her 7 tables.'	Un laṛkíõ ne kahá, ki ham usko sát mezẽ dengí. (13)
The women said, 'They will give us 8 pence.'	Auratõ ne kahá, Wuh ham ko áṭh áne denge. (14)
The men said, 'They will give us 9 books.'	Ádmíõ ne kahá, Wuh hamko nau kitábẽ dengí. (15)
They all said, 'We will give you Rs. 15.'	Un sabhõ ne kahá, ki ham ápko pandrah rúpae denge. (15)

The pupil should persevere until these can be given in any order in 25 seconds.

Wuh baṛí hai. Wuh barí hai. Wuh bharí hai. Wuh baṛhí húí hai.

Note.—One class did this much work in thirty hours, another in nearly forty.

LESSON X.

X. On this Jesus said to the woman, Go call thy husband and bring him hither. The woman replied, I have no husband (I am husbandless).

Is par Yisú' ne 'aurat se kahá, Jáo, apne shauhar ko yahã' bulá láo. 'Aurat ne kahá, Maĩ be-shauhar hũ'. (33)

Suwál aur Jawáb.—Pahle pahal Yisú' ne 'aurat se kyá kahá ? P. p. Y. n. 'a. s. kahá, ki Mujhe páni pilá. Jab us 'aurat ne kahá, Yih páni mujh ko de, to Khudáwand ne kyá kahá ? Jab us 'aurat ne yih bát kahí, to Khudáwand ne kahá, ki apne shauhar ko buláo. Jab Khudáwand ne shauhar buláne ko kahá, to us 'aurat ne kyá jawáb diyá ? Is bát par us 'aurat ne jawáb diyá, ki maĩ be-shauhar hũ'. Kyá yih 'aurat achchhí thí? Nahĩ', wuh achchhí nahĩ' thí.

Apní kitáb mujh ko díjiye. Maĩ apní kitáb áp ko detá hũ'. Apná qalam dúsre ko de do. Maĩ apná qalam unko detá hũ'. Apní kápí us 'aurat—laṛke, laṛkí—ko do. Maĩ apní kápí detá hũ'.

Distinguish between *yahã'* and *wahã'*, here and there.

Yahã' mez par kyá hai? Wahã' mez par kitáb hai. Wahã' kyá hai? Wahã' darwáza hai. Call for lists of verbs in V and VI and also ask for futures in all persons and genders. Note relation of future and subjunctive. Count to 20. Review all interrogatives thus far introduced.

Note the higher pitch of the first syllable in *pahle*, also the full vowel sounds of *áo*, in *buláo*, *jáo*, *láo*. Review Charts I and II.

LESSON XI.

XI. Jesus said to the woman, Thou hast well said I have no husband, for thou hast already had five husbands and he with whom thou now art, he is not thy husband. This thou saidst truly.

Yisú' ne 'aurat se kahá, Tú ne k͟húb kahá ki maĩ be-shauhar hũ', kyũ'ki tú pánch shauhar kar chukí hai, aur jis ke pás tú ab hai, wuh terá shauhar nahĩ' hai. Yih tú ne sach kahá. (49)

Sámari 'aurat kahã' rahtí thí? S. 'a. shahr mẽ rahtí thí. Kis ke pás rahtí thí? Wuh kisí ádmí ke pás rahtí thí. Us ke kitne shauhar ho chuke the? Us ke pánch shauhar ho chuke the. Kitne shauhar kar chukí thí? Wuh to pánch shauhar kar chukí thí. Ab kis ke pás hai? Ab wuh chhaṭe ádmí ke pás hai.

Review all previous questions bearing directly on the text.

Laṛkí pání píegí ? Laṛki pání pí chukí hai. Laṛke, tú yih bát kah degá ? Janáb, maĩ to kah chuká hũ'. Bahin, tum us ádmí ko pilá dogí ? Huzúr, maĩ to pilá chukí hũ'. Bahin, tum pání bharne játí ho ? Garíb-parwar, Maĩ pání bhar chukí hũ'. Munshí jí, áp ne yih bát sach sach kahí ? Hã', sáhib, maĩ ne yih bát sach sach kahí hai.

Write on the board **Jis ne yih kúã' ham ko diyá**, and substitute new subjects, new direct and indirect objects, one at a time, with the resulting verb changes, until the pupils can do this exercise readily in 30 seconds. It might be put on a chart and reviewed for many weeks.

I		you	a pen
thou		me	1 book
he		thee	3 tables
she		him	4 pencils
we	gave	her	5—10 curtains
you		us	
you polite		the boys.	11—15 doors
they		you polite	boots
the boys		them	chairs
the girls		the men	16—20 coats.

After perfect familiarity is attained with these, add the verb *brought*, **láyá, láí, láe**; then a week or two later add the verb **bhejá**, or **bhej diyá**.

Review the Charts. Practise particularly *Wuh baṛí gáṛí mẽ baiṭhtí thí*, and note the intonation, and the comparative pitch of the last three syllables.

LESSON XII.

XII. When it became known to the Lord that the Pharisees had heard that Jesus was making more disciples than John, and was baptising, then, leaving Judea, he went away to Galilee.

Jab Khudáwand ko ma'lúm húá ki Farísíõ ne suná ki Yisú' Yuhanná se ziyáda shágird kartá aur baptisma detá hai to Yahúdiyá ko chhoṛkar, wuh Galíl ko chalá gayá.

Learn first *Yahudiyá . . . chalá gayá.*

K͟hudáwand kahán thá ? Kh. Yisú' Yahúdiyá men̲ thá. Yahúdiyá ko chhoṛkar kidhar (kahán̲ ko) chalá gayá ? Y. ko chh., wuh Galíl ko chalá gayá.

Now learn **Yisú' Yuhanna se . . . detá hai** (John iv. 1).

Kaun baptisma detá thá ? Yuhanna baptisma detá thá, Aur kaun ? Yisú' ke shágird baptisma dete the. Farísion̲ * ne kyá suná ? Farísion̲ * ne suná ki Yísú' áp baptisma detá thá. Kyá Yisú' áp baptisma detá thá ? Nahín̲ *, wuh áp baptisma nahín̲ detá thá, balki uske shágird dete the. Kaun ziyáda shágird kartá thá, Yisú' yá Yuhanná ? Yisú' ziyáda shágird kartá thá. Farísion̲ ne suná ki Yisú' k͟hud baptisma detá thá, kyá yih bát sach thí ? Nahín̲ yih ġalat bát thí. Yisú' ne áp baptisma na diyá, balki uske shágirdon̲ ne diyá. K͟hudáwand Yisú' ko kyá ma'lúm húá ? Usko ma'lúm húá ki Farísion̲ ne yih ġalat bát suní hai. Yih bát sunkar K͟hudáwand ne kyá kiyá ? Y. b. s. K. ne Y. ko chhoṛá. Yahudiyá ko chhoṛkar wuh kidhar gayá ? Y. ko chh. wuh Galíl ko chalá gayá. Go † Yisú' áp baptisma nahín̲ detá thá, tau bhí ‡ Farísion̲ ne suná kí wuh logon̲ ko baptisma detá hai, is liye wuh Y. ko chhoṛ gayá.

Exercise in Active Past Tense.

Write on individual slips and learn, one at a time, the following, adding a new slip as speed is attained on the preceding.

I gave you the table. (7)	Main̲ ne áp ko mez dí.
They gave me the book. (8)	Unhon̲ ne mujh ko kitáb dí.
He gave them the books. (8)	Us ne unko kitáben̲ dín̲.

---

* A nasalised vowel is usually indicated by a following n̲. It is more correct to write ŏ than on̲, but the latter is commoner.

† Though. ‡ Still, nevertheless.

She gave us two tables. (7)	Usne hamko do mezẽ dĩ'.
You gave him both books. (10)	Áp ne usko dono kitábẽ dĩ'.
We gave her the three handkerchiefs. (10)	Ham ne usko tínon rúmál díe.
The boys gave the girls all four tables. (13)	Laṛkon ne laṛkíon ko cháron mezen dĩ'.
The girls gave the boys this handkerchief. (12)	Laṛkíon ne laṛkon ko yih rúmál díyá.
The women gave the men these handkerchiefs. (13)	'Auraton ne ádmíon ko yih rúmál díe.

Each pupil should be able to give the nine slips in 18 secs. More than 22 secs. cannot be allowed.

Shall I, we, go ? Main jáún * ? Ham jáen ?

May I, we, come ? Main áún ? ham áen ?

May I, we, stay ? Main rahún ? Ham rahen ?

What shall I, we, do ? Main kyá karún ? Ham kyá karen ?

Shall I shut the door ? Main darwáza band karún ?

Shall we draw water ? Ham pání bharen ?

Shall the boy get up ? Kyá wuh laṛká uṭhe ?

Shall I eat dinner now ? Main ab kháná kháún ?

The pupil may now read in the Roman New Testament the familiar verses in John 4.

LESSON XIII.

XIII. And he had to go by way of Samaria. So he came to a city of Samaria, which is called Sychar. This is near the plot of ground that Jacob gave his son Joseph.

Aur usko Sámaría se hokar jáná zarúr thá. Pas wuh

---

* A nasalised vowel is usually indicated by a following n. It is more correct to write õ than on, but the latter is commoner.

Sámaría ke ek shahr tak áyá, jo Sukhár kahlátá hai. Yih us qita' ke nazdík hai jo Ya'qúb ne apne beṭe Yúsuf ko diyá. (41)

Learn to speed, writing first on three slips, then on one.*

By what way did he go? Wuh kis ráste se gayá? Wuh kahán se hokar gayá? Wuh S. se hokar gayá. Wuh us ráh se kyún gayá? Us ráh se jáná zarúr thá. Játe játe kahán tak áyá? J. j. wuh S. ke ek shahr tak áyá. Wuh shahr kyá kahlátá hai? Wuh Sukhár kahlátá hai. Us shahr ká kyá nám thá? Us shahr ká nám Sukhár thá? Sukhár shahr kahán thá? Wuh Sámaría men thá. Hán, S. men thá, magar kis ke nazdík thá? Wuh us qit'a ke nazdík thá, jo Ya'qúb ne apne beṭe Yúsuf ko diyá. Y'aqúb ne kis ko diyá thá? Y'aqúb ne apne beṭe Y. ko diyá thá. Ya'qúb ke kitne beṭe the? Y. ke bárah beṭe the. Kyá uskí koí beṭí thí? Hán, ek beṭí thí.

Us qit'a men kyá thá? Us q. m. ek kúã' thá. Wuh kis ká kúã' kahlátá thá? Wuh Ya'qúb ká kúã' kahlátá thá. Yúsuf ke báp ká kyá nám thá? Y. k. b. k. n. Ya'qúb thá. Shahr ke nazdík kyá thá? S. k. n. ek kúã' thá.

Masíh Yisú' ko kyá zarúr thá? M. Y. ko z. thá ki S. se hokar jáe. Kyá yih zarúr hí thá? Hán, Sámaríá se hokar jáná zarúr thá. Kahán tak áyá? Wuh kúẽ tak áyá. Wahán ákar wuh kahán baiṭhá? Wahán ánkar wuh kúẽ par baiṭh gayá. Jab wuh baiṭhá thá, kaun áí?

Review Ex. in Past Tense bringing up to speed. Count 1–20 in turn, write each no. on the board, and as the teacher points let one pupil ask and another answer to *kitne, kitni*?

* *N.B.* While XI—XII and other slip exercises are being mastered to speed, review I—X.

LESSON XIV.

Exercise in Intransitive Past Tense.

The girl said, I came from the city.	Laṛkí ne kahá ki, maiṉ shahr se áí.
The boy said, I came from the city.	Laṛke ne kahá ki maiṉ shahr se áyá.
The girl said, Mary you came from the city yesterday.	Laṛkí ne kahá, Mariam, tu kal shahr se áí.
The boy said, John you came from the city yesterday.	Laṛke ne kahá, Yuhanná tú kal shahr se áyá.
We (women) came from the city yesterday.	Ham kal shahr se áíṉ.
We (men) came to the city day before yesterday.	Ham parsoṉ shahr meṉ áe.
They (men) came home yesterday.	Wuh kal ghar áe.
They (women) came home day before yesterday.	Wuh parsoṉ ghar ko áíṉ.
Men, did you come home yesterday.	Ai ádmío, kyá tum kal ghar áe ?
My boy came home day before yesterday.	Merá laṛká parsoṉ ghar áyá (á gáyá).
Your girl came the day-before-day-before-yesterday.	Tumhárí laṛkí atarsoṉ áí.
Did you come yesterday or not ?	Kyá áp kal áe ki nahíṉ ?

Review charts. Majors I–X may be laid aside for a week.

LESSON XV.

Accordingly Jesus tired and worn from the journey just sat down on the well, and it was about the sixth hour.

Chunánchí Yisú' safar se thaká mándá hokar yún hí kúẽ par baiṭh gayá, aur yih chhaṭe ghanṭe ke qaríb thá. (32)

Suwál o Jawáb.—Sukhár shahr ke nazdík kyá thá ? S. sh. k. n. ek kúã' thá. Us kúẽ ke pás kaun áyá ? Us k. k. p. Khudáwand Yisú' áyá. Wahán par ánke * us ne kyá kiyá ? W. p. áke wuh baiṭh gayá. Kyún baiṭh gayá ? Wuh thaká thá. Kyún thaká thá ? Wuh safar se thaká thá. Kahán se safar karke áyá thá ? Wuh Yahúdiyá se safar karke áyá thá. Jab baiṭh gayá to kaunsá ghanṭá thá ? Yih chhaṭe ghanṭe ke qaríb thá. Kyá Yisú' akelá † thá ? Hán akelá thá, uske shágird shahr gaye the.

Jab wuh baiṭh gayá to shahr se kaun á gayí ? J. w. b. g. to sh. s. ek Sámarí 'aurat á gaí. 'Aurat ke nazdík ‡ yih ádmí jo kúen par baiṭhá thá kaun thá ? Wuh usko Yahúdí jántí thí. Jab wuh á gayí, to Yisú' ne kyá kahá ? J. w. á. g. t. Y. n. kahá, Mujhe páni pilá. Use Yahúdí jánkar 'aurat ne kyá jawáb diyá ? U. Y. j.' a. n. jawáb diyá, ki tú mujh se páni kyún mángtá hai ?

LESSON XV. B.

Gintí 1-25, ek se lekar pachís tak. Ordinals, pahlá, dúsrá, tísrá, chauthá, pánchwán, chhaṭá, sátwán, áṭhwán, nawán, daswán.

---

* Either *ánke* or *áke*.

† Alone.

‡ Near ; in one's view or opinion.

He went into the city.	Wuh shahr men gayá.
She went into the city.	Wuh shahr men gaí.
We (men) went into the city.	Ham shahr men gaye.
We (women) also went into the city.	Ham bhí * shahr men gaín.
You went into the city (polite).	Áp shahr men gaye.
You went into the city.	Tum shahr men gaye.
I went into the city.	Main shahr men gayá.
Said she, I too went into the city.	Usne kahá, ki main bhí shahr men gaí.
They went into the city.	Wuh shahr me gaye.
They (women) too went into the city.	Wuh bhí * shahr men gayín.

Write on five or ten slips and recite in 11 secs.

Review Charts.

LESSON XV. C.

The Samaritan woman said to him, Thou, being a Jew, why askest water from me a Samaritan woman, for the Jews have no dealings with the Samaritans.

Sámarí' aurat ne us se kahá, Tú Yahúdi hokar mujh Sámari 'aurat se pání kyún mángtá hai ? kyúnki Yahúdí Sámaríon se kisí tarah ká bartáo nahín rakhte. 50)

Teach in breath-groups according to the spacing of the words.

Suwál o Jawáb.—Yih' 'aurat kaun thí ? Wuh Sámarí thí. Yisú' kaun thá ? Wuh Yahúdí thá. Yahúdí Sámaríon ke háth † se pání píte the ? Nahín, nahín píte the. Kyá wuh roṭí Sámarí ke háth se kháte the ? Na wuh roṭí

* *Bhí* in Urdu is not stressed emphatically but slurred over.

† Hand.

kháte the, na pání píte the, na kisí tarah ká bartáo un se rakhte the. Kyá Masíh piyásá tha ? Háṉ wuh piyásá thá. Wuh kyúṉ piyásá thá ? Wuh safar karke Yahúdiá se áyá thá. Yisú' us 'aurat ke háth se pání píná cháhtá thá ? Háṉ, cháhtá thá. Yih 'aurat achchhí thí ? Nahíṉ, wuh achchhí nahíṉ thí. Kyúṉ nahíṉ ? Wuh yúṉ hí ek ádmí ke pás rahtí thí, jo us ká shauhar na thá. Masíh ne us se pání kyúṉ mángá ? Kyúṉki wuh piyásá thá, aur is liye bhí ki wuh us se báteṉ karná cháhtá thá. Naját kaháṉ se hai ? Naját Yahúdíoṉ se hai. Kaun naját detá hai ? Khudáwand Masíh naját detá hai.

Áp kis tarah áe haiṉ ? Tum kal kis tarah Láhaur gaye ? Wuh kis tarah áí hai ? Ham kis tarah jáeṉ ? Áp ne yih kitábeṉ kitne meṉ líṉ ? Maiṉ ne áṭh áṭh áne ko líṉ. Áp ne yih kursí kis tarah se dí ? Maiṉ ne yúṉ hí dí. Yih kis tarah ka ádmí hai. Yih kaise log haiṉ ? Yih bahut achchhe log haiṉ ? Yih kaisá pání hai ? Yih kis tarah kí bát hai ?

Take a clock and ask the time—*Kyá bajá hai?* or *Kitne baje haiṉ?* and practise from time to time, till the pupil can readily answer.

Compare Interrogatives VIII.

Review Charts.

LESSON XVI.

Our fathers worshipped in this mountain and you say that the place where one ought to worship is in Jerusalem.

Hamáre bápdádoṉ ne is paháṛ par parastish kí, aur tum kahte ho ki wuh jagah jaháṉ parastish karní cháhiye Yarúsalem meṉ hai. (40)

Suwál o Jawáb.—Sámarí log parastish kaháṉ karte the ? S. l. us paháṛ par p. k. t. Yahúdí log parastish kaháṉ karte the? Wuh Yarúsalem men p. k. t. Yarúsalem kin logon ká shahr thá? Y. Yahúdíon ká shahr thá. Sukhár kin logon ká shahr thá? S. Sámarí logon k. sh. t. Yahúdí kyá kahte the? Y. k. t. ki Yarúsalem men parastish karní cháhiye. Parastish kahán karní cháhiye? Parastish har jagah karní cháhiye, kyúnki Khudá har jagah hai. Masíhí log girjagharon men, Hindú log mandiron men, Mussalmán log Makka men aur apne apne masjidon men parastish karte hain. Aur sab log apne apne gharon men bhí karte hain.

Pání bharná cháhiye. Kursí láná * cháhiye. Roṭí khāná cháhiye. Yih bát kahná nahín cháhiye. Itne rúpaë dene nahín cháhiye Yih rúpayá dená nahín cháhiye. Yih khará nahín hai. Ham ko pání bharná cháhiye. Tum ko bímár † honá nahín cháhiye. Use yih ṭopí mol lená nahín cháhiye. Áp ko dúdh ‡ píná nahín cháhiye. Yahán mere pás rahná § cháhiye. Chha baje uṭhná cháhiye. Cháhiye ki yih 'aurat apná shauhar buláe.

Review Charts.

LESSON XVII.

Woman, believe me, the hour is coming when you shall worship the father neither on this mountain, nor in Jerusalem.

Ai 'aurat, merí bát ká yaqín kar, ki wuh waqt átá hai ki tum na to is pahár par báp kí parastish karoge, aur na Yarúsalem men. (39)

Suwál o Jawáb.—Kis ne yih bát kahí? Khudáwand Y. M. ne y. b. k. Kis se kahí? Us ne us Sámarí 'aurat se kahí. Wuh 'aurat usko kyá jántí thí? Wuh usko Yahúdí nabí jántí thí. Wuh log Khudá kí parastish kahán karte the?

---

* To bring. † Ill. ‡ Milk. § To stay.

Wuh ek hí jagah karte the. Masíh ne is bát kí bábat kyá kahá ?

Khudá kí parastish kis jagah karní cháhiye ? Kh. k. p. har jagah karní cháhiye. Kis waqt karní cháhiye ? Har waqt k. ch. Pandit jí, áp log Khudá kí parastish kahán karte hain ? Janáb, ham log to mandiron men karte hain Bihishtí, tum log kahán parastish karte ho ? Huzúr, ham to masjidon men karte hain.

Main ne tumhen wuh khet kátne ke liye bhejá.

Us ne barí mihnat kí. Us ne bari minnat kí.

He labored very hard. He implored very hard.

Wuh chhate ghante ke qarib uthá thá.

LESSON XVIII.

You worship you know not what (you perform his worship whom you do not know). We perform his worship, whom we know, for salvation is (out) from the Jews.

Tum jise nahín jánte, us kí parastish karte ho. Ham jise jánte hain, us kí parastish karte hain, kyúnki naját Yahúdíon men se hai. (40)

Suwál o Jawáb.—Yahúdí kis kí parastish karte the ? Y. Khudá kí parastish karte the. Sámarí log kis kí parastish karte the ? S. l. uskí para stish karte the, jise wuh nahín jánte the. Wuh kaun thá ? Wuh Khudá kí aur buton kí bhí parastish karte the. Naját kahán se hai ? N. Yahúdíon men se hai. Kaun naját degá ? Khudá n. degá. Kis ke wasíle * se degá ? Wuh Khudáwand Yisú' Masíh ke wasíle se detá hai. Kis ko degá ? Mángnewále ko degá. Kaun mánge ? Jo koí cháhe mánge aur lewe bhí.

Let the pupil give also the positive forms :—*Main usko jántá hún*, etc.

---

* By whose means ?

Main usko nahín jántá.	Wuh usko nahín jántí.
Áp usko nahín jánte.	Main usko nahín jántí.
Ham usko nahín jánte.	Ham usko nahín jántín.
Wuh usko nahín jánte.	Wuh usko nahín jántín.
Wuh usko nahín jántá.	Áp usko nahín jántín.

Ginti.—10—100, 500, 1000, das, bís, tís, chális, pachás, sáṭh, sattar, assí, nawwe, sau yá saikṛá. Ek sau, pánch sau, das sau, yá hazár.

Review time.

Kyá bajá hai ? or, Kitne baje hain ? Ek bajá hai. Do baje hain, tín baje hain, waġaira, waġaira, etc., etc.

See Interrogs. VIII.

Practise for rhythm, *Uskí parastish karte hain*, and also with particular care for the Urdu quality of the s's, r's, and non-aspirate k's and t's.

LESSON XIX.

But the time is coming, rather is now, that true worshippers shall perform the worship of the Father with spirit and truth, for the Father seeks for himself such worshippers.

Magar wuh waqt átá hai, balki ab hí hai, ki sachche parastár Báp kí parastish rúh aur sachchái se karenge, kyúnki Báp apne líe aise parastár ḍhúnḍhtá hai. (47)

Suwál o Jawáb.—Khudá kyá hai ? Khudá rúh hai. Masíh kyá hai ? Masíh sachchái hai. Khudá apne líe kyá ḍhúnḍhtá hai ? K. a. l. sachche parastár ḍ. hai. Sachche parastár kaun hain ? Sachche p. wuh hain, jo rúh aur sachchái se parastish karte hain. Khudá kí parastish kahán karen ? K. kí p. har jagah karní cháhiye. Parastár kyá hai ? Parastár wuh hai jo Khudá kí parastish kartá hai. Parastish karnewále ko parastár kahte hain. Kis tarah se Khudá kí parastish karní cháhiye? Khudá kí p. rúh se karní cháhiye. Agar koí ádmí sachchái se Khudá ko ḍhúnḍhegá, to wuh usko páegá.

Áp apní kitáb ḍhúnḍhte the. Kyá wuh milí? Nahíṉ. Maiṉ ne use bahuterá ḍhúnḍhá, par wuh na milí. Áp apne líe kyá karte haiṉ? Maiṉ apne líe kám kartá húṉ. Masíh Sámaría meṉ apne líe kyá ḍhunḍhtá thá? Wuh apní bátoṉ ke líe jagah ḍhúnḍhtá thá. Kyá koí jagah milí? Háṉ, wuh log achche nikle.

Maiṉ áj shahr jáúngá. Yuhanná abhí gayá. 'Aurat abhí kúẽ ko jáegí. Ham parsoṉ shahr meṉ jáeṉge. Áp chauthe roz na jáeṉge? Nahíṉ parsoṉ tísrá roz hai. Ham parsoṉ hí jáeṉge. Zarúr jáeṉge. Wuh abhí jáeṉge.

Maiṉ uskí bát ká yaqín nahíṉ kartá.	Áp unkí bát ká yaqíṉ nahíṉ karte.
Wuh merí bát ká yaqín nahíṉ kartá.	Wuh tumhárí bát ká yaqín nahíṉ kartí.
Ham is bát ká yaqín nahíṉ karte.	Laṛkíáṉ merí bát ká yaqín nahíṉ kartíṉ.

Ginti—1 $1\frac{1}{4}$ $1\frac{1}{2}$ $1\frac{3}{4}$ 2 $2\frac{1}{4}$ $2\frac{1}{2}$ $2\frac{3}{4}$ 3 $3\frac{1}{4}$ $3\frac{1}{2}$ $3\frac{3}{4}$ 4 $4\frac{1}{4}$ $4\frac{1}{2}$ $4\frac{3}{4}$ 5 $5\frac{1}{4}$ $5\frac{1}{2}$ $5\frac{3}{4}$ 6 $6\frac{1}{4}$ $6\frac{1}{2}$ $6\frac{3}{4}$ 7 $7\frac{1}{4}$ $7\frac{1}{2}$ $7\frac{3}{4}$ 8 $8\frac{1}{4}$ $8\frac{1}{2}$ $8\frac{3}{4}$ 9 $9\frac{1}{4}$ $9\frac{1}{2}$ $9\frac{3}{4}$ 10 $10\frac{1}{4}$ $10\frac{1}{2}$ $10\frac{3}{4}$ 11 $11\frac{1}{4}$ $11\frac{1}{2}$ $11\frac{3}{4}$ 12 $12\frac{1}{4}$ $12\frac{1}{2}$ $12\frac{3}{4}$ $\frac{1}{4}$ $\frac{1}{2}$ $\frac{3}{4}$. Cf. Interrogs. VIII.

Have pupil omit the negative and give it.

Sachchã, sachche, sachchí sachchái. Ḍhúnḍhná, ḍhúnḍhá, ḍhúnḍhtá, ḍhúnḍhtí, ḍhúnḍhte.

LESSON XX.

The woman said, I know that Messiah who is called Christ is coming—When he will come, he will tell us all things. I who speak unto thee am he.

'Aurat ne kahá, Maiṉ jántí húṉ ki Masíh jo Kristus kahlátá hai ánewálá hai—jab wuh áegá to wuh hame<u>n</u> sab báte<u>n</u> batá degá. Mai<u>n</u> jo tujh se bol rahá hú<u>n</u> wuhí hú<u>n</u>. (51)

Suwál o Jawáb.—Masíh ke áne kí bábat Yahúdí kyá kahte the? Wuh kahte the ki Masíh ánewálá hai aur ánkar (ákar) naját degá. Sámaríon ko bhí is bát ká yaqín thá? Ha<u>n</u> wuh bhí is bát ko jánte the. Masíh ákar kyá karegá? Masíh ákar sab báte<u>n</u> batá degá. Is bát ke kahne par Masíh ne kyá kahá? Is par Masíh ne kahá, Mai<u>n</u> jo tujh se báte<u>n</u> kar rahá hú<u>n</u> wuhí hú<u>n</u>. 'Aurat ko yaqín áyá ki Yisú' wuh Masíh hai? Há<u>n</u> yaqín áyá. Yahúdí us ánewále nabí ko kyá kahte the? Wuh usko Masíh kahte the. Yúnání * usko kyá kahte the? Yúnání usko Kristus kahte the.

a. Wuh bol rahá hai. Wuh kám kar rahí hai. Ham pání bhar rahe hai<u>n</u>. Wuh roṭí khá rahe hai<u>n</u>. Wuh báte<u>n</u> kar rahí hai. Áp kyá kar rahe hai<u>n</u>? Ham ge<u>n</u>d † ḍhú<u>n</u>ḍh rahe hai<u>n</u>. Tum kyá kar rahe ho? Main ek 'aurat se báte<u>n</u> kar rahá hú<u>n</u>. Ham shahr me<u>n</u> já rahí hai<u>n</u>. Mai<u>n</u> is ádmí ko pání pilá rahí hú<u>n</u>.

b. Practise all hours of the clock by quarters.

Review Charts.—Practise the above verse with special reference to the dental t's.

N.B.—Review I—X again. Periodically lay by, and periodically review, all familiar material until it cannot be forgotten.

LESSON XXI.

In the meantime his disciples came and began to wonder that he is talking with a woman, still any one did not say anything regarding the matter.

Itne me<u>n</u> us ke shágird á gaye aur ta'ajjub karne lage ki

---

* Greeks. † Ball.

wuh 'aurat se báten kar rahá hai, táham kisí ne is bát ke báre men kuchh nahín kahá. (45)

Suwál o Jawáb.—Us ke shágird kahán gaye the? Wuh shahr men gaye the. Kis líe gaye the? Wuh khání mol lene gaye the. Jab Yisú' 'aurat se báten kar rahá thá to kyá húá? Jab Yisú' 'aurat se báten kar rahá thá uske shágird áe. Jab áe, to unko kyá ma'lúm huá? Unhen ma'lum ho gayá ki Yisú' Sámarí 'aurat se bát chít kar rahá hai. Kyá karne lage? Unhon ne ta'ajjub kiyá. Is bát ke báre men kisí ne kuchh kahá? Kuchh nahín. Kisí ko itní jur'at * thí? Kitná pání cháhiye? Itná bas hai.

'Auraten pání bhar rahí hain. Do tín larke hamárí taraf á rahe hain. Ek larkí bhí shahr kí taraf se á rahí hai. Áp ká larká hamárí taraf dekh rahá hai. Mán apne bachche ko dúdh pilá rahí hai. Ustád larkon se suwál kar rahá hai. Larke jawáb de rahe hain. Larkíán qalam se likh rahí hain. Ek na ek din sab log Khudá kí parastish karenge. Qulí log mujh se ziyáda paise máng rahe the, aur main ne sab ko thorá thorá diyá. Take *dálná*, *nikálná*, *jáná*, *bharná*, *lená*, *dená*, *kháná*, *kahná*, *píná*, *baithná*, *banná*, and form the continuative present tense of each according to this model, using different subjects, pronouns and nouns.

Repeat the above verse with particular attention to the quality of the trilled r's, and to the final vowels.

LESSON XXII.

So the woman left her water-jar and went into the city and began to say to the people, Come see a man who told me all my deeds. Is it possible that this is Messiah?

Pas 'aurat apná ghará chhorkar shahr men chalí gayí aur

* Temerity.

logon se kahne lagí. Áo ek ádmí ko dekho jis ne mere sab kám mujhe batá diye. Kyá mumkin hai ki Masíh yihí hai? (53)

Suwál o Jawáb.—Shahr se kaun á gaye? Shágird shahr se áe. Jab wuh áe, to 'aurat ne kyá kiyá? Jab áe, 'aurat ne apná ghára chhorá aur shahr men chalí gayí. Wahán jákar kyá kiyá? Wahán logon se kahne lagí, Áo, *wagaira*. Yih 'aurat Yisú' ko kyá kahtí thí? Wuh usko Masíh kahtí thí. Yih 'aurat shahr men kyá kar rahí hai? Wuh shahr men logon se bát kah rahí hai ki áo aur dekho. Wuh kis bát se usko Masíh jántí thí? Usne 'aurat ko us ko sáre kam dikháe, is líe wuh usko Masíh jántí thí.

Áo, do ádmíon ko dekho, jinhon ne apne sab kám mujhe batá diye. Áo, tín 'auraton ko dekho jinhon ne hamáre sab kám ham ko batáe hain. Áo, sát larkíon ko dekho jo kúẽ par baithí hain. In logon ko dekho jo shahr se áe hain. Is Sámarí 'aurat ko dekho, jis ne logon ko buláyá thá. Áo, in Sámaríon ko dekho jo shahr kí taraf se á rahe hain. Áiye, is nabí ko dekhiye jo kúẽ par baithá thá. Un Shágirdon ko dekho jo kháná mol lene ko gaye the. Áo, un ádmíon ko dekho jinhon ne kháná mol liyá thá.

Review the Charts.—Watch the rhythm of the above verse.

LESSON XXIII.

They went out of the city and began to come to him. Meantime (in this much [time]) his disciples began to beg him, Sir, eat something, but he said to them, I have for eating such food as which you do not know.

Wuh shahr se nikalkar uske pás áne lage. Itne men uske shágird us se yih darkhwást karne lage, ki Ai Rabbí, kuchh khá le, lekin usne un se kahá, Mere pás kháne ke liye aisá kháná hai jise tum nahín jánte. (63)

Suwál o Jawáb.—Shahr men kaun gayí? Logon se kyá kahne lagí? Shahr se kaun nikle? Log shahr se nikle. Wuh kidhar jáne lage? Wuh Masíh ke pás jáne lage. Us waqt Masíh kahán thá? U. w. M. kúẽ ke pás thá. Us ke sáth kaun the? Uske shágírd uske sáth the. Itne men wuh kyá darkhwást karne lage? Unhon ne yih darkhwást kí, ki Rabbí kuchh khá le. Masíh ká kyá jawáb thá? Masíh yih jawáb dene lagá, Mere pás kháne ke liye hai. Kaisá khánά uske pás thá? Usne kahá, ki aisá khánά hai jise tum nahín jánte.

Wuh roṭí kháne lagí. Laṛká dúdh píne lagá. Itne men ádmí shahr se áne lage. Masíh kúẽ ke pás 'aurat se báten karne lagá. Wuh ham ko dene lage. Wuh gend ḍhúnḍhne lagín. Jis waqt wuh ham ko dekhtá hai wuh ham se paise mángne lagtá hai. Mán ko dekhkar bachcha rone lagtá hai. Laṛke bárah bajne par áne lagenge.

Synopsis of *karná.*—Karke, karo, main kartá hún, main kartá thá, main ne kiyá, main ne kiyá hai, main ne kiyá thá, karún, karúnga. So with *ḍálná, chhoṛná, dená, lená.*

Rabbí, dabbi, batti, bachcha, bachá, kachchá. Báġ, bág bhág. Review previous words.

LESSON XXIV.

So the disciples said among themselves, Has any one brought him something to eat? Jesus said to them, My food is this, that I do works according to the will of my sender and fulfil his work.

Pas shágirdon ne ápas men kahá, Kyá koí uske kháne ke liye kuchh láyá hái? Yisú' ne un se kahá, Merá khánά yih hai ki apne bhejnewále kí marzí ke muwáfiq 'amal karún aur us ká kám púrá karún. (48)

Suwál o Jawáb.—Masíh ke na kháne ke sabab se shágirdon ne ápas men kyá kahá? Uske na kháne se unhon ne ápas men kahá, Kyá koí uske pás kuchh kháne ko láyá hai? Masíh ká kháná kyá thá? Khúdá kí marzí púrí kární. Kis ne Masíh ko bhejá? Khudá ne. Kis liye bhejá? Is liye ki wuh Khudá kí marzí ke muwáfiq 'amal kare. Bhejnewálá kaun hai? Bhejnewálá Khudá hai. Bhejá húá kaun hai? Masíh bhejá húá hai. Khudá kí marzí kyá hai? Khudá kí yih marzí hai ki Masíh naját ká bandobast (arrangement) púrá kare. Naját ke bandobast ke liye kyá zarúr thá? Yih zarúr thá ki Masíh markar zinda hojáe (dying become alive).

Mistrí, aisí kursí lení cháhiye? Huzúr kí marzí; yih kursí achchhí hai. Achchhí bát, yihí de do. Is ke muwáfiq do aur lá do. Kaun kháná láyá thá? Main kháná láyá thá. Kis ne kháná kháyá? Áp ke larke ne kháná kháyá. Us ne kab kháyá? Us ne chha baje se pahle kháyá thá. Larke ke líe kaun roṭí láyá? Us kí mán láí. Un larkon ke líe kaun láyá? Un kí bahinen láín. Un ádmíon ke líe kaun kaun roṭí láí hai? Un kí larkíán apne apne báp ke líe láí hain.

Ágá Khán, Gází Khán, Bág, kágaz, bálig.

LESSON XXV.

Do you not say, In the coming of harvest there are left four months? Behold I say unto you, Lift up your eyes and look on the fields that the harvest is ripe.

Kyá tum kahte nahín ki fasl ke áne men chár mahíne báqí hain? Dekho, main tum se kahtá hún ki apní ánkhen uṭhákar kheton par nazar karo ki fasl pak gayí hai. (50)

Suwál o Jawáb.—Fasl ke áne kí bábat log kyá kahte the? Log kahte the ki fasl ke áne men chár mahíne báqí hain. Masíh ne fasl ke báre men kyá kahá? Us ne kahá, ki fasl pak gayí hai. Áṉkheṉ uṭhákar kyá dekhná cháhiye thá? Khetoṉ ko dekhná cháhiye thá. Khetoṉ ke kyá ma'ní (meaning) haiṉ? Kyá khet ke ma'ne yaháṉ zamín ke khet, yá ádmíoṉ ke khet haiṉ? Yaháṉ khetoṉ ke ma'ní log haiṉ. Jab Masíh ne kahá ki fasl pak gayí hai, us ká kyá matlab thá? Uská yih matlab thá ki Sámarí log Khudá par ímán láne ko taiyár haiṉ.

Dekho ji, bárah bajne meṉ kítní miniṭ báqí haiṉ? Janáb, das pandrah miniṭ báqí haiṉ. Is kitáb par nazar (karo) kijiye ki kaisí hai. Us ádmí ko dekho ki kyá kar rahá hai. Garíb-parwar, wuh fasl ko káṭ rahá hai Roṭí pak gayí hai? Huzúr, pak gayí. Tum mujhe kyá kahte the? Maiṉ áp se yih kah rahá thá ki Áp ke khetoṉ meṉ fasl bahut achchhí hai. Háṉ, ṭhík hai, aur tumháre khetoṉ meṉ bhí. Háṉ janáb, ab kí daf'a * sabhoṉ kí fasl baṛí achchhí hai.

Ápní kitáb uṭhákar mez par rakkho. Janáb, maiṉ apní kitáb uṭhákar mez par rakhtá húṉ. Ab phir uṭhákar kursí par rakkho—farsh par; khiṛkí, darwáze, Sáhib ke pás, waġaira, waġaira.

Chár bajne meṉ kitní miniṭ báqí haiṉ? Chár bajne meṉ 1–30 miniṭ báqí haiṉ. Cháhiye ki ustád yih suwálát bahut daf'a púchhe.

Apní áṉkheṉ uṭhákar khetoṉ par nazar karo. Particular attention to pronunciation and rhythm.

LESSON XXVI.

The reaper receives wages and gathers fruit for eternal life, that the sower and the reaper both together may rejoice, for on this occasion the proverb is correct that one

---

* Time, occasion, times.

sows another reaps (the sower is another the reaper another).

Káṭnewálá mazdúrí pátá, aur hamesha kí zindagí ke líe phal jam'a kartá hai, táki bonewálá aur káṭnewálá, dono milkar, khushí karen. Kyúnki is par yih masal ṭhík átí hai ki bonewálá aur hai, káṭnewálá aur. (53)

Suwál o Jawáb.—Káṭnewálá kaun hai? Káṭnewálá wuh ádmí hai jo ki fasl ko káṭtá hai. Mazdúrí ke kyá ma'ní hain? Wuh dám jo kám karne ke líe milte hain, mazdúrí kahláte hain. Mazdúr kaun hai? Mazdúr wuh ádmí hai jo paise ke líe kám kartá hai. Kyá yahán is bát men Masíh ke yihí ma'ní hain? Yahán to nahín. Yahán us ke matlab men bonewálá wuh hai jo logon ko Khudá ki báten batáe, aur káṭnewálá wuh hai jo logon ko ímán dilákar Khudá ke pás láwe. Phal ká kyá matlab hai? Phal wuh log hain jo ímán láte hain. Fasl ke waqt kaun khushí karte hain? Bonewálá aur káṭnewálá dono milkar khushí karte hain. Mazdúr kyá pátá hai? Mazdúr mazdúrī pátá hai. Bonewálá aur káṭnewálá ek hí ádmí hain? Nahín, bonewálá aur hai, káṭnewálá aur. Yih kis kí masal thí? Yih Yahúdíon kí masal thí, aur is mauo'e * par yih masal ṭhík átí hai.

Yih dekhnewále kaun hain? Wuh Lahaur ke rahnewále hain. Bolnewále áp hain, aur sunnewálá main hún. 'Aurat bolí, ki main gawahí denewálí thí. Áp ke gáon kí 'auraten kidhar já rahí hain? Wuh Dihlí ko jánewálí hain. Larke mele men jánewále hain. Yih gáonwále shahr men já rahe hain. Is kí gharwálí bahut achchhí 'aurat hai.

Gintí.—Count to 20 by quarters, until the figures can be read as quickly as in English.

Wuh baiṭhtá thá. Wuh káṭṭí thí, wuh kátti thí, us ne káṭí thí, us ne kátí thí.

LESSON XXVII.

I sent you to reap that field on which you have performed no labour. Others did the labour and you became partners in the fruit of their labour.

Main̲ ne tumhen̲ wuh khet káṭne ke líe bhejá jis par tum ne mihnat nahín̲ kí, auron̲ ne mihnat kí, aur tum unkí mihnat ke phal men̲ sharík húe. (41)

Suwál o Jawáb.—Khet kyá hai ? Khet wuh zamín hai jahán̲ bíj * boyá jáe. Yahán̲ khet ká matlab (meaning, intention) ádmí hai yá zamín hai ? Yahán̲ khet ká matlab zamín nahín̲, balki ádmí hai. Káṭne se kyá murád † hai ? Káṭne se murád hai ki ádmíon̲ ko Masíh kí k̲habar dekar us ke pás láná. Mihnat se kyá murád hai ? Ádmíon̲ ko K̲hudá kí báten̲ kahná, yá Masíh kí k̲habar sunání mihnat se yih murád hai. Is khet par kis ne mihnat kí ? Is khet par, Masíh ne kahá, auron̲ ne mihnat kí. Wuh aur kaun the ? Wuh nabí the. Wuhí bonewále the. Unkí mihnat ke phal men̲ kaun sharík húe ? Masíh ke shágird unkí mihnat ke phal men̲ sharík húe.

Main̲ shahr kí taraf já rahá thá—rahí thí.	Ham shahr kí taraf já rahe the—rahí thín̲.
Tú shahr kí taraf já rahá thá—rahí thí.	Tum shahr kí taraf já rahe the—rahí thín̲.
Wuh shahr kí taraf já rahá thá—rahí thí.	Áp shahr kí taraf já rahe the—rahí thín̲.
Áp shahr kí taraf já rahe the—rahí thín̲.	Wuh shahr kí taraf já rahe the—rahí thín̲.

Kí taraf, toward, in the direction of. Write out the English of these on 16 slips, and repeat to speed.

Form similar sentences with subjects *Laṛká, laṛkí, láṛke,*

---

* Seed. † Intent, purpose.

laṛkíán, *'auraten*, *mán*, and others, using the verbs *kahná*, *jáná*, *áná*, *láná*, *karná*, *bolná*, *batáná*, *kháná*, waġaira, in both Present and Imperfect.

Deke, dekkhe, dekhe. Us ne us garíbo ko dekkhe, aur use rupaia deke us kí khushí dekhí. Wuh gore á rahe hain. Wuh ghoṛe á rahe hain.

N.B.—He who can pronounce the verses of this lesson rapidly and well can not fail on many Urdu sentences.

LESSON XXVIII.

And many of the Samaritans believed on Christ because of the woman's saying, and coming to him they began to make request, Stay with us. Accordingly he remained there two days.

Aur bahut se Sámarí us 'aurat ke kahne se Masíh par ímán láe aur uske pás ákar kahne lage, Hamáre pás raho. Chunánchi wuh do roz wahán rahá. (45)

Suwál o Jawáb.—'Aurat kidhar gayí? Kyá kahne lagí? Uske kahne se kyá natíja (result) húá? Uske kahne se bahut se Sámarí log Masíh par ímán láe. Jab Sámarí log ímán láe to kyá karne lage? Wuh Masíh ke pás jákar darkhwást karne lage. Unhon ne kyá darkhwást kí? Un kí yih darkhwást thí, kí hamáre pás rah. Wuh kitne roz unke pás rahá? Wuh do din rahá. Wahán rahkar Masíh ne kyá kiyá? Us ne logon se Khudá kí bahut báten kahín.

Yisú' ne yih bát apne shágirdon se kahí. Shágirdon ne apne ustád se kahá. Shágird apne ustád se baṛá nahín. 'Aurat ne apná ghaṛá chhoṛá. Main apne bhejnewále kí marzí púrí karne áyá hún. Ham ne yih bát apne bápdádon se suní. Ya'qúb ne apne beṭe Yúsuf ko diyá. Main apná pinsil tum ko dúngá. Tum ne apní ṭopí kis ko dí?

Laṛke apní kitábeṉ áp ko deṉge. Laṛkí apní kitáb áp ke bhái ke líe láegí. Laṛko, apní apní kitáb band karo. Ham apná apná kám kar rahe haiṉ. Tum log apná apná karo.

Do, dho, ḍho. Review Charts.

LESSON XXIX.

On account of his word many others also believed on him and began to say to the woman, Now we believe not merely from thy telling, for we have heard him ourselves and we know that this is indeed the Saviour of the world.

Uske kalám ke sabab aur bhí bahutere ímán láe aur 'aurat se kahne lage, Ab ham tere hí kahne se ímán nahíṉ láte, kyúṉki ham ne k͟hud sun liyá aur jánte haiṉ ki yih f'ilhaqíqat dunyá ká munjí (naját denewálá) hai. (62)

Suwál o Jawáb.—Waháṉ rahkar Masíh ne kyá kiyá? Waháṉ rahkar us ne logoṉ se kalám kiyá. Kalám karne se kyá húá? Kalám karne se yih natíja húá ki aur bhí bahutere ádmí ímán láe. Ímán lákar log kyá kahne lage? Log kahne lage ki ab ham apne sunne se ímán láe haiṉ, kisí ke kahne se nahíṉ. Logoṉ ne 'aurat se kyá kahá? Unhoṉ ne kahá, ki sirf tere kahne se nahíṉ balki us kí sunne se hameṉ yaqín hai. Kis sabab se log ímán láe? 'Aurat ke kahne ke sabab aur Masíh kí bát sunne ke sabab se ímán láe. Ímán kis tarah se átá hai? Ímán K͟hudá ke kalám ko sunne se átá hai. Wuh log sunne se kyá jánte the? Wuh sunne se jánte the ki Masíh dunyá ká munjí hai. Munjí kyá hai? Naját denewále ko munjí kahte haiṉ; ya'ne munjí ke ma'ne naját denewálá hai.

Kitne ádmí 'aurat ke kahne se ímán láe? Masíh ke sunne se kitne? Masíh kitne din rahá?

Other exercises with *kitná, cf.* Interrog. IX.

Ginti.—Ek se lekar chális tak, 1–40.

She, he, they, I, you, we, both genders, started to go, come, say, send, bring, speak, tell, call, draw, eat, drink, give, take.

Sát, sáth, sáṭh. Review Charts.

LESSON XXX.

After two days Christ started from there and went to Galilee, for he himself gave testimony that a prophet gets no honour in his own country.

Do dinon̲ ke ba'd Masíh wahán̲ se rawána hokar Galíl ko gayá, kyúnki us ne k̲h̲ud gawáhí dí ki nabí apne watan men̲ 'izzat nahín̲ pátá. (43)

Suwál o Jawáb.—Masíh aur uske shágird kitne din wahán̲ rahe ? Masíh apne shágirdon̲ ke sáth wahán̲ do din rahá. Do roz ke ba'd kyá kiyá ? Wuh do din ke ba'd rawána húá. Kidhar gayá ? Galíl ko chalá gayá. Kyá hai jo nabí apne watan men̲ nahín̲ pátá ? Nabí apne mulk men̲ 'izzat nahín̲ pátá. Kis ne yih bát kahí ? Masíh ne is bát kí gawáhí dí. Masíh ká mulk kaunsá thá ? Uská watan Yahúdiyá thá. Nabí kis ko kahte hain̲. Nabí usko kahte hain̲ jo K̲h̲udá ká kalám logon̲ ko sunáe.

Main̲ das miniṭ ke ba'd áún̲gá. Sáhib pandrah miniṭ ke ba'd áen̲ge. Gáṛí das bajne ke bárah miniṭ ba'd áegí. Fasl chár mahíne ke ba'd pak jáegí. Khána kitní der ba'd taiyár hogá ? Koí das pandrah miniṭ ba'd, janáb.

Wuh Galíl ko gayá. Usne gawáhí dí. 'Aurat shahr men̲ gayí. 'Aurat ne yihí gawáhí dí. Shágird gáon̲ men̲ gaye. Shágirdon̲ ne kalám kiyá. Laṛká kál rawána húá. Laṛke ne us ká kalám suná.

K̲h̲ud, 'izzat, kí, ke, ki, laṛkí gáí, laṛke gaye. Practise Homonymic Sentences.

LESSON XXXI.

So when he came to Galilee, the Galileans received him, for as many works as he had done in Jerusalem at the time of the feast, they had seen them, for they too had gone to the feast.

Pas jab wuh Galíl men̲ áyá to Galílíon̲ ne us ko qabúl kiyá, is líe ki jitne kám us ne Yarúsalem men̲ 'íd ke waqt kiye the, unhon̲ ne un ko dekhá thá, kyún̲ki wuh bhí 'íd men̲ gaye the. (58)

Suwál o Jawáb.—Masíh Sámaria ko chhoṛke kahán̲ áyá ? Masíh Samária ko chhoṛke Galíl men̲ áyá. Kin logon̲ ne use qabúl kiyá ? Galíl ke logon̲ ne us ko qabúl kiyá. Kis sabab se use qabúl kiyá ? Is sabab se ki wuh log bhí 'íd men̲ gaye the. Wuh 'íd karne ko kahán̲ játe the ? Yarúsalem men̲ 'íd karte the. Wahán̲ unhon̲ ne kyá kyá dekhá ? Unhon̲ ne wahán̲ Masíh ke kám dekhe. Kitne kám dekhe ? Jitne kám us ne kiye the unhon̲ ne sab ko dekhá. Dekhne se kyá natíja * húá ? Yih natíja húá ki unhon̲ ne Masíh ko qabúl kiyá.

Us ne yih kám kiyá. Unhon̲ ne baṛá kám kiyá. Us ne baṛe baṛe kám kiye. In ádmíon̲ ne kitná kám kiyá ? Un laṛkon̲ ne kaisá kám kiyá ? In laṛkíon̲ ne achchhá kám kiyá. Kis ne yih bát kí ? Kinhon̲ ne yih báten̲ kín̲ ? Sabhon̲ ne yih kám kiyá.

Ginti.—Ek se lekar pachás tak, 1–50.

Qabúl, waqt, faqír. Gayí, gayín̲, gaye, gayá, gáe, gáen̲.

Wuh gayí thí. Wuh gayí thín̲. Wuh gae the. Wuh gáe thí. Wuh gáen̲ thín̲.

N.B.—The lessons up to this point should require all the students' time for four to six weeks, and then the student

---

* Result.

should be able to tell the story, or to ask and answer any sort of textual question without the book. He should read thus far, Jno. iv. 1–45, readily in Roman and he may begin now to read this in character.

In the following lessons, use a map and any pictures that are available to give vividness to the work. Let the teacher first tell the story off hand, though he will of course make his previous preparation, introducing the new words and explaining them. Then he will read the text, the pupils listening, as they follow on their books. The next day he will ask the indicated and other questions from the pupils. Pupils should compare the English version to note how the same idea is differently rendered into the two languages, and to get the idiomatic equivalents. Previous work should be kept under constant review as hereinafter indicated. No construction should remain unfamiliar to the pupil. Each must have a ready mastery of every construction.

Pupils should regularly be required, with open English text, to ask questions on every incident.

LESSON XXXII.

John iv. 46–54.

The pupil will be able to answer, without the Urdu book, the following questions :—

Kis ne pání ko mai banáyá ? Kahán̲ banáyá thá ? Kafarnahúm men̲ kaun rahtá thá ? Wahán̲ kaun bímár thá ? Mulázim ne kyá suná ? Yih k̲h̲abar sunkar usne kyá kiyá ? Yisú' ke pás jákar kyá dark̲h̲wást kí ? Yisú' ne kyá jawáb diyá ? Kyá mulázim ne apní dark̲h̲wást ko chhoṛ diyá ? Phir kyá kahá ? Us ke beṭe kí kyá hálat thí ? Uskí dark̲h̲wást ('arz) dobára sunkar Masíh ne kyá kahá ? Mulázim ne is par kyá kiyá ? Kidhar ko rawána húá? Us ke naukar use kahán mile? Unhon ne kyá khabar dí? Báp ne kyá suwál kiyá? Naukaron ne kyá jawáb diyá? Is se báp kyá ján gae? Mu lázim ke gharáne ne is mu'jize ke sabab kyá kiyá? Qáná men Masíh ká pahlá mu'jiza kyá thá? Dúsrá kyá?

Let the pupils write and hand in the Urdu of the following, and then let the same be gone over rapidly in class until all have it at command.

This is the well, place, city, house, room, where I first saw him, the boy, girl, man, woman, boys, men, women, girls—at least nine sentences.

In the following sentences, substitute, one at a time, the alternate words and phrases as indicated by the capital letters.

Yih wuh (A) hai jis, jin, ká, ke, kí, (B) bímár thá.

A. shakhs, mulázim, naukar, bádsháh, ádmí, 'aurat, sing. and pl.

B. beṭí, laṛkí, laṛke, laṛkíán, bachcha, báp, mán, bachche, 'aurat, 'auraten, ghoṛá, ghoṛíán.

Stay here until, etc. Yahín raho jab tak... na... tap utre, bachche ko árám ho, sárá gharáná ímán láe, sáhib paise bakhshe, use mile, mu'jiza dikháe, koí baṛá nishán dekho, bímár ho, tum se púchh le.

Dictation in Roman Urdu should be regularly practised now, and the marking of all vowels and consonants required. Do it at the blackboard, if possible.

New words may now be frequently reviewed backwards and forwards from English to Urdu and vice versa, as well as requiring their use in sentences.

Let the pupils count in turn first, second, third, fourth, fifth—tenth, in the form *pahlá*, later *pahlí*, then *pahle.*

Pahlá, dúsrá, tísrá, chauthá, panchwán, chhaṭá, sátwán, áṭhwán, nauwán daswán.

LESSON XXXIII.

John ix. 1–12.

Suwálát.—Masíh kahán játá thá? Játe men us ne kis ko dekhá? Masíh ke sáth kaun the? Us ke Shágirdon ne kyá kahá? Masíh ne kyá jawáb diyá? Wuh ádmí kis líe andhá paidá húá? Masíh ko kis ne bhejá? Masíh ko kyá zarúr thá? Din men log kyá karte hain? Rát ko kyá karte hain? Dunyá ká núr kaun hai? Masíh ne zamín par kyá kiyá? Phir us ne thúk se kyá kiyá? Andhe kí ánkhon par kyá lagáí? Miṭṭí lagákar kyá kahá? Shilokh ká tarjuma kyá hai? Jab andhe ne dhoyá, to kyá húá? or, Andhe ne jo dhoyá to kyá húá? Kis kis ne us ko dekhá? Yih ádmí jo andhá thá pahle kyá karta thá? Use bíná dekhkar ba'z ne kyá kahá? Ba'z ne kyá? Us ne kyá kahá? Logon ne kyá suwál kiyá? Us ká jawáb kyá thá? Jab log púchhte the ki wuh kahán hai, to us ne kyá jawáb diyá?

N.B.—Pupils will be able with the English version to ask these and all succeeding questions and to answer them with or without such assistance.

Ginti.—Ek se lekar sáṭh tak, 1–60, bárí bárí gino.

Customary action.—Wuh bhíkh mángá kartá hai. Wuh bhíkh mángtá hai. Us ne bhíkh mángí. Us ne qalam mángá. Wuh andhá haikal ke pas baiṭhke bhíkh mángá kartá thá. Yih 'aurat kúë se pání bhará kartí thí. Munshí ṭhík ṭhík kahá kartá hai. Laṛká yihí jawáb diyá kartá hai. Apne báp se púchhá karo. Yih ádmí achchhá kám kiyá kartá hai. Aisí aisí kháne kí chízen hamáre pás bhejá karo. Yahán kyún áyá karte ho? Yih dhobí áp ke kapṛe dhoyá karegá. Form similar sentences with *jáná* (irregular *jáyá*), *ḍálná*, *kháná*, *píná*, *dekhná*, *lená*, *uṭhná*, *banáná*.

Bhejá húá. Yih bhará húá ghaṛá le jáo. Yih dhoe húe kapṛe kis ke hain? Main ne usko kúẽ par baiṭhá húá dekhá.

Let the pupil copy out all examples in vss. 1–12 of subjects with *ne*, with their verbs and their objects, and deduce the rule of this tense. Seventeen examples.

Review briefly Chapter IV.

No further regular references, but daily practice of pronunciation exercises.

LESSON XXXIV.

John ix. 13–23.

Suwálát.—Log us shakhs ko kahán le gaye? Farísíon ne kyá púchhá? Us shakhs ne kyá jawáb diyá? Wuh kaunsá din thá ki jis men wuh bíná húá? Is wáste ba'z Farísí kyá kahte the? Aur ba'z ba'z ne kyá kahá? Pas un men kyá húá? Yih shakhs Masíh ke haqq men kyá kahtá thá? Kyá Farísíon ko yaqín áyá ki yih pahle andhá thá? Is sabab se unhon ne kis kis ko buláyá? Kyá kyá suwál púchhe? Uske mán báp ne kyá jawáb diyá? Wuh kin se ḍarté the? Kis wáste ḍarte the? Kahán se khárij kiyá jáegá? Yih shakhs chhoṭá thá yá baṛá? Yahúdíon ne kyá eká kiyá thá?

Note the forms *píná*, to drink, *piláná* to give another drink; *dekhná* to see, *dikháná*, to make one see, show; *khulná*, to come open, *kholná*, to make open; *banná*, to be made, *banáná*, to make; *nikalná*, to go out, *nikálná*, to put out or take out; *uṭhná*, to rise, *uṭháná*, to raise, lift up; *pakná*, to become ripe or to cook (intransitive); *pakáná* to cook (transitive); *kahná*, to say, *kahláná*, to make or cause or have another say. Use these forms in appropriate sentences in various tenses. Use also the forms for customary action and with *chukná* and *sakná*. See below.

Vss. 4, 16, end, *nahín kar saktá, dikhá saktá hai*, both in present tense, though the former has no hai, apparently. Really the hai is in the nahín, so that ordinarily hai is omitted when nahín occurs. *Us ne nahín diyá*, He has not given; *Us ne diyá hai*, He has given; *Us ne na diyá*, He did not give; *Us ne diyá*, He gave.

Express ability, with **sakná**, in present tense, using **áná, jáná, karná, kháná, púchhná, baiṭhná**, waġaira.

Use the same forms with **kyúnkar** and **kis tarah**.

LESSON XXXV.

John ix. 24-41.

Suwálát.—Farísí us shakhs ko dobára bulákar kyá kahne lage? Wuh Masíh ke haqq men kyá kahte the? Wuh shakhs kyá kahne lagá? Sibára unhon ne kyá suwál kiyá? Us ne is tísre suwál par kyá kahá? Unhon ne use burá bhalá kis wáste kahá? Farísí kis ke shágird the? Kyún kahte the, ki Ham Músá ke shágird hain? Unhon ne Masíh ke haqq men phir kyá kahá? Us ádmí ke nazdík ánkhon ke kholne se kyá ma'lúm hotá thá? Khudá kin kí nahín suntá hai? Kis kí suntá hai? Kaun sí bát dunyá ke shurú' se sunne men nahín áí? Jo shakhs Khudá kí taraf se nahín hai, wuh kyá kar saktá hai? Unhon ne use kis wáste báhar nikál diyá? Is ke ba'd kaun us ádmí ko milá? Milkar kyá kahne lagá? Us ne kyá suwál kiyá? Use kyá jawáb milá? Us ne sijda karne se pahle kyá kahá? Masíh dunyá men kis wáste áyá? Kyá Farísí andhe the? Andhá hone se kyá hotá? Gunahgár kaun ṭhahrtá hai? Kis ká gunáh qáim rahtá hai?

Grammar.—Conditional sentences. Cf. vi. 10, ix. 31, 33, 41, and note the similarity and difference. *Agar mángtí. . . to detá, hotá to kar saktá, hote. . . to ṭhahrté* and *Agar ho aur chale, to suntá* hai. The last is a simple condition, the three former indicate it as contrary to fact. With the former the negative is always *na*.

Agar áp na áte, to main̲ játá. Agar yih kitáben̲ achchhí hotín̲ to main̲ wápas na kartá. Agar shágird sab báten̲ pahlí bár síkhte, to ustád ko dobára sikháná na hotá. Agar áp shurú' se Urdú bolte, to ab achchhí tarah se bol sakte. Agar áp Hindustán men̲ paidá hote to Urdú bolná ásán (*easy*) hotá. Agar Masíh us ádmí se na miltá, to wuh andhá hí rahtá. Agar laṛká kisí se púchhtá to wuh yih bát na kahtá. Agar laṛkí in logon̲ ko jántí, to wuh unkí bát kabhí na mántí. Agar wuh andhá mujh se bhíkh mánge, to main̲ de saktá hún̲. Agar koí ádmí K̲h̲udá kí marzí par chale (*or*, marzí ke muwáfiq 'amal kare) wuh achchhá ádmí hogá. Agar áp kahen̲ to merá naukar áp ke pás rah sakegá.

Note the verb form that follows *táki*, *ki*, of purpose in vss. 36, 39.

LESSON XXXVI.

The teacher will tell the story of Jno. vi. 1-11, and then assign it for the next day's reading. So for future lessons. The teacher should tell the incidents briefly and then explaining as many new words as possible in Urdu, assign the lesson for further study.

Review.—Tell the story of chapter iv.

Chhaṭe báb * ke shurú' (*beginning*) men̲ Yisú' kahán̲ gayá thá ? Us jhíl ká kyá nám thá ? Us ke píchhe kaun áe ? Bhíṛ us ke píchhe kyún̲ ho lí ? Kaunsí 'íd nazdík thí ? Yisú' ne apní taraf kyá áte dekhá ? Ise dekhkar Filippus se kyá kahá ? Yih bát kyún̲ kahí ? Filippus ne kyá jawáb diyá ? Kitní roṭíán̲ lení cháhiye thín̲ ? Wahán̲ ek

* Chapter.

aur shágird kaun thá? Us ne kyá kahá? Us laṛke ke pás kyá thá? Kitne ádmí wahán̲ the? Yih roṭián̲ itne ádmíon̲ ke líe káfí hongín̲? Yisú' ne kyá hukm diyá? Wuh kahán̲ baiṭh gaye? Roṭí lekar Yisú' ne kyá kiyá? Us ne kis qadr un ko machhlián̲ bánṭ dín̲?

Observations.—Note direct discourse in vss. 5 and 6. *Bhíṛ ho lí*, not *bhíṛ ne*, and cf. vs. 11, *Yisú' ne roṭián̲ lín̲*. Why? Cf. i. 37, 40, 43. Ho lená is intrans. Vs. 10 us jagah, locative, or else men̲ is omitted. Note the indefinite use of jo, vs. 2. Note the use of *uṭhákár*, vs. 5, and *shukr karke*, vs. 10, the participle in *kar* instead of "when." Fix these idioms in mind.

Grammatical Drill.—Put as many as possible of the verbs in the present progressive, as *Yisú' jhíl ke pár já rahá hai*. Make as many short sentences with infinitives of purpose as possible, and translate, as *pár jáne ke liye kahá*, said to go across; *mu'jiza karne ke liye buláyá*, called him to work a miracle.

Gintí.—Ek se lekar sattar tak gino, 1–70.

No further reference will be made to the Charts, but the teacher should give daily drill in those particular sounds and sentences which the individual pupils find most difficult. Words that are mispronounced in conversation or reading should be noted and used in this drill also. Dictation to and by the pupils should also be a part of the daily or semi-weekly drill.

LESSON XXXVII.

vi. 1-12.

Review.—Write the story of iv. 1-15 briefly. Tell the story of iv. 46-54.

Suwálát.—Kitne ádmí ser húe? Jab wuh ser ho chuke to Masíh ne apne shágirdon̲ ko kyá hukm (*order*) diyá? Jama' karne ká hukm kyún diyá? Kitní roṭíán thín? Kitní machhlíán bhí thín? Kitní ṭokríán bharín? Yih ṭukṛe kahán se bache? Wuh log yih mu'jiza dekhkar kyá kahne lage? Dunyá men ánewálá kaun thá? Yih mu'jiza dekhkar logon ne kyá karná cháhá? Masíh ne kyá kiyá? Shágird kidhar gaye? Kis waqt jhíl ke kináre gaye? Kis par chaṛhe? Kis shahr ko chale gaye? Kyá yih din ká waqt thá, yá rát ká? Maujen kyún uṭhne lagín thín? Kitní dúr gaye the jab Yisu' unke pás áyá? Kis tarah áyá? Kishtí kis tarah se chaláte the? Jab unhon ne dekhá to kyá kahá? Kyún? Us ne kyá kahá? Wuh kis bát par rází húe? Kishtí kahán pahunchí? Kab?

Observations.—Note vs. 12, *bache húe*, vss. 14, 15, 17, *dekhkar*, *ákar*, *chaṛhkar*; vs. 19, *khete*, *chalte*, *áte*, and their English value. Note locatives, vss. 16, 21, *jhíl ke kináre*, and *us jagah*. Note simple and causative forms, vss. 17, 21, *chaṛhná*, and *chaṛháná*.

Grammatical Drill.—Put all possible verbs in the past progressive, as *bach rahe the*. Note that *játá hai*, and *já rahá hai*, *játá thá* and *já rahá thá*, may be used with identical meanings. Use these verbs also with *lagná*, and *chukná*, in different gens. and nos.

Idioms to be mastered.—*Ham jama' kar chuke hain. Main ma'lúm kar chuká hún. Wuh kursí baná chuká hai. Wuh ghoṛe ko pakaṛ chuká hai. Áp kitáb dekh chuke hain? Main kal tak dekh chukúngá. Kyá, áp sáhib ko rází karte hain? Wuh to rází ho chuke hain. Daryá ke kináre kaun hain? Do ádmí us jagah khaṛe hain.*

Das das karke pachás tak gino. Ek ek karke pachás se lekar assí tak gino.

Jis tarah cháho usí tarah karo. Jis qadr cháho usí qadr kháo. Jis jagah cháho, usí jagah baiṭho. Itne ádmí áe ki ham gin na sake.

Wuh mere pás hai. Sáhib ke pás le jáo. Sáhib ko de do. Mere pás á rahí hai. Main áp ke pás áún? Wuh mere pás áyá hai. Merí kitáb áp ke pás hai? Shahr ke nazdík kúã' hai.

See further exercises in Interrogative Exercises, and follow them until all are mastered, but in conjunction with these lessons.

LESSON XXXVIII.

vi. 22-29.

Review.—Tell the story of iv. from the standpoint of a disciple.

Dúsre din bhír kahán thí? Agle* din kitní kishtíán roṭí kháne kí jagah thín? Usí ek kishtí men kaun sawár húe? Yisú' us waqt kidhar gayá thá? Âur chhoṭí kishtíán kahán se áín? Kidhar ko áín? Log un chhoṭí kishtíõn men kyún sawár húe? Log kidhar ko áe? Yisú' se milkar kyá kahne lage? Yisú' ke kahne ke muwáfiq, log use kyún ḍhúnḍhte the? Mu'jize ke sabab yá roṭí kháne ke sabab? Kis ke líe mihnat karní cháhiye? Fání khurák kyá hai? Dúsrí khurák kab tak ṭhahrtí hai? Ġairfání khurák kaun detá hai? Kis ne Ibn-i-Ádam par muhr kar dí hai? Unhon ne Khudá ke kám karne kí bábat kyá suwál kiyá? Khudá ká kám Yisú' ke kahne ke mutábiq (muwáfiq) kyá hai? Khudá ne kis ko bhejá?

Observe above **Dúsre din**, and in the same case **agle din**, indicating *time when*. vs. 24 *na . . . na.* Make a list of verbs in past tense which agree with their subject and of those agreeing with their object.

Drill.—Put all these verbs in present, past and future tense, of different genders and both numbers.

---

* Previous.

Ginti.—Ek ek karke sáṭh se nawwe tak, and das das karke sáṭh tak.

Exx. with *ke siwáe, ke nazdík, ke ba'd.* See Drill Table, Nouns.

LESSON XXXIX.

Read vss. vi. 30-40.

Review the story of ix. Tell the story in class.

Wuh log kyá dekhná cháhte the? Unke bápdádon̲ ko kyá nishán milá thá? Kitáb-i-muqaddas men̲ (Baibal men̲) kyá likhá hai? Kis ne wuh roṭí ás̲mán se dí thí? K̲h̲udá kí roṭí kyá bak̲h̲shtí hai? Jab unhon̲ ne suná ki K̲h̲udá kí dí húí roṭí zindagí bak̲h̲shtí hai to unhon̲ ne kyá dark̲h̲wást ('arz) kí? Kis ne kahá ki zindagí kí roṭí main̲ hún̲? Bhúkhá aur piyásá kaun na hogá? Masíh ke pás kaun á jáegá? Kyá wuh kisí ko nikálegá? Masíh kahán̲ se utrá? Kyún̲ utrá? Uske bhejnewále kí marzí kyá hai? Apne logon̲ ko kab zinda karegá?

Observations.—Note the subjunctives of purpose after *ki* and *táki*, vss. 30, 38–40, and of possibility in vs. 35, *jo áe, jo ímán láe.* Also vs. 34, *diyá kar.* Cf. *líe* vss. 31 with *ke* as preposition and 38 without *ke* with conjunction force. Cf. vss. 35, 37, *hargiz* and *kabhí.*

Drill.—Put all these verbs in the pres. subj. and future ind. tenses, and note the relation between the two tenses. They are sometimes distinguished as indefinite and definite future.

Das das karke sau tak gino. Ek ek karke sau tak gino.

Exx.—ke líe, ke pás, se, men̲ se, ko.

LESSON XL.

Read vss. vi. 41-71.

Review ix.—Write out the story briefly.

Log kyúṉ buṛbuṛáne lage ? [41]. Yisú' kis ká beṭá thá ? [42]. Nabíoṉ ke sahífoṉ meṉ kyá likhá thá ? [45]. Zindagí kí roṭí kaun hai ? [48]. Masíh ne apná gosht dene kí bábat kyá kahá ? [51]. Yih sunkar Yahúdí kyá kahne lage ? [52]. Gosht kháne aur k͟hún píne kí bábat Masíh ne kyá kahá ? [54]. Us ne yih báteṉ kaháṉ kahíṉ ? [59]. Yih báteṉ uske shágirdoṉ ko kaisí ma'lúm húíṉ ? [60]. Masíh kí yih báteṉ jismání thíṉ yá rúhání ? [63]. Yisú' shurú' se kyá jántá thá ? [64]. Kitne shágird ulṭe phir gaye ? [66]. Masíh ne bárahoṉ se kyá suwál kiyá ? [67]. Kyá jawáb milá ? Masíh ne kin ko chun liyá ? Uská pakaṛwánewálá kaun thá ? [71].

Observations.—Note ix. 17, **haqq** and vss. 32, 55, **haqíqí** and **haqíqat** from same root. vs. 59, **ta'lím dete waqt,** *meṉ* understood. 45, *ta'lím páe húe,* past participle agreeing with what ? Cf. *jab tak . . . na,* in vss. 44, 53, "As..so," *jis tarah, isí tarah.*

Drill.—Use these verbs with **sakná** in present and future tenses.

Exx.—ke ba'd, ke sáth, ke pás, kí nisbat, ke sabab, tak, par.

LESSON XLI.

v. 1-23.

Review.—Tell the story of vi.

Pánchweṉ báb meṉ jo bímár ádmí ko achchhe karne kí bábat likhá hai, wuh bayán karo. 1–9. Logoṉ ke nazdík kyá bát rawá na thí ? Kyúṉ ? 10. Us ádmí ko kyúṉ ma'lúm na thá ki Yisú' ne mujhe shifá bak͟hshí ? Ba'd meṉ us ne kis tarah ma'lúm kiyá ki merá shifá bak͟hshnewálá Yisú' hai ? 13, 14. Yisú' ne us se haikal meṉ milkar kyá kahá ? 14. Yahúdí Sabt ke sabab kyá karne lage ? 16. Yisú' ne apne haqq meṉ kyá bát kahí ? 17. Yih bát un ko burí kyún lagí ? 18. Yahúdí us ko kyún qatl karná cháhte the ? 18.

Báp beṭe ko 'azíz rakhne ke sabab kyá dikhátá hai ? 20. Masíh ne murdon aur zindon kí bábat kyá kahá ? 21. 'Adálat kis ke sipurd hai ? 22. Báp kí aur Beṭe kí 'izzat men kyá ta'alluq (attachment, relationship) hai ? 23.

New words.—Bheṛ, sheep; *pazhmurda-adhmúá*, half-dead; *mubtilá*, involved in; *muddat*, length of time; *hálat*, state, condition; *tandurust*, body-right, well; *hiláná*, to shake; *rawá*, permissible; *chárpái*, "four-leg," the light Indian bedstead; *chárpáe*, four-footed animals; *ṭalna*, to slip away; *áfat*, calamity; *aisá na ho*, lest; *aisá*, such; *khabar*, news; *satáná*, persecute; *koshish*, endeavour; *faqat*, only; *kháss*, special, particular; *barábar*, equal; *toṛná*, to break; *'azíz*, dear, beloved; *'adálat*, judgment, court; *sárá*, whole; *sipurd*, charge, care; *'izzat*, honour.

Tujhe chárpái uṭháná rawá nahín hai. Mujhe aisí kitáb paṛhná wájib nahín hai. Ham ko aisá kám karná rawá nahín hai. Aise logon ko pák jagah áná rawá nahín hai. Ádmíon ko Sabt ke din shifá dená rawá hai. Tumhen bachchon ko satáná wájib nahín hai. Yih na karná, aisá na ho ki bímárí tum ko lage. Wuh áp ke pás áná cháhtá hai. Wuh apne rúpaë * áp ke sipurd karná cháhte hain. Usne mujh se kahá, Koí kháss bát na thí, ek † ma'múlí bát thí. Agar áp ko manzúr hai, main chauthe roz ánke khabar dúngí. Mujhe áp se kuchh kahná hai. Jis tarah wuh 'azíz húá, usí tarah áp bhí 'azíz ho jáenge. Wuh do din ke ba'd gayá. Mere sipurd karo. Tumháre liye mere siwá koí Khudá na ho. Us ne sáhib ke sipurd kar diyá.

* Rupaë is, possibly, the only word with a short penult which takes the accent thereon.

† Common.

Us ne ek ke siwá sab bhej díe. Yih khabar áp ko kis se milí ?

Observations.—In vs. 3 **se** is not prep., but an intensive affix. There is also a **se** which is an affix of likeness, **kále se ádmí**, blackish men. This **sá, se, sí** is of different origin, i.e. from *sárá* or *sár*, and we have in *Panjábí*, *kálá sárá ádmí*. The prep. **se** has many meanings, and each one must be fixed in mind. Make a list of them. Note vs. 6 **pаṛá húá**, and vs. 19 **karte** after **dekha**. Both common. Vss. 7, 8, **utarná, utárná**, and *uṭhná*, *uṭháná*. Vss. 10, 13 *jis ne* and *jo*—Why ? Note the direct discourse in 13 and 15. In 14, 20 note the comparison of adjectives, **is se ziyada, in se baṛe.** Regular form.

Exx.—*ke ba'd, ke sipurd, ke siwá*, with nouns and pros. of Drill Tables in sings. and pls.

Put *achchhá, bímár, baṛá, burá, khush, rází, gahrá, thaká, sachchhá, chhoṭá*, according to vs. 14 in the comparative. The superlative is **sab se achchhá**, the best, etc.

LESSON XLII.

v. 24–47.

Review.—Write out the story of vi.

New Words.—*'Arsa* space of time ; *raushní*, or *roshní*, light ; *manzúr*, acceptable ; *dákhil*, entering ; *sazá*, punishment ; *áwáz*, voice ; *nekí*, goodness ; *badí*, evil ; *rást*, right ; *shikáyat*, complaint ; *samajhná*, to understand ; *jíná*, to live ; *jalná*, to burn ; *chamakná*, to shine ; *chirág*, a lamp ; *ya'ní*, i.e., that is ; *súrat*, form ; *payám*, message ; *mahabbat*, love ; *maqaddas*, holy ; *wáhid*, one, single ; *qabúl k.*, to receive ; *ummed*, hope ; *lagáná*, to apply, to attach, to plant ; *rahhná*, to put ; *nawishta*, writings, scripture ; *ádám-zád*, man-born, son of man.

Observations.—Note **sazá ká hukm**, punishment-order,

condemnation, vs. 24. In vs. 35 jaltá húá and chamaktá húá, húá is omitted with the first when the two are united, though it might be used. In 29 the verb kí has a higher pitch than kí, cf. Kuchh 'arse tak, kuchh is not declinable, khush rahná subject of manzúr húá, tum ko dative after *húá*. Cf. vss. 14, 39, milná, with ko and dat., also used with men̲ and se, but with slightly different meanings. Persons meet one another, with se; but if more incidentally then ko. A thing meets a person, ko c. person, or dat., *chiṭṭhì mujh ko milí*; dúdh pání men̲ milá, the milk united with the water. Make a list of and compare the "*agars*," and "*jabs*." Note various uses of se in this chapter.

Drill.—Make a synopsis of verbs *qabúl**, *manzúr"*, *dák̲h̲il" baṛá"*, *honá*, *karná*, *karáná*, to be big, to make big, to have made big, etc., in pres., past, fut., in all persons, gens., nos.

Exx.—If he come, I will go; give, take; give, bring; say, write; ask, do; send, go.

Also, If he had come, I would have gone, etc.

Ginti.—Ek ek karke sau tak.

* Suwálát.—Sazá ká hukm kis par na hogá? 24. Maut aur zindagí kis ke ik̲h̲tiyár men̲ hain̲? Murde kyá sunke jíen̲ge? 25. 'Adálat karne ká ik̲h̲tiyár kis ne kis ko diyá? 27. Qiyámat ke waqt kyá hogá? 29. Qiyámat kyá hai? Masíh (hán̲, har ek sachchá munsif) kis tarah 'adálat kartá hai? 30. Masíh kí gawáhí kaun detá hai? 32. Yuhanná ne kyá gawáhí dí? 33. Masíh kis kí gawáhí manzúr kartá hai? 34, 36. Yúhanná kaisá chiráġ thá? 35. Yahúdíon̲ ko kuchh 'arse tak kyá manzúr húá thá? 35. Masíh ke kyá kyá gawáh the? 36. Kis tarah ma'lúm húá ki Yahúdí K̲h̲udá ke kalám ko apne dilon̲ men̲ nahín̲ rakhte the?

---

* Pupils should be able to ask these from the key.

38. Yahúdí zindagí ke líe kahán ḍhúnḍhte the? 39. Zindagí kahán mil saktí thí? 39, 40. Dunyá men kaun qabúl hotá hai? 43. Yahúdí ímán kyún na láe? 44. Yahúdíon kí shikáyat kaun karegá? 45. Músá ne kyá likhá? 46 Yahúdíon ne kis par ummed lagá rakkhí thí? 45.

Áp ne kitne 'arse tak kamre men baiṭhná manzúr kiyá? Jab naukar darwáze men dákhil húá, málik ne áwáz dí. Har ádmí ne nekí badí kí hai. Us ne mujhe baṛá be-'izzat kiyá. Agar áp is bát ko samajhte, to mujh ko rást jánte. Ek jaltá húá chirág mere pás láo. Jis tarah áp cháhte hain, main usí tarah karúngá. Pulis (police) kí gawáhí sachchí hai, jhúṭhí nahín hai. Janáb kí gawáhí mujhe manzúr hai. Ímán, ummed, mahabbat yih tínon insán men cháhiye. Is bát kí kuchh ummed nahín hai. Jab insán be-ummed ho játá, wuh achchhí tarah kám nahín kar saktá.

LESSON XLIII.

vii. 1-24.

Review.—Tell stories of iv., v., vi.

New words.—*Rawána*, starting; *mashhúr*, widely known; *chhipná*, to hide (intrans.); *bháí*, brother; *'adáwat*, enmity; *burá*, bad, evil; *goyá*, as if; *poshída*, secret; *chupná*, to keep quiet; *chup cháp*, quietly; *guftgú*, conversation; *ráh*, way; *gumráh*, out of the right way; *sáf*, clean, clear; *ádhá*, half; *guzarná*, to pass; *haikal*, temple; *bagair*, without; *sharí'at*, law, religious law; *khatna*, circumcision; *ṭúṭná*, to break (intrans.), be broken; *bilkull*, altogether; *taubhí*, still, nevertheless; *nárástí*, unrighteousness; *hálánki*, although; *faisala*, decision; *'ilm*, knowledge; *ma'lúm*, known; *ta'lím*, instruction, all three from the same root, as also *mua'llim*, instructor; *'álim*, a wise man. The three radicals of the Arabic root *'ilm* are present in each.

Suwálát.—Yisú' ne Yahúdiya men phirná kyún na

cháhá? 1. 'I'd-i-Khiyám men jáne ke báre men uske bháíon ne kyá kahá? 3. Kyún kahá? 5. Masíh ne kyá jawáb diyá? 6. Phir 'íd men kaun kaun gaye? 10. 'I'd men log kyá kahte the? 11. Kyún? 12. Masíh kab záhir húá? 14. Kahán? Usne apní ta'lím kí bábat kyá kahá? 16. 'Izzat kí nisbat kyá bolá? 18. Músá ke báre men kyá farmáyá* (kahá)? 19, 22.

Honá: Wuh roz isí waqt bímár ho játá hai. Áp yih roṭí kháne se bímár ho jáenge. Kyá húá? Áp ká bháí bímár hokar gir paṛá (fell down). Yih bát mashhúr ho jáegí. Kal mere báp ghar se rawána húe. Chup cháp baiṭho, bát na karo. Unhon ne do ghanṭe tak ápas men guftgú kí. Unkí 'adáwat poshída na rah sakí. Wuh unkí ánkhon se chhip gayá. Us ne mere bháí ko gumráh kar diyá. Wuh ta'lím páe baġair kis tarah sharí'at jántá hai? Khatna karná Mussalmánon ká dastúr hai. Yih kursí kis tarah se ṭúṭí? Sáf bát to yihí hai, kí yih faisala bilkull burá hai. Jab áṭh din guzre to unhon ne laṛke ká khatna kiyá.

Note in vs. 5 **na** and vs. 6 **nahín** with past perf. and pres. perf. tenses. **Baġair paṛhe**, without having read, studied. Fix this idiom in mind. In vs. 23, **ġusse** is not, as one might suppose, an adj. in mas. pl., but a noun with *men* understood, so that we say **'aurat ġusse húí, ádmí ġusse húá,** and **ádmí ġusse húe. Sabt ke din,** locative of time.

Drill.—Use the infinitives with *lagná* in pres., past fut. Use all verbs in simple past tense with object or prepositional modifier.

Exx.—Make a list of the ten or twelve prepositions and use them with various nouns till they are readily handled.

---

* To use *farmáná* (to speak; from Persian *farmán*, a command) indicates marked respect for the one speaking. No one should ever use it of himself, e.g., *Ápne kyá farmaya*? What did you say?—and one replies *Main ne kahá*, etc.

Ginti.—Pahlá, dúsrá, tísrá, chauthá, pánchwán̲, chhaṭá, sátwán̲, áṭhwán̲, nauwán̲, daswán̲.

LESSON XLIV.

vii. 25-52.

Review.—Write the story of v.

New words—*Sardár*, chief; *pukárná*, to call; *káhin*, priest; *piyáda*, footsoldier, ; *já ba já*, place after place; *ak͟hír*, last; *andar*, inside; *nadí*, stream, river; *názil*, come down; *pahunchná*, to arrive; *be-shakk*, without doubt; *nasl*, seed, race; *gáon̲*, *gán̲w*, village; *ik͟htiláf*, a division; *bhalá*, well, good; *'ámm*, common; *la'nat*, curse; *la'natí*, cursed; *mujrim*, guilty; *háth ḍálná*, to lay hands on.

Suwálát.—Us kí sunkar Yarushalemí kyá kahne lage? 25-7. Masíh ne unke jawáb men̲ kyá kahá? Piyádon̲ ko kyá hukm milá? 32. Aur unhon̲ ne kyá jawáb diyá? 46. Masíh ne ḍhúnḍhne aur na páne kí bábat kyá kahá. 34. 'I'd ke akhír din kí báton̲ ko batáo. 37-44. Farísíon̲, piyádon̲ aur Nikudemus kí báten̲ bayán karo. 45-52. Logon̲ men̲ Masíh ke watan kí bábat kyá ik͟htiláf húá? 53.

Observations.—*Cf.* **dekhná,** 52, **and dikháná,** 31, **dinon̲ tak,** 33, **do tín din tak; já ba já,** 35, **din ba din.**

Master the idioms.—Koshish ho rahí hai, 25; sáf sáf kahtá hai, 26; sach sach ján liyá, kahán̲ ká, jahán̲ ká, 27, 42; ta'lím dete waqt, 28; chupke chupke, 32; chalá jáún̲gá, 33; 'I'd ke ak͟hír din, 37; názil na húá thá, 39; jise wuh páne ko the, nahín̲ uṭhne ká, 52.

Yih bak͟hshish K͟hudá kí taraf se áí hai. Sáhib ne yih kitáb áp kí taraf bhejí hai. Haikal ká sardár kahne (pukárne) lagá. Kyá chha din nahín̲ hain̲ jin men̲ ánke shifá pání cháhiye? Káhin qurbání par háth ḍálte the? Yih ádmí shahr ke andar jákar já ba já paisá mángtá phirtá hai. Panjáb men̲ pánch nadíán̲ hain̲. Gangá baṛí nadí hai. Pák Rúh Pintekust ke din názil húá thá. 'Arabí nasl ke achchhe achchhe ghoṛe ís gáon̲ men̲ hain̲. In baton̲ men̲ ikh̲tiláf nahín̲ hai. 'Ámm log is bát ko jánte hain̲. Jo mujrim hai wuh la'natí hai. Wuh jáne ko the.

Drill.—*Ho saktá hai*, in all persons and genders and nos. of pres. synopsis of *sakná* in pres., past, fut. with *kahná, jánná, áná, pukárná, bhejná, karná, háth ḍálná, dekhná, pakaṛná, dená.*

Run through the verbs of the lesson, putting them in the past tense, and where already in that change gender or number or person.

Gintí.—Pahlí (á, e) dúsrí, tísrí, chauthí, pánchwín̲, chhaṭí, sátwín̲ áṭhwín̲, nauwín̲, daswín̲.

LESSON XLV.

viii. 1-30.

Review.—Write the story of vi.

New words.—*Zaitún*, olive ; *subh*, morning ; *sawere*, early ; *ziná*, adultery ; *a'in fe'l*, very act ; *faqíh*, scribe ; *bích*, middle ; *Tauret*, the Mosaic Law ; *sangsár*, stoned ; *ilzám*, accusation ; *jhukná*, to stoop ; *sídhá*, straight ; *be-gunáh*, sin-less ; *patthar*, stone ; *hukm*, order ; *hákim*, ruler ; *mu-kh̲átib*, addressing ; *pair*, foot ; *paîrawí*, following ; *agar-chi*, although ; *jism*, flesh, body ; *chhoṛná*, to let go ; *chhúṭ-ná*, to escape ; *chhuṭkárá*, escape ; *marná*, to die ; *márná*, to kill, to beat ; *már ḍálná*, to kill ; *Bait-ul-Mál*, house of treasure ; *ún̲che*, high ; *pasand*, pleasing ; *dunyá*, world ; *núr*, light.

Cf. vii. 33-38, and write out the future of *jáná* and *dená* in both genders, all persons.

Suwálát.—Yisú' ke kahán̲ jáne ká bayán áṭhwen̲ báb ke shurú' men̲ hai ? Faqíh Farísí kis ko láe ? Unhon̲ ne kyá suwál kiyá ? Yisú' ne kyá kiyá ? Jab unhon̲ ne dobára suwál kiyá to Yisú' ne kyá kahá? Is bát ká kyá asar (influence) húá? Masíh ne 'aurat ko kyá hukm diyá? Núr kí bábat Masíh ne kyá kahá? 12. Gawáhí dene kí bábat kyá? 14. Faisala karne kí bábat kyá kahá? 15, 16. Us ne yih báten kahán aur kis waqt kahín? 20. Logon ne usko kyún na pakṛá? Yahúdíon ne kis bát se samjhe ki Masih apne áp ko már ḍalegá? 21. Gunáh se chhúṭne ke líye kis bát kí zarúrat hai? Masíh kyá kahtá áyá? 25. Us ne apne bhejnewále kí nisbat kyá kahá? 26, 29.

Observations.—Note pakṛí gayí thí, regular passive form, *pakṛá jáná*, was caught, to be caught. In vss. 3, 5, 7, *khaṛá*, *sangsár*, *sídhá*, with **honá** and **karná** exhibits the regular form of the "Nominal Verb" formed by adj., or noun, and verb, with **honá, karná, karáná, sídhe** not **sídhá**, to agree with *us ne*. In 7, **us ke** [*badan* (body) *men*] **patthar máre.** In 14 the regular correlatives of **agarchi** and **go** are **taubhí** and **táham.** In 25 **kahtá áyá** denotes that the saying is contemporaneous with *the coming*, as I came saying, I have continued saying.

Drill.—All forms of *khaṛá honá* in present, past and future, imp., and subj.

Exx.—Ke mutábiq, ke bích men, ke níche, ke úpar.

Áj subh ek chor 'ain f'el men pakṛá gayá. Us ko sazá dení cháhiye. Jhukkar is darwáze se dákhil honá cháhiye. Ánkh jism ká núr hai. Músá kí pánch kitáben Tauret kahlátí hain. Áp ko akelá baiṭhná pasand hai? Agarchi chor andhere men chorí kare, tau bhí pakaṛá jákar sazá páegá. Laṛko, khaṛe ho jáo. Sídhe hokar baiṭho. Ek ek karke mere pás áo, aur jo jo mewa * pasand hai do do karke le jáo. Chúnki (since) is ne mere bháí ke patthar márá, is ko sazá dení zarúr hai. Shurú' karná ásán (easy) bát hai;

---

* Fruit.

púrá karná aur bát hai. Agar us ne apne áp ko már ḍálá hai, to áp ko yád hogá ki maiṉ yihí bát kahtá áyá húṉ. Mujh par ilzám lagáne ká koí sabab nahíṉ hai.

Ginti.—Pahle, dúsre, tísre, chauthe, pánchweṉ, chhaṭe, sátweṉ, áṭhweṉ, nauweṉ, dasweṉ.

LESSON XLVI.

viii. 31-59.

Review.—Write out the story of vii. Tell the stories of iv., v., vi. briefly.

New words.—*Qáim*, established ; *ṭhahrná*, to stand, stop, be stationary, be determined (arranged, fixed) ; *ṭhahráná*, to cause to stand, to determine, appoint, fix, settle ; *wáqif*, acquainted ; *ázád*, free ; *gulám*, slave ; *gulámí*, slavery ; *wáqa'í*, truly ; *harám*, forbidden, unlawful ; *jhúṭh*, lie ; *jhúṭhá*, false, lying ; *ke yaháṉ*, place, neighbourhood ; *farzand*, son, sons ; *jagah*, place ; *sábit*, firm, established, proved ; *subút*, proof ; *maza*, taste ; *banná*, to become, be made ; *'umr*, age ; *baras* year, years ; *peshtar*, before ; *be-'izzat*, without honour, disgrace ; *khún*, blood ; *khúní*, murderer ; *khush*, happy ; *khushí*, happiness ; *bad*, bad, evil ; *badí*, badness, evil ; *khúb*, excellent, good ; *khúbí*, goodness ; *khúbsúrat*, beautiful ; *buzurg*, noble, honorable, aged ; *buzurgí*, honour, old age ; *baṛá*, great ; *baṛáí*, greatness.

Observations.—Note how adjs. form nouns by adding í and how nouns become adjs., in the same way, or if of Hindi origin á and í, as from jhúṭh we get jhúṭhá, jhúṭhí. Passive ázád kiye jáoge. 33. ke se kam karte, 39, 41. Memorise idioms of vs. 40.

Drill.—He, she, I, we, thou, you, you (polite), they (in both genders) have (and, have not), one (or, two-ten) books, hands, eyes, tables, dollars, rupees, clocks, horses.

Also the boy-s, girl-s, man, men, woman, women, have, have not books, etc. Also, have you two books, etc.

Exx.—With above subjects use alternately *kahá*, *bolá*, *bolí*, *bole* (said—will come to-morrow).

Suwálát.—Ádmí kis tarah Masíh ká shágird ban saktá hai? 31. Sachcháí ke wáqif hone se kyá bantá hai? 32. Kyá suwál o jawáb "ġulám ázád" kí nisbat húá? 33–36. Báp aur farzandon kí nisbat kyá guftgú húí? 38–44. Yahúdí Ibráhím kí bábat kyá kahte the? 39. Yisú' ne kyá kahá? 39. Usne Iblís kí bábat kyá kahá? 44. Badrúh ká ilzám kyún húá? 48. Ibráhím kí bábat kyá kalám húá? 52–57. Yahúdíon ne Yisú' ko sangsár karná kyún cháhá? 58.

Ġulám Muhammed Mussalmánon men 'ámm nám hai, Ba'z ádmí jhúṭh bolne se khush hote hain, lekin haqíqat men yih bahut burí bát hai. Sachcháí jhúṭh bolne se sábit nahín hotí. Ya'qúb ká beṭá Yúsuf Misr kí ġulámí men bahut baras rahá. Wuh ġulám rahne se apne bháíon se baṛá ho gayá balki bádsháh ká sá ikhtiyár payá. Peshtar us se ki us ke bháí Misr men á gaye, us ne bádsháh ke líe bahut kuchh ánáj (grain) jama' kiyá. Us waqt us kí 'umr chálís baras se kam thí, ya'ní wuh chálís baras tak na pahunchí * thí. Aġar Yúsuf haqq par qáim na rahtá to wuh qaid kháne men na paṛtá, aur aġar qaid men na paṛtá, to wuh bádsháh ke pás na pahunchtá. Is se sábit hotá hai ki taklíf se fáida miltá hai. Yih jhúṭhí bát nahín hai. Bachche dúdh ke maze se khush hote hain. Khudá ke logon kí khwáhish yih hai ki ham gunáh se ázád ho jáen (bach jáen).

Dictation.—iv. 38.—Dictate the difficult words to the munshi in irregular order.

LESSON XLVII.

iii. 1-21.

Review.—Write the story of viii.

New words.—*Rát*, night; *Rabbí*, *ustád*, teacher; *nayá*, new; *sirá*, end; beginning; *paidá*, born; *bádsháhat*, kingdom; *búṛhá*, old; *peṭ*, belly, stomach, womb; *hawá*, wind, air; *jidhar*, whither; *ásmán*, heaven; *utarná*, to descend, to go down; *sámp*, serpent; *bayábán*, wilderness, desert; *hamesha*, always; *mahabbat*, love; *iklautá*, only-born; *halák*, destroyed; *wasíla*, means; *tárík*, dark; *táríkí*, darkness; *dushman*, enemy; *dushmaní*, enmity; *malámat*, reproach, blame, scolding.

Observations.—Note **rát ko**, at night; so din ko, by day, **ustád hokar**, as a teacher. Note the use of *jab tak. . . na*, till, when, or while. . . not, i.e., unless. What tense form follows purpose conjunctions? See 14–17, 20, 21. *Note passives at end of* 14, 20, 21.

Suwálát.—Rát ko Yisú' ke pás kaun áyá? 2. Wuh kaun thá? 1. Us ne kyá kahá? 2. Kyá jawáb use milá? 3. Sardár ne kaun sá ta'ajjub ká suwál kiyá? 4. K͟hudá kí bádsháhat men̲ dák͟hil hone ke líe kyá zarúr hai? 25. Jo jo paidá hotá hai, wuh kyá hai? 6. Yisú' ne hawá ke chalne ke báre men̲ kyá kahá? 8. Yisú' ne kis bát par ta'jjub kiyá? 10. Masíh kin kin báton̲ ká zikr (account) kartá hai? 1 2. Ásmán par kaun chaṛh gayá hai? 13 Músá ne kyá kiyá? 14. Usí tarah se kyá zarúr hai? Tísre báb kí solah wín̲ áyat (3, 16) sunáo (recite). K͟hudá ne apne beṭe ko kyún̲ bhejá? 16. Sazá ke hukm kí bábat kyá likhá hai? kis par hai? Kis par nahín̲ hai? kyá sabab hai? 17-19. Núr aur táríkí kí do chár báten̲ batáo. 19–21.

Jab tak main̲ na áún̲, tum yahín̲ baiṭhe raho. Jab tak pání na paṛe is daryá par kishtí já na sakegí. Jab tak sáhib shahr men hain tum log bhí ṭhahro. Jab tak Masíh dobára na áwe (áe) is dunyá kí hálat kyúnkar achchhí hogí? Jis tarah us ádmí ne apne beṭe ko ta'lím dí, usí tarah kí ta'lím ap log bhí apne apne beṭon ko den. Merá kám Huzúr ke wasíle se ho jáegá. 'Aurat ke siwá sab nikal gaye, aur wuh akelí Masíh ke pás rah gayí. Naját dunyá ko Masíh ke wasíle miltí hai. Do laṛke máre gaye. Do kitában áp ke pás bhejí gayín. Yih kursí kahán baní? Wuh Lakhnau men ban gayí. Yih kám kab kiyá gayá? Wuh tín roz se taiyár hai.

Drill.—Use verbs of the lesson with *saknā* in present and past, all persons and genders.

Exx.—*Ke wasíle, ke siwá*, with all personal pros.

Ginti.—100 ; 500 ; 1000 ; 10,000 ; 1,00,000. Sainkṛá, pánch sau, hazár, das hazár, lákh.

LESSON XLVIII.

iii. 22-36.

Review.—Write story of ix.

New words.—*Mulk*, country ; *qaidkhána*, jail ; *tahárat*, purification ; *bahs*, dispute ; *insán*, man (generic) ; *dúlhá*, bridegroom ; *dulhan*, bride ; *dost*, friend ; *dostí*, friendship ; *khush*, happy ; *khushí*, happiness ; *baṛhná*, to increase ; *ghaṭná*, to decrease ; *muhr*, seal, gold, coin ; *náp*, measure ; *nápná*, to measure ; *chíz*, thing ; *mánná*, to believe, obey ; *gazab*, wrath.

Observations.—Note the passives at end of 24, 27, 28. zamín hí kí* kahtá hai. 31. **Us kí* suntá. Beṭe kí* mántá,** 29, 36. **Náp nápkar**, measuring measuring, i.e. by measure.

Suwálát.—Yisú' apne shágirdon ke sáth kis mulk men áyá? 22. Wahán kyá karne lage? 22. Yúhanná kahán

* Bát

thá? Kyá kartá thá? Kyún? 23. Ba'd is ke Yúhanná kis jagah ḍálá gayá thá? 24. Kis kis kí bahs húí? Kis bát kí bábat húí? 25. Logon ne Yúhanná ko kyá kahá? 26. Insán kyúnkar kuchh pátá hai? 27. Yúhanná ne apne báre men ki main Masíh hún yá nahín kyá kahá? 28. Yúhanná ne baṛhne aur ghaṭne ke báre men kyá kahá? 30. Jo zamín se hai wuh kyá kahtá hai? 31. Ham kin báton ki gawáhí de sakte hain? 32. Kaun Khudá ko sachchá ṭhahrátá hai? 33. Kaun Khudá kí báten kahtá hai? 34. Khudá ká ġazab kis par hai? 36.

Merí us ke sáth bahut bahs húí. Merí suno. Un ká laṛká baṛá ho gayá hai. Yih laṛká báp kí nahín mántá. Insán baġair dostí khush rah nahín saktá. Agar rúpae baṛhen to ham is ko khushí kí bát samajhte hain; aġar ghaṭen to ham ko afsos (sorrow) hotá hai. Is ġaríb ádmí ko do man * dána nápke dená. Is kamre men áp kitní chízen gin sakte hain? † Shádí men dúlhá aur dulhan ke baġair thoṛe ádmí na honge. Jab áp apne mulk men khush the, to kyún us ko chhoṛke gair mulk men chale áe? Ham is líe áe ki yahán ke logon ko tá'lím den.

Drill.—I (you, we, she, he, they) heard, him (them, us, me, you, you).

Exx.—Daryá, jhíl ke par, ke áge—ghar, koṭhí, bangla, shahr, kúán, mere, tumháre.

Ginti.—Review the time of day, all quarters.

LESSON XLIX.

ii. 1-12.

Review.—Write the story of iii., and tell it in class.

New words.—*Da'wat*, invitation; *khádim*, servant; *khidmat*, service; *khidmatgár*, servant, table-servant; *dastúr*,

---

* Weight of 82 lb. † Wedding.

custom; *maṭka*, large-mouthed jar; *man*, 40 qts. or 82 ℔; *gunjáish*, capacity; *mír majlis*, chief of the assembly; *náqis*, defective; *jalál*, glory; *pesh*, before; *rakhná*, to place, to keep; *chand*, some; *buláná*, to call.

Suwálát.—Yisú' ká pahlá mu'jiza kyá thá? Us ká zikr karo. Us shádí men kyá chíz ghaṭ gayí? 3. Kis ne Yisú' ko is bát kí k͟habar dí? 3. Yisú' ne kyá jawáb diyá? 4. Mariam ne k͟hádimon̲ se kyá kahá? 5. Kitne maṭke wahán̲ the? 6. Kis kám ke líe the? Un men̲ kitní kitní gunjáish thí? Yisú' ne un k͟hádimon̲ ko kyá hukm diyá? 7. Unhon̲ ne kyá kiyá? Masíh ne dobára kyá hukm diyá? 8. Jab mír majlis ne mai chakí to us ne kis ko buláyá? 8. Us ne dúlhá se kyá kahá? 10. Kyá mír-majlis ko patá thá ki yih mai kahán̲ se áí thí? 9. Kaun jánte the? Is mu'jiza se kyá záhir húá? 11. Yisú' apní mán̲ aur apne shágirdon̲ ke sáth kahán̲ gayá? 12. Wuh kitne din tak wahán̲ rahe?

Jo dastúr kí bát ho, us ke k͟hiláf (contrary) chalná baṛá mushkil (difficult) hai. Patthar ke maṭke bahut kam (few) hain̲, lekin miṭṭí ke bahut hain̲. Tahárat ke bahut dastúr Mussalmánon̲ men̲ hain̲. Is bartan kí gunjáish do tín ser kí hogí. Ma'lúm hotá hai ki Yahúdíon̲ ká dastúr thá ki ek ádmí shádíon̲ men̲ mír-majlis banáyá játá thá, aur k͟hádim sab chízen̲ us ko dikháte the; aur wuh ūn chízon̲ ko chakhá kartá thá.

Kal shám ke kháne men̲ áp kí da'wat hai. Da'wat kis kí taraf se hai? Da'wat hamárí taraf se hai. Main̲ yih chiṭṭhí áp kí k͟hidmat men̲ láyá hún. Bahut achchhá. Abhí is ko memsáhiba ke sámne pesh karo. K͟hudá ká jalál dunyá se záhir hotá hai. Yih chízen̲ bilkull náqis hain̲.

Drill.—Use a half dozen mas. and fem. nouns with past tenses of verbs of lesson, as subjects and objects.

Exx.—Chhaka, chakha. Chor chorí chhoṛo. Ai choro, chori chhoṛo.

LESSON L.

ii. 13-35.

Review.—Tell briefly the stories of iv. and ix.

New words.—*'Id-i-Fasah*, Pascal Feast; *kabútar*, pigeon; *bechnewálá*, seller; *bechná*, to sell; *bikná*, to be sold; *bikwáná*, to sell through another; *sarráf*, money-lender; *rassí*, rope; *koṛá*, scourge; *takhta*, plank; *ulṭáná*, to turn over (intrans.); *ulṭá*, upside down; *farosh*, seller (in compounds only as *kutub farosh*); *tajárat*, commerce; *gairat*, zeal; *nishán*, sign; *maqdis*, temple; *ḍháná*, to cast down; *badan* body; *murda* (n. or adj.) dead; *yád áná*, to come to mind; *qaul*, saying; *i'tibár*, trust; *hájat*, need; *dil*, heart.

Suwálát.—Yahúdion̲ kí baṛí 'íd kaunsí thí? 'I'd kahán̲ karte the? 13. Masíh ne kin kin ko haikal men̲ se nikálá? 14. Logon̲ ne us se kyá suwál kiyá? Unhen̲ kyá jawáb milá? 18, 19. Yih bát shágirdon̲ ko kab yád áí? 22. Wuh maqdis kitne baras men̲ baná? 20. Us waqt log ímán kyún̲ láe the? 23. Yisú' ne un par i'tibár kyún̲ na kiyá? 24. Yisú' ko kis bát kí haját na thí? 25.

Main̲ ne sarráfon̲ ko baiṭhe húe dekhá. Us ne ádmion̲ ko bechte húe páyá. Khudáwand kabútar-faroshon̲ ko tajárat karte húe dekhkár ġussa húá. Us ne logon̲ ko maqdis men̲ tajárat karte húe dekhá. Us ne mez ko ulaṭ diyá. Main̲ ne rassíon̲ ká koṛá paṛá húa dekhá. Maqdis ke ḍháne se aur us ke khaṛá karne se Masíh ká nishán púrá húá. Yih bát mujhe us waqt yád áí. Is bát kí baṛí ġairat mere dil men̲ thí, lekin áp ke na i'tibár karne se wuh ġairat na rahí. Merí jitní hájaten̲ hain̲ sab áp ko yád hon̲gí. Murda apná qaul kis tarah púrá karegá? Jab Masíh murdon̲ men̲ se jí uthá, tab uskí báten̲ i'tibár ke láiq * (worthy) sábit húín̲.

Drill.—Put all verbs in participle-wálá and use with

preps. *se, ko, ke, sabab, ke wasíle, ke bích men, kí nisbat*, in all nos. and gens.

Exx.—Use synopsis table, with half dozen verbs from the lesson.

LESSON LI.

i. 29-50.

Review.—Tell the stories of v. and vi.

New words.—*Nigáh*, glance, sight; *barra*, lamb; *phirná*, to turn (intr.); *sagá*, of the same father and mother, own; *báshinda*, inhabitant; *makr*, deceit; *anjír*, fig; *darakht*, tree; *májara*, wonder; *firishta*, angel.

Suwálát.—Dúsre din kaun kaun khaṛe the? 35. Yúhanná ne kis ko dekhá. 36. Wuh do shágird kidhar gaye? 37. Yisú' ne un se kyá púchhá? 38. Us roz wuh kahán rahe? 39. Yih shágird kaun the? 40. Yisú' kidhar jáne lagá? 43. Kis ko apne sáth buláyá? Filippus ne kis ko buláyá? 45. Natan'el kahán thá? 46. Masíh ne us ke haqq men kyá kahá? 47. Natan'el ne Yisú' se kyá kahá? 49. Us ká ímán dekhkar Masíh kyá bolá? 50.

Observations.—Note in 47, 51, **áte dekhkar**, and **khulá húá**, and **játe utarte dekhná. Is se pahle ki**, before (first) of time, but **sámne**, of place; **áge**, of time or place. **Baṛe baṛe májare**, the repetition of the **baṛe** is distributive, many different, great wonders. In 37, **yih kahte sunkar**. Master these.

Drill.—I saw (so and so) seeking, etc. *ḍhúnḍhte, áte, chalte, milte, sunte, láte, nikalte búláte*. Use all pros. as subj. and as objs.

Phiro aur báen (left) háth ki taraf ho jáo. Ḍhúnḍho to páoge. Yih merá sagá bháí hai. Merí do sagí bahinen bhí hain. Wuh ádmí kis mulk ká báshinda hai? Unhon ne shahr ko makr se halák kiyá. Anjíron kí fasl mausami garma men hai. Do darakht bare aur do chhote hain. Áp ne yih májara kahán dekhá? Baġair chábí ke darwáza khulá. Firishta áyá aur Patrus ke áge áge chalá, phir wuh darwáza áp se áp khul gayá, aur dono ke dono qaid-kháne se báhar nikal gaye.

Exx.—Take subjs., *Yúhanná*, *Patrus*, *Imám-ud-Dín*, *Ramzán*, *Rání*, *Mumtáz Bíbí*, with a dozen verbs of this lesson after the form in 36, *já rahá thá*. Also write with *aur*.

LESSON LII.

i. 19-34.

Review.—Tell the story of ii.

New words.—*Lewí*, Levites; *iqrár*, confession; *inkár*, denial; *pukár*, a call; *pukárná*, to call; *darmiyán*, in the midst, amid, among; *tasma*, a strap or strip of leather; *Láiq*, fit, worthy; *wáqi'*, occurred; *muqaddam*, prior, also headman of a village (Kashmir); *muqaddama*, law-suit; *pahchán*, recognition; *pahchánná*, to recognise; *quds*, holy; *maqdis*, holy place; *ma*, indicating place, as in masjid, place of *sijda*, worship; *quddús*, holy; *maqaddas*, holy, from one root.

Suwálát.—Farísion ne kis ke pás ádmí bheje? 19. Yih ádmí kis bát ke púchhne ke líe bheje gaye the? Yúhanná ne apne haqq men kyá kahá? 23. Jab unhon ne púchhá ki tú baptisma kyún detá hai, to Yúhanná ne kyá jawáb diyá? 26. Dùsre din Yúhanná ne Yisú' ko dekhkar kyá kahá? 29. Yúhanná pání se baptisma kyún detá thá? 33. Masíh ke haqq men Yúhanná ne kyá gawáhí dí? 31. Yúhanná kis tarah se baptisma detá thá? Yisú' kis tarah se? 33.

Observations.—Note mere ba'd ká ánewálá, like is men

ká páni pío. *Cf.* the three occurrences of apná, in three persons. In 31 detá húá áyá, two contemporaneous actions. Passive bheje gaye the. 24. Note the dif. in 30 between kahá thá and *pahchántá na thá*, the latter continuous past progressive tense, whereas *kahá thá* has the significance of a simple past, as it frequently has, or a past which is long distant, or, may be, a past that is previous to some other action.

Drill.—There is (a man) standing in (your) midst whom (you) do not know.

Substitute men, woman, women, and our, their, the city's, village's, and I, you, you, p,* we, he, they, the boys, the girl.

Exx.—Ke darmiyán, ke pár, ke láiq.

LESSON LIII.

i. 1-18.

Review.—Tell the story of i. 35-51.

New words.—*Ibtidá*, beginning; *kalám*, word; *maujúd*, present; *maujudagí*, presence; *farzand*, son; *k͟hwáhish*, wish; *iráda*, purpose; *mujassam*, in the flesh, become flesh; (*jism*, body); *fazl*, grace: *ma'múr* filled, built up with; *ma'múrí*, fullness; *ma'rifat*, means, knowledge; *god*, lap.

Suwálát.—Shurú' men̲ kalám kí babat kyá likhá hai? [1]. Us ke wasíle se kyá kyá paidá húá? [3]. Zindagí kahán̲ thí? [4]. K͟hudá kí taraf se kaun bhejá gayá? [6]. Us ká kyá kám thá? [7]. Kis ko K͟hudá ne farzand banne ká haqq bak͟hshá? [12]. Yih farzand kis se paidá húe? [13]. Kalám kab mujassam húá? Mujassam hokar wuh kalám kahán̲ rahá? [14]. Wuh kis se ma'múr thá? [14]. Músá kí ma'rifat

* Polite.

kyá dí gayí ? [17]. Yisú' Masíh kí m'arifat kyá pahunchí ? [17]. Khudá dunyá men kis tarah se záhir kiyá gayá ? [18]. Yuhanná ne us kí bábat kyá gawáhí dí ? [16].

Observations.—**Apnon** is used as noun ; so **jitnon**, else they would have the ending e. The different uses of se are partly owing to the fact that two distinct words, one meaning *with* and the other *from* and another *like*, have been corrupted into the same pronunciation, se. Make a list of the preps. of this chapter. Also of the uses of honá, **húá**.

Drill.—From i. 6, 17, 24 ; iii. 14, 20, 21, 24, 27, 28, make a study of the passives, and write out—I have been sent, thou has been sent, he has been sent, etc., both gens. and nos.

Exx.—Kí ma'rifat, ke bagair, ke wasíle se, ke sáth.

LESSON LIV.

Review.—Tell the story of iii.

Read x.

New words.—*Ḍákú*, robber ; *dar-bán*, door-keeper ; *báhar*, outside ; *gair*, strange ; *bhágná*, to flee ; *tamsíl*, parable ; *chárá*, grazing, fodder, food ; *charwáhá*, grazer, shepherd ; *chor*, thief ; *churáná*, to steal ; *kasrat*, abundance ; *málik*, master ; *bheṛiyá*, wolf ; *paráganda*, scattered : *fikr*, thought, anxiety ; *ján*, life ; *galla*, flock ; *chhínná*, to snatch ; *ikhtiyár*, authority ; *diwána*, mad ; *diwánagí*, madness ; *Tajdíd*, renewal ; *jáṛá*, cold, (n). winter ; *mausim*, season, corrupted into "monsoon" ; *gird*, around ; *ḍánwáḍol*, back and forth ; *sáf*, clean ; *kufr*, blasphemy ; *ṭahalná*, to walk about ; *bátil*, futile ; *áyá*, whether ; *bakná*, to talk foolishly ; *kufr bakná*, to blaspheme.

Suwálát.—Tamsíl sunáo. 1-5. Kyá unhon ne yih tamsíl samjhí? Darwáze kí bábat Masíh ne kyá kahá? Chor kí bábat kyá? 10. Mazdúr kyá kartá haí? 12, 13. Achchhe charwáhe kí do chár bátei̱ batáo? 11, 15. Ján dene lene ke báre mei̱ kyá kahá? 11, 15, 17, 18. Yahúdíoi̱ mei̱ ikh̲tiláf kyúi̱ húá? 'I'd-i-Tajdíd kab aur kahái̱ hotí thí? Yis'u' kahái̱ ṭahal rahá thá? 23. Masíh ke gird kaun ho gaye? 24. Kyá púchhte the? Yisú' apne apne haqq mei̱ kyá gawáhí pesh kartá thá? Wuh log us kí kyúi̱ na sunte the? 27. Use sangsár kyúi̱ karná cháhá? 33. Masíh ká kyá jawáb thá? Yisú' kahái̱ chalá gayá? 40. Log us ke haqq mei̱ kyá kahte the?

Observations.—Note the repetition in vs. 4, indicating repeated action, **áge áge, píchhe píchhe. Un ká láná,** vs. 16, where the obj. is in the poss. vs. 29, **wuh dí haii̱.** Why dí? Vs. 36, **áyá,** whether, often used to introduce an indirect question. *Chalá gayá* in 40 has the form of the passive, but not its signification. In 37 **nahíi̱** with **kartá** shows the verb is in the Indf. pres, while **na kartá** would be either subj. past or ind. prest.

Drill.—As in 9, **áyá jáyá karegá,** and 40, **diyá kartá thá,** use these two tenses with the customary form of verbs in 1-6. Note that it is not **gáyá karegá,** but **jáyá.** Hooper says this is because *jáyá* is an old infinitive form, and that all these forms, used to denote customary action, are ancient infs., not past participles.

Exx.—Ke andar, ke gird, ke sabab.

Under Observations.—Note the direct discourse in vs. 6.

LESSON LV.

Read xi.—Tell the story in brief.

Review.—Tell the story of ii.

New words.—*Bahin,* sister; *pái̱w* or *páoi̱,* foot; *'itr, attar*, perfume ; *bál*, hair ; *ponchhná*, to wipe, rub ; *'azíz*, dear ; *maut*, death ; *ṭhokar*, stumble ; *soná*, to sleep ; *suláná*, to put to sleep ; *jágná*, to wake ; *jagáná*, to waken one ; *bachná*, to escape danger ; *bacháná*, to save ; *fásila*, space, distance ; *tasallí*, comfort ; *qiyámat*, resurrection ; *khayál*, thought, idea ; *qadam*, footstep ; *girná*, to fall ; *niháyat*, exceedingly ; *ranjída*, grieving ; *ranj*, grief ; *ghabráná*, to be confused, agitated (also transitive) ; *ánsú*, tear, tears ; *bahná*, to flow ; *gár*, a cave ; *dharná*, to place ; *bad-bú* stench ; *khushbú*, perfume ; *bá'is*, reason ; *baland*, lofty ; *kafan*, winding-sheet ; *bandhná*, to be bound ; *bándhná*, to bind ; *chihrá*, face ; *rúmál*, handkerchief ; *lipatná*, to be rolled up ; *sadr*, chief ; *qaum*, nation, tribe ; *qabza*, possession ; *ummat*, people of a faith or sect ; *nubúwat*, prophecy ; *nabí*, prophet ; *sál*, year, years ; *mashwara* conference ; *'alániya*, openly ; *jangal*, woods, waste land ; *'iláqa*, district ; *dihát*, country, as opposed to city ; *ittilá'*, intimation, information ; *nínd*, sleep.

Suwálát.—Kinhon ne kis bát kí khabar kahlá bhejí ? 3. Jab Masíh jáne lagá, to kyá guftgú húí ? 7-14. Tomá ne apne sáth ke shágirdon se kyá kahá ? 16. Un ke áne par La'zar ko qabr men rakkhe húe kitne din ho gaye the ? 17. Masíh se milte hí dono bahinon ne kyá kyá kahá ? 21, 32. Marthá ne kis tarah se apní bahin Mariam ko buláyá ? Is par Mariam ne kyá kiyá ? Us ke sáth kaun gaye ? 29, 31. Yisú' ke ánsú dekhkar log kyá kyá kahne lage ? 36 37. Jab Masíh ne patthar haṭáne ko kahá, to us mare húe kí bahin ne kyá kahá ? Wuh kaisí qabr thí ? 38. Masíh ne kis bát ká shukr kiyá ? 41, 42. Shukr karke kyá pukárá ? 43. La'zar kis tarah se nikal áyá ? 44. Masíh ne kyá hukm diyá ? 44. Is mu'jize se kyá do natíje húe ? Sadr 'adalat men kyá mashwara húá ? 47-53. Yisú' 'alániya kyún na phirá ? Kyá hukm diyá gayá thá ? 54-57.

Observations.—Note the particular idioms in the questions and their textual answers. Master these. In 28, 54, yahín, wahín, are intensive forms of yahán, wahán. In 9, 10, din ko, rát ko, bárah baje ko, do pahr ko, shám ko, points of time at which, or during which, the event takes place. In vs. 6 do din aur, measure of time, without the prep. Compare the sentences with agar. As at end of 11 and 14, note the two ways of expressing purpose. In 44, háth páon bandhe húe might be construed as an accusative absolute, "his hands and feet being bound"—with the shroud.

Drill.—Vs. 29. Substitute *bolte, kahte, uṭhte, buláte, dekhte* with any other proper changes. Use these verbs with the synopsis table.

Exx.—Ke ás pás, ke bá'is.

Chand ek báten. Ek laṛká is gáon kí taraf á rahá hai. Ek laṛkí us ke sáth hai. Wuh uskí bahin hai. Uske lambe lambe bál 'itr se khushbúdár hain. Wuh apní mán ko baṛá 'azíz hai. Agar us laṛke par maut áe to us kí mán ko baṛá sádma (shock, grief) hogá. Ab bachcha thak gayá hai aur laṛkí apne bháí ko suláne lagí hai. Ab wuh so gayá hai. Laṛkí chalí gayí hai. Tum chupke se chalo, usko mat jagáo. Agar wuh jáge to kaun usko tasallí de sakegá?

Us ne yih bát kal mujhe kahlá bhejí. Kyá tum din ko jáoge, yá rát ko? Tum apne sáth ke logon ko is bát ká 'ittilá' do. Do qadam áge barho. Kyún ghabráte ho? Ham sab bach jáenge. Jáne do. Áne do. Rahne do. Marne do. Kahne do. Kholne do. Karne diyá. Uṭháne diyá. Apne naukar ko hukm do, ki baland pahár par chahṛ jáo. Merí kyún nahín sunte ho?

LESSON LVI.

Read xii.—Tell the story.

Review.—Tell the story of xi.

New words.—*Jíná*, to live; *jiláná*, to make to live; *taiyár*, ready; *khidmat*, service; *khádim*, servant, *khidmatgár*, servant (among English table-servant); *jatámasí*, spikenard; *ádh*, half; *ser*, two pounds, quart; *khális*, pure; *besh-qímat*, priceless; *qímat:* price, worth; *qímatí*, valuable; *mahakná*, to exhale perfumes; *dínár*, shilling, denarius; *garíb*, pl. *gurba*, poor; *'ám*, pl. *'awám*, common; *thailí*, bag; *sirf*, only; *khajúr*, date (s. and pl.), date-palm; *dálí*, branch; *mubárak*, blessed; *gadhá*, *gadhí*, ass; *sawár*, rider; *beṭí*, daughter; *sulúk*, treatment; *sochná*, to think, consider; *ban paṛná*, to be made, attained; *pairau*, follower; *gehún*, wheat; *dáná*, grain, *Janáb*, sir; *phal*, fruit; *khona*, to lose; *'adáwat*, enmity; *mahfúz*, guarded; *bádal*, cloud; *garajná*, to thunder; *khenchná*, to draw; *ishára*, sign, hint; *paigám*, message; *sakht*, hard; *ruj'ú*, turning towards.

Observations.—Note price in vs. 5 with *men*. In 6 **nikál lená**, where **lená** gives the signification of *for one's self*; **nikál dená** would be to take out and give to another. **Gurba** and **'awámm** are Arabic pls. **'Awám un nás**, men in general, all men; **Yúnán**, Greece, and **Yúnání**, Grecian. In 19 **ban paṛná** belongs to a class of verbs, where the second member does not apparently add any especial meaning to the first part. The last word of 27, **bachá**, has the accent on the last syllable, which is owing to the fact that it is from **bacháná**, not from **bachná**. It illustrates that one must know a language before he can pronounce it. Note the direct discourse in 33, and the passives in 31, 32, 34, 42. In 46, **núr hokár**, "being a light," as a light.

In 47, *mujrim* (from *jurm*, a crime, offence, charge), a criminal, one charged with crime.

Suwálát.—Yisú' Bait'anniyáh men̲ kab áyá ? 1. Wahán̲ kaun the ? Wahán̲ logon̲ ne uske wáste kyá taiyár kiyá ? 2. Kaun kaun us waqt maujúd the ? 'Itr kí bábat batáo. 3-8. Wuh 'itr kitne men̲ bik saktá thá ? 5. Yahúdah ne yih bát kyún̲ kahí ? Log Báit'anniyáh ko kyún̲ aé ? 9. Yarúshalem men̲ Yisú' ké dák̲h̲il hone ká zikr karo. 12-18. Farísí kyá kahne lage ? 19. Masíh se milne ke líe kaun áe ? 20. Kis kí ma'rifat milná cháhá ? 21, 22. Yisú' ká jawáb kyá thá ? 24-26. Ásmán se kyá áwáz áí ? 28. Logon̲ ne kyá kahá ? 29. Charháe jáne ke báre men̲ Masíh ne kyá kahá ? aur kyún̲ ? 32. Itne mu'jizon̲ se kyá húá ? 37. Yasha'yáh ne yih báten̲ kís líe kahín̲ ? 41. Sardáron̲ ke ímán kí bábat kyá zikr hai ? 42, 43. Kaun Masíh par ímán na lánewálon̲ ko mujrim ṭhahráegá ? 47, 48. Masíh kyá kahtá aur boltá thá ? 49. Hamesha kí zindagí kyá hai. 50.

Drill.—Yih (*ádmí*) *is kí nisbat* (*achchhá*) *hai.* Substitute *lambá, bará, burá, chhoṭá, bhárí* (heavy), *sak̲h̲t, sídhá, patlá, moṭá.* Also, table, book, man, men, woman, women, *shahr, qabr, gadhá, gehún̲, dáná, 'itr, phal.*

Exx.—Main̲ charháyá jáún̲gá, tú, wuh, ham, tum, áp, wuh, in both genders.

LESSON LVII.

Read xiii. and tell the story.

Review.—Write story of xi.

New words.—Ruk̲h̲sat leave, dismission; *Iblís, Shaitán*, Satan, *dastark̲h̲wán*, table-cloth; *bartan*, dish; *shurú'* commencement; *naháná*, to bathe; *sarásar*, wholly; *pahinná*, to dress, to put on one's clothes; *pahináná*, to put clothes on another; *dhoná*, to wash; *dhuláná*, to cause to wash; *namúná*, pattern; *ba-sharte*, on condition; *nawishta*, scripture; *lát márná*, to kick; *shubha*, doubt; *síná*, breast; *chhátí*, breast, bosom; *sahára*, support; *niwála*, morsel; *ḍúbná*, *ḍuboná*, to sink; *samáná*, to be contained in; *jald*, quickly; *darkár*, necessary; *muhtáj* poor, needy; *murg̲*, cock; *murg̲í*, hen; *báng*, voice, call; *bár*, time; *ján*, life; *farz*, obligation, duty.

Observations.—Note that jaisá in 1 and 15 does not have the correlative as it does in 33. Urdu rather more than Hindi, inclines to omit the correlatives. Why at the end of vs. 5 is it **kiye** and not kiyá? In 7, ba'd men̲, shows that ba'd is really a noun. **Dhone na páegá** is the regular permissive form, inflected inf. with *páná*. In 10 **sab ke sab** means all of all, every whit, *Koṭ pahino*, put on your coat. *Bábá ká koṭ pahináo*, put the child's coat on him. In 14 **mujh Khudáwand ne dhoe** seems inexplicable, where we should expect *main̲ K̲hudáwand ne*, but we have as we might expect in Lk. xviii. 13, Be merciful to me a sinner, **mujh gunahgár par rahm kar.** Note **dhoyá karo** and **kiyá karo**, next vs. **Naukar baṛá nahín̲ hotá**, *is never*, as a rule, but **nahín̲ hai** would mean *is not*, in this particular instance. **Jatáe detá hún̲** expresses authority in the form *jatáe*, as compared with the thought of the form *jatátá hún̲*. In 33, *bachcho*, *o* is the regular vocative pl. ending.

Suwálát.—Masíh dunyá se ruk̲hsat hokar kidhar játá thá? Wuh apnon̲ se kaisí muhabbat rakhtá thá? Yahúdah ke dil men̲ kyá bát thí? Masíh ne kis taríqe (tarah) se unke pair dhoe? 4-10. Un par kyá farz thá? 14. Us ne kyá namúna diyá? 15. Kaun baṛá nahín̲ hotá? 16. Kaunsá nawishta Masíh ke haqq men̲ púrá húá? 18. Jo koí bheje húe ko qabúl kartá hai, wuh kis ko qabúl kartá hai? 20. Apne pakṛe jáne ke báre men̲ Masíh ne kyá kahá? 21. Is men Patrus aur Yuhanná kí taraf se suwál kaise kiyá gayá? 23-26. Masíh ne Yahúdáh se kyá kahá aur báqí shágirdon ne kyá samjhá? 29. Kyá nayá hukm shágirdon ko milá? 34. Patrus ke báre men kyá bát húí? 36-38.

Drill.—Dhoyá karo. Yih kitáb liyá karo. Waqt par pahunchá karo. Bárah baje rukhsat diyá karo. Ustád ke pás jáyá karo. Ek dúsre se mahabbat rakkhá karo. Is men pání dálá karo. Golí pakará karo. Shám ká áṭh baje khánâ kháyá karo. Rukhsat gyárah baje húá kare. So with the verbs in the vss. 3-11.

E.G.—Mujhe rukhsat hai? Dastarkhwán bichhá húá hai. Yih bartan kharíd lo, achchhe hain. Áp ne Urdú paṛhná kab shurú' kiyá? In kapṛon ko dhoo. Dhulái kitní hogí? Wuh Hindú roz nahátá hai. Yih ádmí sarásar jhúṭhá hai. Bábá ká koṭ pahináo. Janáb, main ne bahuterá pahináyá magar wuh pahintá nahín. Yihí namúna kursí ká hai. Isí ke mutábiq banáyá karo. Is kamre men das ádmí mushkil se samá sakte hain. Yih murġíán moṭí hain. Bihtar ki áp kharíd len, basharte ki darkár hon. Is lakṛí ká sahára lo, nahín to tum ḍúbke maroge. Yih murġ bahut sawere báng diyá karte hain.

LESSON LVIII.

Read xiv.

Write the story of xiii.

New words.—*Makán*, place, dwelling; *madadgár*, helper; *madad*, help; *hásil*, produce, gain; *yatím*, orphan; *thoṛá*, little; *der*, lateness, delay; *chúnki*, since; *piyárá*, dear, beloved; *sukúnat*, dwelling; *sákin*, dweller; *maskin*, dwelling-place; *sukúnat-gáh*, dwelling-place; *yád diláná*, to remind; (*dená*) *diláná*, to cause to give; *itmínán*, assurance; *káfí*, sufficient; *muddat*, length of time; *báqí*, left, remaining.

Observations.—Note the Subjunctive mood in **ghabráe**, also at end of 27. After **táki**, we always have it, and as **ki** is frequently used with the same meaning as **táki**, we have the Subj. frequently after **ki**, as in end of 16, and in 31 **ki jáne, ki** of purpose, and a little farther on **ki** introducing the direct object clause of **jáne**. **Wahán̠ kí ráh**, as *Ágrá kí ráh*, the road to Agra, **Dihlí kí ráh**, the road to Delhi. In 7 **Agar jáná hotá** is an infrequent past perf. conditional, equivalent to the common *agar jántá*. Cf. 13 : 19 with 14 : 27 **diye játá hun̠** and **jatáe detá hun̠**. Collate the "*agars*" and note the difference in meaning, according to mood and tense.

Drill.—Use all the verbs of vss. 25-31 in sentences with **sakná** and **chukná**, varying the subjects through persons and genders, by Synopsis Table.

E.G.—Áp kitní muddat se Hindustán men̠ hain̠? Yih kahán̠ kí ráh hai? Itne rúpae káfí hon̠ge? Koí ádmí is ádmí ke wasíle ke baġair Baṛe Sáhib ke pás já nahín̠ saktá. In se baṛe makán áp ke pás nahín̠ haín̠. Áp ko is kám men̠ koí madadgár cháhiye. Us ne kitne rúpae hásil kiye? Is yatím laṛke ke mán̠ báp kab mar gaye? Main̠ thoṛí der b'ad jáún̠gí. Yih laṛká áp ko bahut piyára hai. Gáṛí abhí áyá cháhtí hai. Kitní der hogí? Der kuchh nahín̠. Do miniṭ men̠ áwegí. Áp kí sukúnatgáh kahán̠ hai? Main̠ do mahíne se Ágrá men̠ sukúnat kartá hún̠. Main̠ áp ko itmínán detá hún̠ ki yih kám kal tak zarúr ho jaegá.

Exx.—I did it before (after) he came, went, read the book, sent it, bought it. All pronouns.

LESSON LIX.

Read xv.

Review.—Write the story of v., in class.

New words.—*Angúr*, grape; *bág̲bán*, gardener; *darbán*, door-keeper; *phal*, fruit; *chháṉṭná*, to sift, prune; *judá*, separate; *pheṉkná*, to throw; *súkhná*, to dry (intr.); *sukháná*, to cause to dry; *ág*, fire; *jhoṉkná*, to stoke, throw; *jalná*, to burn (intr.); *jaláná*, to make burn; *dost*, friend; *dostí*, friendship; *chunná*, to choose; *muqarrar*, appointed; *'adáwat*, enmity, hatred; *satáná*, to persecute; *'uzr*, excuse; *muft*, gratis, free; *kaṭná*, to be cut; *káṭná*, to cut; *kaṭáná*, to have cut.

Observations.—Vs. 4, **Jis tarah... isí tarah**, so in 9 **Jaise ... waise**, but in 12 the correlative is omitted. In 13 end, **de de**, shows an idiomatic use of **de** as an auxiliary to the root of some other verb, which in this case happens to be **dená**, and here is Subj. Why? Cf. 15 end. and 14 : 28 mid. So is **lená** used, with rather the force of the Greek Middle, i.e. reflexive, as in 16, **chun liyá.** In 9 **jab hí** appears to have the force of **tab hí**, and is often so used, *then indeed.* In 20 **yád rakkho**, remember; **yád áná**, to come to mind; **yád diláná**, to remind; **yád-gár**, a memorial; **yádgárí**, a token; **gunáh**, sin; **gunahgár**, sinner. In 6, passive voice.

Sentences.—Do ser angúr bázár se láná. Hamáre bág̣ ke lie koí achchhá bág̣bán [málí] buláná cháhiye. In darak̲h̲toṉ se ḍálíoṉ ko káṭ do táki phal ziyáda lage. Is ko achchhí tarah se chháṉṭ lo. Wuh judá hokar kyúṉ baiṭhe haiṉ? Gend pheṉko. Kapṛe súkhne ko ḍálo. Yih ádmí ág meṉ lakṛíáṉ jhoṉk rahe haiṉ. Wiláyat se mere do dost á gaye haiṉ. Us ká kyá 'uzr? Us ne mujhe muft satáyá. Jisko áp chuneṉge, maiṉ us ko muqarrar karúṉgá. Is kamre meṉ ág k̲h̲úb jal rahí hai. Gol-kamre meṉ bhí ág jaláo.

Drill.—Change all the verbs with *agar* to the "contrary to fact" form.

Exx.—*Ke lie, ke sabab, kí tarah*, with all pronouns, and dost, phal, ḍálí, angúr, darakht, ág, naukar, bát, both singulars and plurals.

LESSON LX.

Read.—xvi.

Review.—Tell the story of xi, then write it.

New words.—*Gumán*, thought, idea ; *g̠am*, sorrow ; *g̠amgín*, sorrowful ; *fáida*, profit, advantage ; *fáidamand*, advantageous ; *rást*, righteous ; *rástbází*, righteousness ; *qusúr*, fault ; *qusúrwár*, faulty ; *bardásht*, endurance ; *tamám*, entire ; *áyanda*, future, coming ; *mátam*, weeping, wailing ; *janná*, to bring forth ; *dukh*, pain ; *ghaṛí*, hour, time ; *bachcha*, young (noun) ; *dard*, bodily pain ; *chhínná*, to snatch away ; *musíbat*, trouble ; *g̠álib*, overcoming, victorious ; *k̲h̲átir*, heart, sake ; *k̲h̲átirjama' rakkho*, keep up heart, lit. keep together heart.

Observations.—Note direct discourse in 2, end, and 19, second line. In 12, learn, aur bhí bahut sí bátein̲ kahní hain̲. The subj. of *hain̲* is baten̲ kahní, the inf., as a gerundive agreeing with its obj. In 32 apne apne, each his own.

Sentences.—Gumán na karo ki Urdú bag̣air koshish hásil kiyá jáegá, warna (else) afsos hogá. Rástbáz honá fáidamand hai, magar ná-rást ádmí g̣amgín hon̲ge. Má báp apne bachchon̲ ke qusúron̲ kí bardásht karte hain̲. Áyanda ko tum in qusúrwáron̲ se alag raho, nahín̲ to (warna) musíbat men̲ paṛoge. Is bachche ko dukh na dená. Mere háth men̲ baṛá dard ho rahá hai. Us laṛke ne apní ṭopí mere háth se chhín lí. Jo laṛke laṛ (fight) rahe the, un men̲ kaun g̣álib áyá? Merí k̲h̲átir ek ghaṛí yahán̲ par ṭhahro.

Drill.—Put the verbs of 25-38 in the future, all pers. and nos.

Exx.—*Kí khátir, kí tarah, ke pás, ke báre,* with nouns of new lesson, sings. and pls.

LESSON LXI.

Read xvii.

Review.—Write story of v. in class.

New words.—*Har,* every; *bashar,* mankind, humanity; *wáhid,* single, alone, singular number (grammar); *barhaqq,* true, very truth; *paidá,* born; *paidáish,* birth; *peshtar,* before; *jalál,* glory; *jalálí,* glorious; *pahuncháná,* to cause to arrive; xiv. 26, *quds, quddús, muqaddas,* holy; *nigahbání,* guard; *nigáh,* sight; *nigahbán,* watchman; *hifázat,* preservation; *halákat,* destruction; *halák karná,* to destroy; *sharír,* wicked; *biná,* foundation; *'álam,* world; *'ádil,* just; *'adálat,* justice; *wáqif,* knowing; *waqúf,* knowledge; *bewuqúf,* a fool.

Observations.—Use **peshtar** with either **se** or **ke,** as in 5 and 24. In 8 and 13, **sach sach,** and **púrí púrí,** the doubling gives an intensive idea. Collate the objects of *diyá* in vss. 2-9, 22, 24, and explain why always *diyá.*

Sentences.—Kyá yih lafz wáhid haí yá jama'? Yih lafz wáhid hai, kyúnki us ke sáth hai milá hai. Jo bashar paidá hotá hai, so hí mar játá hai. Jalálí farishte maqaddas logon kí nigahbání karte hain. Khudá hamárí hifázat karke hamen halákat se bachátá hai. Agar yih ádmí be-wuqúf na hotá to sharír na bantá. Biná-e-'álam se peshtar Khudá thá.

Drill.—Put all verbs of 22-26 in past tense, retaining same subjects.

Exx.—Jo (kuchh) us ne mujhe diyá wuh sab terí hí taraf se hai.

Substitute.—*Ghoṛe, ghoṛíán, ádmí, laṛkíán, laṛke, shágird, zindagí, zamín, kalám, jalál, paisa,* for *kuchh.*

LESSON LXII.

Read xviii.

Review stories of i., and tell in class.

New words.—*Nálá*, water-course, small stream; *aksar*, usually; *sipáhí*, sepoy, soldier; *palṭan*, battalion; *mash'ala*, torch; *hathyár*, weapon, tool; *talwár*, sword; *dahina*, right; *kán*, ear; *uṛná*, to fly; *uṛáná*, to make fly; (*chalná*) *chaláná*, to make go, drive; *miyán*, sheath; *súbadár*, officer; *piyáda*, footsoldier; *susar, susrá*, father-in law; *saláh*, advice; *bihtar*, better; *jánpahchán*, acquaintance; *diwán-kháná*, office, court, hall; *darbání*, doorkeeper(ess); *launḍá*, servant; *launḍí*, servant-girl; *koelá*, charcoal; *dahkáná*, to light a fire; *tap*, fever; *tapná*, or *tápná*, to get warm by a fire; *tamáncha*, slap or blow; *rishta*, relationship; *rishtedár*, relation; *qal'a, qilá*, fort; *nápák*, unclean; *faryád*, petition, complaint; *bad-kár*, evil-worker; *kárkhána*, workshop; *taríq*, fashion, manner; *hawála*, charge, custody; *nazar*, sight; *manzúr*, seen, i.e. accepted; *chilláná*, to scream, cry out.

Observations.—In vs. 3 **mash'alon, aur chirágon, aur hathyáron**, are joined by *aur*, which is sometimes inserted where in English we would say torches, lamps and weapons. In some connections *aur* is omitted, where we would use it, as **roṭí makkhan**, bread and butter, **beṭe betíon** *ke líe*, for his sons and daughters [*beṭon beṭíon ke líe*, would not be idiomatic]. In 4 *honewálí* means the *things about to happen.* In 14 *marná* is the subj., a common use of the inf. In 21 *kyá kyá* means what different things I have done. In 23 *burái* is the abstract noun formed from *burá*. Note the participle *bandhá húá* used with use. In 33, **ján** se márná is a regular idiom for már ḍálná, to kill. **Bádsháh,** king, gives us the noun **bádsháhat,** kingdom; it is of Persian origin, though we do have also *bádsháhí.* In 36, we have the rather unusual passive past subjunctive, *kiyá játá,* after a clause of purpose, "that I should not have been put in charge of." In 33 the unusual order of the words in Pilate's question strongly emphasises the **kyá.**

Suwálát.—Yisú' kidhar gayá? 1. Wuh jagah us ke pakaṛwánewále ko kis tarah ma'lúm thí? 2. Yahúdáh kin kin ádmíon̲ ko sáth lekar áyá? 3. Yisú' ne un se kyá púchhá? 4. Jab us ne kahá ki Main̲ hí hún̲, to un ko kyá húá? 6. Masíh ne apne shágirdon̲ ke líe kyá darkh̲wást kí? 8. Patrus ne kyá kiyá? 10, 11. Masíh ko wuh kahán̲ le gaye? 12-14. Darbání ne Patrus se kyá púchhá? 17. Jáṛe ke sabab log kyá kar rahe the? 18. Hanná ne Masíh ke sáth kyá kiyá? 24. Yahúdí use Pílátus ke pás kyún̲ le gaye? 31. Agar Masíh kí bádsháhat is dunyá kí hotí to kyá hotá? 36. Pílátus ne kyá cháhá aur kyún̲? 39. Bhíṛ ne kis ko chuná? 40.

Drill.—We eat breakfast, dinner, supper, lunch, at six, twelve, two, eight, ten o'clock. In all pers., nos., gens., of the **kháyá karte hain̲** form.

Exx.—*Nálí, nálá,* also *daryá, jhíl, samundar, hauz, táláb,* both nos. with *ke pár.*

All pros., and man, men, boy, boys, girl, girls, soldier, soldiers, women, *-ke hawále* and *ke sabab.*

LESSON LXIII.

Read xix. 1-37.

Review story of xviii. and tell story in class.

New words.—*Kánṭá,* thorn, fork; *táj,* crown; *arg̲awání,* scarlet; *poshák*, clothing; *ádáb*, respect; *salíb*, cross; *ahl*, people; *qatl*, killing; *khair-khwáh*, well-wisher; *mukhálif*, opponent; *taiyárí*, preparation; *chabútara*, a mound or terrace to sit on; *Qaisar*, Cæsar; *'Ibrání*, Hebrew; *khopṛí*, skull; *kitába* or *katba*, motto, inscription; *maqám*, place, encampment; *kurta*, shirt; *hissa*, part; *bin-silá*, un-sewn; *bunná*, to knit, weave; *pháṛná*, to tear, split; *qur'a*, lot; *bánṭná*, to divide; *bíwí*, wife; *sirká*, vinegar; *bhígná*, to get wet; *bhígoná*, to wet; *isfanj*, sponge; *zúfa*, hyssop; *shákh*, twig, branch; *jhukáná*, to bend something; *ṭáng*, leg; *lásh*, body, corpse; *toṛná*, to break; *utárná*, to take down; *maslúb* (from salíb cross), crucified; *bhálá*, spear; *chhedná*, to pierce; *paslí*, rib; *haḍḍí*, bone.

Observations.—Koṛe lagwáe, had some one lagáná koṛe, and so koṛe lag gaye. In 3 us ke [*badan men*] tamánche máre. Note the participles in 5, rakkhe; 17 uṭháe húe, pahine 19, 20, likhá húá 23, buná húá, and 29, bhará húá, bhigoe húe. In 12 it is hard to see what difference it would make if the common form chhoṛ detá were used. Collate the passives.

Suwálát.—Sipáhíon ne Yisú' ko kyá kyá pahináyá? 2. Pílátus ne salíb dene ke báre men kyá kahá? 6. Jab Pílátus ne chhoṛná cháhá to Yahúdíon ne kyá kahá? 12. Sipáhíon ne us ke kapṛon ke sáth kyá kyá kiyá? 23-24. Unhon ne Masíh ko kyún aur kis tarah se piláyá? 28-29. Yahúdíon kí kyá darkhwast Pílátus se thí? 31. Kaunse do nawishte kis tarah púre húe? 34-36.

Drill.—The (table) was given to him. Substitute tables, book, crown, clothing, *kitába*, *khopṛí*, shirt, vinegar, body, *shákh*, also in pls.

Exx.—Put verbs of 31-37 into present tense.

LESSON LXIV.

Read xix. 33—xx. 31. Tell the story.

Review.—Write the story of xviii.

New words.—*Khufya*, secret; *taur*, manner; *ijázat*, permission; *murr*, myrrh; *'úd*, incense; *súti*, linen; *khushbúdár*, fragrant; *kafnáná*, to enshroud; *dafn*, burial; *tarke*, early; *hatná*, to push aside, put out of the way; *daurná*, to run; *baṛhná*, to go forward, to get ahead; *bamújib*, according to; *safed*, white; *sirháná*, pillow, bed-head; *páenti*, bed-foot; *miyán*, sir, friend; *chhúná*, to touch; *salámatí*, peace, prosperity; *mekh*, peg, big nail; *surákh*, hole; *i'tiqád*, trust; *be-i'tiqád*, faithless.

Observations.—In 39 and 26, ser and roz as measures do not take the ending on. In 4, **Patrus ke áge**, if it were at rest, but se áge, since it is motion. In 5 nazar kí, you will note the higher pitch of kí, as compared with kí, of, in 42. See also vs. 11. In 4, 6, 11, the repetition of the word indicates a repeated act or condition. Collate participles, and passives. Master participial idioms of 29.

Suwálát.—Kis ne Yisú' kí lásh mángí? Kis kis ne kafnáyá? 39. Kahán dafnáyá? 42. Kaun taṛke qabr par áí? 1. Us ne shágirdon ko kyá khabar dí? 1, 2. Dauṛke unhon ne kyá kyá dekhá? Kaun pahle pahunchá? 4, 6. Mariam ne kyá kuchh dekhá? 11-17. Usí shám ko shágird kahán the? 19. Masíh ne pás áke kyá kiyá? 19-23. Kaun us waqt gair-házir thá? 24. Us ne kyá kahá? 25. Áṭh roz ke ba'd kyá húá? 26, 27, 29. Yih báten is kitáb men kyún likhí gayín 30, 31.

Drill.—This, these book-s, table-s, chair-s, thing-s, cloth-s, person-s, boy-s, girl-s, were sent, will be sent, are being sent.

Exx. Sentences.—Khufya sipáhi (the secret police) ko

buláná cháhiye. Us taur se likhná nahín cháhiye, is taur se likho. Is qaida ke bamújib us ko barí sazá milegí. Mujhe ijázat hai ki main jáún? Kafn dafn ke líe kuchh rúpaya cháhiye. Hat jáo, dauro, dauro, tab hí barhoge. Jis ko ádmí 'izzat dená cháhtá hai, usí ko wuh sirháne bithátá hai. Áp salámatí se áe hain? Kal tak hamen pachás mekhen cháhiye. Mere kapre men yih súrákh kis tarah se áyá hai? Yih ádmí i'tiqad ke láiq nahín hai. Miyán jí, páentí na baitho. Sirháne baitho.

Exx.—Change all verbs of 1-10 into other genders and numbers.

LESSON LXV.

Read xxi.—Tell the story.

Tell story of xx.

New words.—*Shikár*, hunting; *jál*, net; *kasrat*, abundance; *nangá*, naked; *kúdná*, to jump; *dongí*, a boat; *dúr*, far; *báwujúd is ke*, "with this existing," in spite of this; *phatná*, to tear (intr.); *jur'at*, temerity; *gallabání*, herding; *dilgír*, sorrowful; *jawán*, young man; *búrhá*, old; *hál*, state; *gunjáish*, room, capacity.

Observations.—In 4 note **hote hí**, a very common idiom. In 8 **háth,** is cubit. In 11 **kasrat ke báwujúd**, "along with," *i.e.* in spite of, the abundance. In 12 **púchhtá** is past conditional, "to no one became temerity that he should ask him, who art thou?"

Suwálát.—Murdon men se jí uthne ke ba'd Yisú' tísrí bár kahán apne shágirdon par záhir húá? 1, 14. Shágird rát ko kyá karte the? 3. Subh hote hí kaun kanáre par á khará húá? 4. Us ne unhen kyá hukm diyá? 6. Shágird use pahchánkar kis kis tarah se kanáre par á gaye? 7. 8. Kitní machhlián pakrí gayín? 11. Kis bát kí jur'at un ko na húí? 12. Us ne Patrus se kyá suwál kiyá? 16.

Use kyá hukm diyá? 16. Us ke marne kí bábat kyá ishára diyá? 18. Yúhanná kí bábat kyá suwál aur jawáb thá? 21, 22.

Drill.—Vs. 24, Yih wuhí (shágird) hai jo in báton̠ kí gawáhí detá hai aur jis ne in ko likhá hai. Substitute: disciples, girl, girls, boy-s, man, men, woman, women.

Exx.—In use of *báwujúd*: Though poor she gave much money to the poor. I (you, he, she, they) will go in spite of my sickness. Notwithstanding his father's poverty he wasted his (his own) money. Notwithstanding his father's poverty he wasted his (his father's) money. In spite of your prohibition (*mumáni'at*) I will go. (Substitute in both clauses, changing about, man, men, women, boy-s, girl-s, king, soldiers).

LESSON LXVI.

Further Exercises.

Conjugation.

Main̠ apná kám kartá hún̠	I am doing my work.
Tú apná kám kartá hai	Thou art doing thy work.
Wuh apná kám kartá hai	He is doing his own work.
Ham apná kám karte hain̠	We are doing our work.
Tum apná kám karte ho	You are doing your work.
Áp apná kám karte hain̠	You are doing your work.
Wuh apná kám karte hain̠	They are doing their own work.

Main̠ apná kám kartí hún̠.

Etc.

1. Tumhárá nám kyá hai? Áp ká ism mubárak kyá hai? Áp ká ism sharíf kyá hai?	1. What is your name? What is your blessed name? What is your noble name?

2. Merá nám Khudá Bakhsh hai.*	2. My name is K. B.
3. Áiye, janáb, zará baiṭhiye. Sáhib kháná khá rahe hain.	3. Please come and take a seat, sir. Master is eating dinner.
4. Tashríf láiye.	4. Come (respectful; *lit.*, bring your honour).
5. Áp tashríf le játe hain?	5. Are you going? (Respectful.)
6. Áp tashríf kahán rakhte hain?	6. Where do you live?
7. Kyá unhon ne yihí loṭá tum ko diyá thá yá nahín? Yih to unká hargiz nahín, yih to merá hí hai.	7. Did they give you this *loṭá*† or not? This is not theirs at all, it's mine.
8. Áp is kitáb ko paṛhiye, yih merí sab se achchhí kitáb hai.	8. Kindly read this book. It is my best.
9. Áp ne yih loṭá kitne men liyá?	9. How much did you get this *loṭá* for?
10. Main ne yih loṭá ek rúpae ko liyá.	10. I got this *loṭá* for one rupee.
11. Main ne yih chádar chha sát áne gaz lí thí.	11. I got this sheet at six or seven annas a yard.

* The reply is always given thus; the use or even implied acceptance of honorific language concerning oneself being considered bad form. Thus if one inquires, *Áp kab tashríf láe?* no educated Indian would reply simply *kal*, as Europeans often do, as this implies, "Main kal tashríf láyá"!—but he immediately changes the sentence and replies, *Main kal áyá*. So in reply to *Áp ká ism sharíf kyá hai?* one may not reply simply "Khudá Bakhsh" or "John Smith," as this implies "Merá ism sharíf Kh. B. hai," but must reply in full, in the simple form, *Merá nám Kh. B. hai*. [H. F.]

† A small round metal pot.

12. Ḍák-kẖáne se merí (ḍák kí) chiṭṭhíán̲, merá nám lekár, le áo.	12. Get my letters from the post office, giving my name.
13. Áp ke nám kí koí chiṭṭhí ḍák-wále ke pás náhín̲ hai.	13. The postman has no letters for you.
14. Sardár ne ákar kahá hai, ki Sáís ne baggí (bagghí) taiyár kar lí hai.	14. The head-servant has come and says that the syce has the buggy ready.
15. Kyá sáhib ne ab tak khááná nahín̲ kháyá ?	15. Has not the sahib eaten his dinner yet ?
16. Abhí khá rahe hain̲. Áp zará baiṭhen̲.	16. He is just eating. Will you be seated for a little.
17. In áṭh achchhe loṭon̲ ke liye kyá qímat dení cháhiye.	17. What ought one to give for these eight good *lotas* ?
18. Wuh loṭe achchhe nahín̲ hain̲ ; yih un se bahut achchhe hain̲.	18. Those *lotas* are not good ; these are much better.
19. In das jháṛanon̲ ke liye main̲ ne das das paise, ya'ní ḍhái, ḍhái áne diye.	19. For these ten dusters, I gave ten pice each, that is two and a half annas each.
20. Tumháre báp ká kyá nám hai ? Áp ke walíd ká ism mubárak kyá hai ?	20. What is your father's name ?
21. Ma'lum nahín̲, janáb.	21. Don't know, sir.
22. Us laṛke ne tum ko kitní roṭíãn̲ dín̲ ?	22. How many "breads" did that boy give you ?

23. Yih kapṛá chár áne gaz liyá thá.	23. I got this cloth at four annas a yard.
24. Main̲ tumháre liye kitáb láyá hún̲.	24. I have brought a book for you.

Note.—The ceremoniousness of the East, shown in some of the above sentences, is polite usage, and the occidental should accustom himself to using it. The agreement of verb with object in 9, 10, 14, 15, 22, 23, is curious, but it must be accepted and learned so thoroughly that one cannot fail to use it properly. Master these few sentences *absolutely.* Intransitive verbs agree with their subjects, as in 24. *Láyá* is reckoned as intransitive because it is a compound of *le-áná, le-áyá.*

Observe the comparison of adjectives in 24 and 41. It is the regular way of forming the comparative, *un se achchhá*, and the superlative, *sab se achchhá.**

Conjugation—Past Tense.

Main̲ roṭí lene gayá, gayí † .	I went to get bread.
Tú roṭí lene gayá, gayí ..	Thou wentest to get bread.
Wuh roṭí lene gayá, gayí ..	He, she, went to get bread.
Ham roṭí lene gaye, gayín̲..	We went to get bread.
Tum roṭí lene gaye, gayín̲ ..	You went to get bread.
Áp roṭí lene gaye, gayín̲ ..	You (polite) went etc.
Wuh roṭí lene gaye, gayín̲..	They went to get bread.
Main̲ bázár se láyá thá, lái thí.	I brought (or, had brought) it from the bazar.
Tú bázár se láyá thá, lái thí	Thou broughtest it from the bazar.

---

* The teacher should introduce the comparison of a number of adjectives with *se*, *sab se*, and *kí nisbat.*

† Let the pupil get both forms well, but especially learn well one's own gender.

Wuh bázár se láyá thá, láí thí.	He, she, brought it from the bazar.
Ham bázár se láe the, láí thíṉ.	We brought it from the bazar.
Tum bázár se láe the, láí thíṉ.	You brought it from the bazar.
Áp bázár se láe the, láí thíṉ	You, etc.
Wuh bázár se láe the, láí thíṉ.	They brought it from the bazar.
Maiṉ ne apní kitábeṉ un ko díṉ.	I gave them my books.*
Tú ne apní kítáb unko dí.	Thou gavest them thy book
Us ne apní kitáb unko dí.	He gave them his book.
Ham ne apní kitáb unko dí.	We gave them our book.
Tum ne apní kitáb unko dí.	You gave them your book.
Áp ne apní kitáb unko dí.	You gave them your book.
Unhoṉ ne apní kitáb unko dí.	They gave them their book.
Maiṉ ne, tú ne, us ne, ham ne, tum ne, áp ne, unhoṉ ne, uskí kitáb (mujhe) dí thí (tumko).	I gave you his book, thou gavest me his book. [Write each person and gender on a separate slip and so master it.]
Maiṉ ne, tú ne, waġaira, roṭíáṉ unse lí haiṉ.	I, thou, etc. have got bread from them.
Maiṉ ne, tú ne, waġaira, tín roṭíáṉ kháí thíṉ.	I, thou, etc., had eaten (or, ate) three loaves.
Maiṉ ne, tú ne, waġaira, khánáá pakáyá hai.	I, thou, etc., have cooked dinner.

LESSON LXVII.

1. Ab to ma'lúm nahín̲, magar ma'lúm karún̲gá.	1. I do not know now, but I'll find out.
2. Main̲ áún̲ ?	2. May I come ? Shall I come ?
3. Ham á jáen̲ ?	3. Shall we come in ?
4. Main̲ jáún̲ ?	4. May I go ? or, Shall I go ?
5. Main̲ *kyá* karún̲.	5. What *can* I do ?
6. *Ham* kyá karen̲.	6. What can *we* do ? (It's not our fault).
7. Main̲ pahle sadr bázár ko jáún̲gá, aur ummed hai ki wahán̲ se sab chízen̲ sastí mil jáen̲gín̲.	7. I shall go to the big bazar first, and I think that we shall get everything cheap there (all things from there cheap will be met).
8. Mujhe ijázat hai ?	8. May I go ? (Is there to me permission ?)
9. Ab ruk̲h̲sat hai. Kal phir áná.	9. You may go now. Come again to-morrow.
10. Laṛkon̲ ko khaṛá kar do.	10. Make the boys stand up.
11. K̲h̲úb. K̲h̲úb hai. K̲h̲úb kiyá.	11. Excellent. That's good. Well done.
12. Kyá húá ?	12. What's the matter ? (What happened ?)
13. Yih ak̲h̲bár sáhib ko de áná.	13. Go and give this paper to the sahib (giving come).

Conjugation.

Main kaunsá nek kám karúṉ táki maiṉ hamesha kí zindagí páúṉ ?
Tú kaunsá nek kám kare táki tú hamesha kí zindagí páe ?
Wuh kaunsá nek kám kare táki wuh hamesha kí zindagí páe ?
Ham kaunsá nek kám kareṉ táki ham hamesha kí zindagí páeṉ ?
Tum kaunsá nek kám karo táki tum hamesha kí zindagí páo ?
Áp kaunsá nek kám kareṉ táki áp hamesha kí zindagí páeṉ ?
Wuh kaunsá nek kám kareṉ táki wuh hamesha kí zindagí páeṉ ?

What good work can I do, that I may inherit eternal life ?

Note that the future endings coalesce with the root vowels of *lená* and *dená*. All other stems add these endings for the future.

Exercises in "ne."

Note that all transitive verbs in the past tenses take their subjects in the prepositional case form, with "*ne.*" The verbs *bolná, láná, bhúlná,* are used as intransitives. *Lená, dená, karná,* have the perfects *liyá, diyá, kiyá,* while *jáná, marná, honá,* have *gayá, múá, húá.* All other verbs are regular. The transitive verb in its past tenses agrees with its object. The mastery of this peculiarity can be secured only by memorizing these sentences most thoroughly. If your past work is "*kachchá*" be your own master sufficiently to go back and work it up. You cannot afford

* Both genders are the same.

to go on on the supposition that it will come somehow. The only secret of this method is *thoroughness.*

1. Maiṉ loṭá láyá húṉ.	1. I have brought the *loṭá.*
2. Maiṉ ne loṭá bhejá.	2. I sent the *loṭá.*
3. Maiṉ ne loṭá bhejá hai.	3. I have sent the *loṭá.*
4. Ham ne Láhaur meṉ liyá thá.	4. We got it in Lahore (*liya* and *liya tha* are often used indifferently).
5. Us ne yihí kitáb tum ko bhejí.	5. He sent you this very book.
6. Unhoṉ ne mere jáne se pahle yihí kitábeṉ Láhaur se bhejí thíṉ.	6. They had sent you these books from Lahore, before I went.
7. Tum ne achchhí roṭí nahíṉ bhejí.	7. You have not sent good bread.
8. Laṛkoṉ ne achchhá kám na kiyá.	8. The boys did not do good work.
9. Ḍák-wálá wiláyatí ḍák láyá hai ?	9. Has the postman brought the foreign mail ?
10. Ḍák-ghar ke bábú ne wiláyatí ḍák kal yá parsoṉ bhej dí thí.	10. The postmaster sent the foreign mail yesterday or day before.
11. Us 'aurat ne merí laṛkí ko* mårá.	11. That woman beat my girl.
12. Wuh 'auratеṉ kidhar gayí haiṉ ?	12. Whither have those women gone ?
13. Un 'auratoṉ ne yihí loṭá tum ko diyá.	13. Those women gave you *this* jug.

* *Ko* is always used when the object is a person or a definite thing.

14. Wuh laṛkí bolí ki "Ghar se dúr ho jáo."	14. The girl said, "Get away from the house."
15. Us laṛke ne kahá ki "Ham gáe láe hain."	15. The boy said, "We have brought the cow."
16. Mere ádmí ne kal kitáb bhej dí.	16. My man sent the book yesterday.
17. Qulí log hamárá ásbáb le gaye hain̲.	17. The coolies have taken off our luggage.
18. Un laṛkon̲ ne mere liye ek roṭí dí hai.	18. Those boys have given a loaf for me.
19. Kis ne hamáre loṭon̲ ko liyá, or, Kis ne hamáre loṭe liye ? [thí ?	19. Who took our jugs ?
20. Tum ne apní kitáb le lí	20. Did you get your book ?
21. Kyá sab naukar shahr ho áe hain̲ ?	21. Have all the servants been to and returned from the city ?
22. Kin logon̲ ne tum ko chaukíán̲ dín̲ ?	22. What poeple gave you chairs ?
23. Kin logon̲ ne laṛkí ko márá ?	23. What people beat the girl ?
24. Main̲ tín tín rúpae ko do loṭe láí hún̲.	24. I have bought (lit. brought) two lotas at three rupees each.
25. Main̲ das áne gaz kapṛá láyá hún̲.	25. I have brought cloth at ten annas a yard.
26. "Nahín̲," 'aurat bolí, "Laṛká mujh se nahín̲, wuh apní mán̲ se boltá thá."	26. "No," said the woman, "the boy did not speak to me, he was talking to his mother."
27. Kin ádmíon̲ ne yih chorí kí hai ?	27. What men have done this thieving ?

28. Kin laṛkíon̲ ne tum ko gálí dí ?	28. What girls were abusing you ?
29. Kyá tumne chaukí ko liyá ?	29. Did you take the chair ?

Note that *thá*, *thí*, *thín̲* do not always change the sense to past-perfect but are properly translated as simple past. Nevertheless, as in 6, they often give this pluperfect idea.

In 7 and 8 *nahín̲* and *na* are thus regularly used with the present perfect and simple past.

In 21 the emphasis is on the second action, going and *coming*.

Where the object is a thing, there a past transitive verb agrees in gen. and no., unless the concord be broken by "*ko*," when it takes the absolute form in "*á*."

Note how the gender of the subject though unexpressed is carried over into the verb. This is a nicety of speech, that, no matter how difficult, must be well acquired, else one's talk will often be unintelligible. We must learn to think of things in terms of "*á*," "*í*," and "*e*."

Intransitive verbs are much given to using the root with some form of "*jáná*," as in 12, 15, 29. Transitive verbs use "*dená*" in some form, when the action goes toward another, while a reflex termination is often shown by use of "*liya*," "*lená*," like the Greek Middle Voice.

All perfect participles are regularly formed by adding "*á*" to the root.

In 29, as usual, *ko* with *chaukí* makes it definite, and so we translate *the* chair.

LESSON LXVIII.

Sentences.

1. Kyá húá? Tum to isliye paidá nahín húe.	1. What's the matter? You were not born for this.
2. Main ḍák-kháne ho áyá hún.	2. I have been to the post-office (lit. I am come from the p.o., having been there).
3. Tum kahán paidá húe?	3. Where were you born?
4. Yih bachcha das din ká paidá húá hai.	4. This child has been born ten days.
5. Jab billí ke bachche hote the, to baṛá tamáshá hotá thá.	5. When there were kittens, then there was a great show.
6. Kyá tumhárá kám ho gayá hai?	6. Is your work done?
7. Janáb, kháná abhí taiyár ho játá hai.	7. Dinner'll be ready in a minute, sir.
8. Laṛke waqt par házír kyún nahín hote?	8. Why are not the boys present on time?
9. Kal to shahr men baṛá tamáshá húá.	9. There was a great spectacle in the city yesterday.
10. Yih kis tarah ma'lúm húá?	10. How did this become known?
11. Is laṛke ke siwá aur koí naukar házir nahín hai? Nahín, ġaríb-parwar.	11. Isn't there any other servant present but this boy? No, Sir. (No, nourisher of the poor).

12. Bachcha moṭá táza hotá gayá. — 12. The child went on getting fatter.

13. Wahán̲ jákar unke* laṛká paidá húá. — 13. They went there and a child was born to them (in their [house]).

14. Áj munshí ke ghar laṛká húá. — 14. A boy was born to the munshi to-day.

15. Rel par chaṛhná hai aur waqt bahut hí tang hai. Bát karne kí bhí fursat nahín̲ hai. — 15. I have to catch (mount) the train and the time is short (stragit). I have not time to say a word.

16. Shahr ho áe ho ? — 16. Have you been to the city ?

17. Áp ke kitne laṛke laṛkián̲ hain̲ ? — 17. How many boys and girls have you ?

18. Merí kitáben̲ kis ke pás hain̲ ? — 18. Who has my books ?

19. Rel se bahut chízen̲ chorí ho játí hain̲. — 19. Many things are stolen from the railway.

20. Main̲ abhí rawána hotá hún̲. — 20. I am starting at once.

21. Ab kám shurú' húá hai, usko fursat na hogí. — 21. Work has begun now, he'll have no time.

22. Mujhe Panjáb áe das baras húe hain̲. — 22. I have been in the Punjab ten years. (To me, come to the P. ten years have been).

23. Ájkal garmí bahut hotí hai. — 23. It is very warm these days.

---

* In 13 "*unke*," not "*unko*," since "*hán̲*," house, place, is understood and "*hán̲*," is locative.

24. Main̲ áp ke dekhne se baṛá k̲h̲ush hotá hún̲.	24. I am always very pleased to see you.
25. Jab báz ká bachchá tín chár mahíne ká ho jatá hai, wuh uṛ játá hai.	25. When the hawk's fledgling gets to be three or four months old, it flies away.
26. Áj sabhon̲ ká kám ho jáegá.	26. Everybody's work will be finished to-day.

Note that *hai* and *hain̲* are used to state particular facts, while general facts are given by "*hotá hai, hote hain̲.*" While "*honá*" means to become, yet this meaning is more usually expressed by *ho jáná*. There is no Urdu word that can do duty for our *have*.

LESSON LXIX.

Another form of the present, more commonly used to express continuous action.

1. Yih kyá ho rahá hai ?	1. What is this that is going on ?
2. Sáhib kháná khá rahe hain̲ ?	2. Is the Sahib eating dinner ?
3. Main̲ apná kám kar rahá hún̲. Tum apná karo.	3. I'm doing my work. You do yours.
4. Jab main̲ bázár kí taraf já rahá thá to kyá dekhtá hún̲ ki sáhib bhí já rahe hain̲.	4. When I was going to the bazar, what should I see but that the sahib, too, is going.
5. Tum log kal kyá kar rahe the ?	5. What were you fellows doing yesterday ?
6. Sáhib de rahe the, par main̲ ne na liyá.	6. Sahib offered it to me, but I would not take it (was giving it but I took it not).

7. Jab málik báten̲ kar rahá thá (kartá thá) laṛkí ġaur se suntí thí.	7. When the master was talking, the girl listened attentively.
8. Main̲ laṛkon̲ ke liye kháná paká rahá hún̲.	8. I am cooking dinner for the boys.
9. Ham apne laṛkon̲ ke liye khánápaká rahe hain̲.	9. We are cooking dinner for our boys.
10. Áp apne apne laṛkon̲ ke liye khánápaká rahe hain̲.	10. You are cooking dinner each for your own boys.
11. Wuh hamáre laṛkon̲ ke liye paká rahe hain̲.	11. They are cooking for our boys.
12. Wuh ('auraten̲) laṛke laṛkíon̲ ke wáste paká rahí thín̲.	12. They (women) were cooking for the children.
13. Main̲ kutte se bahut ḍartí thí.	13. I was much afraid of the dog.

Though these continuative tenses are never given in the paradigms, yet they are most frequently used. Those in the past tense with "*rahá, rahí*" refer to some *definite* past time; e.g. *Jab bachcha thá, to main̲ kutte se bahut ḍartá thá*, when I was a child, I was much afraid of a dog (for you could not use "*ḍar rahá thá*" in this place); but, *Jab áp ne kal kutte ko márá, main̲ bahut ḍar rahá thá*. When you struck the dog yesterday, I was very much afraid.

LESSON LXX.

Uses of the Infinitive.

1. Uská yahán̲ áná jáná achchhá nahín̲ hai.	1. His coming and going here is not good.

2. Yih bát kahní achchhí nahín hai.	2. It's not right to say that (this).
3. Jhúṭh bolná burá hai.	3. It is evil to speak lies.
4. Is tarah se roṭí khání achchhí nahín hai.	4. It is not well to eat bread thus (in this manner).
5. Mere wápas áne tak len den karná.	5. Trade until I return. (Till my coming back, do taking and giving).
6. Us waqt ján lená ki merá áná nazdík hai.	6. Know then that my coming is nigh.
7. Wahán kabhí na jáná.	7. Never go there (but note "*jáo*" not "*janá*" in 8).
8. Áj wahán unke pas mat jáo.	8. Do not go there to them to-day.
9. Kal usko lekár zarúr áná.	9. You must surely bring him to-morrow.
10. Us ádmí ko sharáb píne kí 'ádat hai.	10. That man has the habit of drinking liquor.
11. Mujh ko abhí jáná hai.	11. I have to go at once. (To me going now is.)
12. Mujhe kal usko khatt likhná hogá.	12. I shall have to write him to-morrow.
13. Golí ká lagná thá ki ghoṛá mar gaya.	13. The horse died the instant the ball struck him.
14. Wuh Bambai jáne ko hain.	14. They are about to go to Bombay.
15. Unke wiláyat jáne par yih kám ho jáegá.	15. This work will be done when they go to foreign parts.
16. Namáz ká burá kahná	16. Why should calling

unko kyún burá lagá? or, Namáz ko burá kahná etc.	prayers "*burá*" (evil) offend her?
17. Mujh ko to zará burá lagne kí nahín.	17. It would never offend me a bit.
18. Na mujh men qudrat kahne kí na tujh men táqat sunne kí rahegí.	18. Neither should I have power to tell you, nor would you have strength to hear.
19. Paṛhne se sabaq yád nahín hotá.	19. A lesson can't be learned by reading.
20. Baiṭhne se mujhe thakáo ho játá hai.	20. I get tired sitting (from sitting to me tiredness becomes).
21. Ham áp ká asbáb bhejne hí ko the.	21. We were just going to send your stuff.
22. Laṛká sabaq yád karne ke wáste áyá hai.	22. The boy has come to learn his lesson.
23. Log uske márne ke liye áe hain.	23. People have come to beat him.
24. Main wahán jáne ká nahín.	24. I'll never go there.
25. Wuh laṛkí marne ke qaríb hai.	25. That girl is near death.
26. Main tumko rakhne ká nahín, magar,—hán, tumhárí madad karúngá.	26. I'll never employ you, but—, yes, I will help you.
27. Áj tum ghar mat jáná.	27. Don't you go home to-day.
28. Áj to shahr jáná hai, na?	28. You have to go to the city to-day, don't you?

29. Áyá bázár se áṭá lene gayí hai.	29. The ayah has gone to get meal from the bazar.
30. Kitáb paṛhní cháhiye.	30. You ought to read the book.
31. Kitáb paṛhná cháhiye thá, *or*, Kitáb paṛhní cháhiye thí.	31. You ought to have read the book.
32. Kháne men̲ yih to bahut achchhá hai, lekin dekhne men̲ nahín̲.	32. This is very good to eat, but not to look at.
33. Sáhib ká likhná thá ki wuh áyá.	33. As soon as the master wrote, he came.
34. "Kal kyún̲ na áí?" Jab laṛkon̲ ko khiláná hotá haí, aur roṭí pakání hotí haí, aur ghar ká sab kám áp hí karná húá, kis tarah áún̲?	34. "Why I did not come yesterday?" When I have to feed the children, and bake the bread, and had to do all the work of the house myself, how could I come?
35. Kal jitne kám karne the main̲ ne kiye.	35. What jobs were to do yesterday, I did.
36. Kitábon̲ ke paṛhne se ánkhen̲ bilkull k̲h̲aráb ho gayí hain̲.	36. (My) eyes are badly injured from reading books.

Note the Urdu infinitive is used as our participle, "reading," called in British grammars "gerund." It may take an object or subject, and the object may be in the absolute form, as in 2, 3, 30, 31 etc., or with "*ko*," as in 9, 16, 26, 34, or it may be with "*ka, ke*," as in 16, 23, 36, but the subject is always in the possessive form, as 6. Where the infinitive has an object, as in 2, 3, 4, 30, 31 etc., the infinitive may, or may not agree with it. If it agrees it is called "Gerundive" by some. If a preposition governs the infinitive, it is always in the masculine form. As in 7 and 8, the future, as contrasted with the present command, takes the infinitive. In 29 is the infinitive of purpose. The "*na*" at the end of 28 is like the German "*nicht wahr?*" *is it not so.*

Master all these forms, as they, or their equivalents, are in constant use.

Diversification.

Practise oral composition by substituting other infinitives in place of those in the sentences. In 11 and 12, use *áná, kahná, bolná, kháná, likhná, roṭí khání, píná, wiláyat jáná, bhejná, márná, lená, dená, paṛhná, pakáná, baiṭhná*, until perfect familiarity is secured. Try it several weeks in succession and do not take it for granted because you did it "last week," you can do it to-day.

In 23, use for *uske, mere, tere, tumháre, hamáre, áp ke, un ke, laṛkon ke, laṛkíon ke, kutton ke, sahib ke, laṛke ke.*

In 24, put in the correct form of the above infinitives, and make other changes as you see your need of *perfect familiarity*, and *ready command* of these words and expressions.

LESSON LXXI.

Repeated Words.

1. Ek ek paisa laṛkoṉ ko do.	1. Give the boys a pice each.
2. Maiṉ ne ádmioṉ ko sáṛhe tín, tín rúpae diye.	2. I gave the men three and one-half rupees each.
3. Maiṉ ne sawá das das rupae ko liye.	3. I got them at Rs. 10/4 each.

4. Yih paune áṭh áṭh áne ko milte hain̲.	4. (You) get these at 7 3/4 annas each.
5. Áp ne áj kyá kyá kám kiye hain̲ ?	5. What various jobs have you done to-day ?
6. Kaun kaun ádmí áyá hai ?	6. Who has come ? (Ans. John, Chas., Thos., etc.).
7. Kaun kaun ádmí áe hain̲ ?	7. Who have come ? (Ans. Hindus, Moslems, etc.).
8. Áge áge mat jáo, píchhe píchhe chalo.	8. Don't go ahead, come along behind.
9. Píchhe píchhe mat áo, mere sáth sáth chalo.	9. Don't come behind, come along with me.
10. Baṛe baṛe laṛke áe, chhoṭe na áe.	10. The larger boys came, the smaller did not.
11. Main̲ ghar ghar gayá par roṭí na milí.	11. I went to house (after) house, but got no bread (bread met not).
12. Usne gáon̲ gáon̲ jákar man̲gá par use na milá.	12. He asked for it at village after village, but did not get it (to him it met not).
13. Ṭhík ṭhík batáo. Ṭhík ṭhík bolo.	13. Tell it exactly. Speak the exact word.
14. Ghoṛe ko már márkar chaláyá thá.	14. He beat the horse again and again to make it go (beating beating made it go).
15. Sawár girte girte bachá. [bachá.	15. The rider almost fell (falling, falling, escaped).
16. Laṛká to mar markar	16. The boy nearly died.

17. Darakht darakht se phal toṛá.	17. (He, They) plucked fruit from every tree.
18. Kuchh kuchh paise mere pás hain.	18. I have some money (coppers).
19. Roṭí woṭí khá lí, bhái? Roṭí ṭukṛá khá liyá, bhái?	19. Have you had dinner, brother?
20. Chá wá pí lí, bhái?	20. Have you drunk tea, brother?
21. Áj áp ne baṛe baṛe kám kiye hain.	21. You've done a number of big pieces of work to-day.
22. Áj achchhe achchhe kháne pakáne hain.	22. Good foods must be cooked to-day.
23. Us ke narm narm bál mujhe achchhe lagte hain.	23. I like the touch of her soft hair. (Her, his, soft hairs touch me nicely.)
24. Kitáben paṛh paṛhkar merí ánkhen bilkull kharáb ho gayí hain.	24. My eyes have been badly injured from much reading (reading and reading books).
25. Jab kabhí (*or*, jab jab) yih karo to merí yád men karo.	25. Whenever you do this, do it in my remembrance.
26. Namáz men koí koí házir hotá hai.	26. A very few come to prayer.
27. Koí na koí namáz men zarúr áwegá.	27. Some one or other will surely come to prayer.
28. Wuh kabhí kabhí átá hai aur main kabhí na kabhí áúngá.	28. He comes sometimes and I shall come some time or other.

29. Jo jo áe do do ám le jae.	29. Whoever comes may take away two mangoes.
30. Kuchh na kuchh mil jáegá.	30. (You) will get something or other.

Note that repetition of the words repeats the idea. This may indicate distribution, as in 1—6, emphasis as in 10, 21—24, or continuance as in 8, 9, 11, 12, 13, 14—17. The repetition of sounds in 19 and 20 is much like our "baby" talk, roly poly, hurly burly, pell mell.

Diversification.—The pupil must take these sentences, after they have been thoroughly committed, and change nouns, pronouns, verbs and adjectives to other persons, tenses, numbers, and genders. The numerals must be at one's tongue's end. Skill in talking can only come as a result of the ability to diversify forms already mastered.

LESSON LXXII.

Conditional Sentences. Shartí Jumle.

1. Agar wuh na átá, to maiṉ usko na mártá.	1. If he had not come, I should not have beaten him.
2. Agar tum usko na márte, to wuh na martá.	2. If you had not struck him, he would not have died.
3. Agar tum isko ṭhík na karte, to maiṉ dám kabhí na detá.	3. If you had not made it right, I should never have given the price.
4. Chíl dekhkar Sahíb ne kahá ki "Agar mere pás bandúq hotí, to maiṉ már detá.	4. Seeing the kite, the master said, "If I had a gun, I would kill it."

5. Agar laṛkí yih na kahtí to wuh us se ná-k͟hush na hotá.

5. If the girl had not said this, he would not have been displeased with her.

6. Agar áp yih ghoṛá mujhe na dikháte, to maiṉ dúsrá zarúr letá.

6. If you had not shown me this horse I'd surely have bought another.

7. Agar mere pás ghoṛí na hotí, maiṉ zarúr paidal játí.

7. If I had not had the mare, I'd surely have gone afoot.

8. Agar maiṉ un se laṛtá, to mujh se ziyáda náláiq koí na thá.

8. If I had fought with him, no one could have been (was) more unworthy than I.

9. Agar áp is ká sabab mujh se na púchhte, to bahut bihtar hotá (*or*, thá).

9. If you had not asked me the reason of this, it would have been much better.

10. Agar log usko chhuṛá na dete, to maiṉ usko adhmúá karke chhoṛtá.

10. If people had not rescued him, I'd have half killed him before I let him go.

11. Mumkin na thá ki Masíh maut ke qabze meṉ rahtá.

11. It was impossible that Christ should remain in the grasp of death.

12. Agar sáhib yaháṉ hote, to tumko ṭhík kar dete.

12. If master were here, he would give you a setting right.

13. Agar wuh mujh se laṛtí to maiṉ usko k͟húb mártí.

13. If she were to fight with me, I'd beat her well.

14. Agar mujhe áná hotá to main̲ be púchhe á játá.	14. If I had been going to come, I'd have come without request.

Note that these conditions are contrary to fact and take that form of the verb, which is called "past conditional" (*mází shartí*), but might better be called, in English, past subjunctive. It is used not only in past conditions that are contrary to fact, but also for a present condition and resulting conclusion, both contrary to reality. If master were here (which he is not) he would set you right (which he does not). If she should fight with me (which she will not), I would beat her (which I shall not).

Hai or *hain̲* never occurs with this form of the verb.

Diversification.

In 1, 2, 3, change one or both verbs by substituting any one of a dozen familiar verbs, until you thus substitute readily.

Exercises in Conditionals.

1. Agar wuh áwe, to main̲ jáún̲?	1. If he come, may I go?
2. Agar main̲ ásmán kí bát-en̲ kahun̲ to tum kyún̲-kar yaqín karoge?	2. If I tell you things of heaven how will you believe?
3. Agar ímán na láoge to tum apne gunáhon̲ men̲ maroge.	3. If you do not believe, you will die in your sins.
4. Agar koí mujh men̲ qáim na rahe, to wuh súkh játá hai.	4. If any one does not abide in me, he dries up.
5. Agar us ko uṭháyá ho, to mujhe batáo.	5. If you have taken him up, then tell me.

6. Agar tum mujhe jante to mere Báp ko bhí jánte.	6. If you had known me you would have known my Father too.
7. Agar tum ne mujhe jáná hotá, to mere Báp ko bhí jánte	7. If they had known me they would have known my Father too.
8. Jab wuh nawishton ká yaqín nahín karte, to merí báton ká yaqín kyúnkar karenge?	8. If they do not believe the Scriptures, how shall they believe my words?
9. Agar tú yih kám kartá hai, to apne áp ko dunyá par záhir kar.	9. If thou doest these works show thyself to the world.
10. Agar main sach boltá hún, to tum merá yaqín kyún nahín karte?	10. If I tell the truth, why do you not believe me?
11. Agar wuh so gayá hai, to bach jáegá.	11. If he has fallen asleep, he will recover.
12. Jab mujh Khudáwand ne tumháre pair dhoe, to tum par farz hai ki ek dúsre ke pair dhoyá karo.	12. If I the Lord have washed your feet, then it is obligatory on you that you should wash the feet of one another.
13. Agar unhon ne mujhe satáyá, to wuh tumhen bhí satáenge.	13. If they have persectuted me, they will persecute you.
14. Jab ham ádmíon kí gawáhí qabúl kar lete hain, to Khudá kí gawáhí us se kahín baṛhkar hai.	14. If we accept the testimony of men, the testimony of God is greater.

15. Jo us ne rúpae diye, to lete áná.

15. If he gives the money, then bring it along.

LESSON LXXIII.

Conditional Sentences.* Shartí Jumle.

1. Agar wuh yahán̲ áe, to main̲ dún̲.

1. If he come here, I may give it.

2. Agar wuh áe to main̲ dún̲gá.

2. If he should come, I'll give it.

3. Agar kuttá phir áe, to usko máro.

3. If the dog come again, kill it.

4. Agar kám darust na karoge, to main̲ paisa na dún̲gí.

4. If you do not set the work right, I shall not give the money.

5. Agar yih bát sach ho, to baṛá nuqsán, baṛá nuqsán hogá.

5. If this be true (which I doubt) it will be a big loss, a big loss.

6. Agar wuh kitáb paṛhtá ho, mat buláná.

6. If he is reading the book, don't call him.

7. Agar sáhib gaye hon̲, to gaye hon̲. Kyá pata hai?

7. If the sahib has gone, why he's gone. What do I know about it?

8. (Agar) Sach púchho, to main̲ use be-wuqúf samajhtá hún̲.

8. To tell the truth, I think him a fool (If you ask truth, I think him senseless).

9. Agar yih chár din kí bát hotí, to mujhe k̲habar na hotí?

9. If this had happened four days ago, should not I know it? (a thing of 4 days).

---

* Where there is doubt, and the thing is assumed as possible, with the pres. subjunctive, 1—8. Other ideas take other forms.

10. Jo (agar) usne rúpae diye, to lete áná.

10. If he gives the money (and he will) then bring it along.

11. Jo (agar) usne kitáb dí, to lení hogí.

11. If he gives the book, you'll have to take it.

12. Jab (agar) main̲ wahán gayá to márá jáún̲gá.

12. If I go there I shall be killed.

13. Jab (agar) wuh is baras k̲hatre se bach gayá, to uskí 'umr baṛí hogí.

13. If he escape danger this year, he'll live long (his life will be long).

14. Agar unhon̲ ne use márá ho, to jald mujhe k̲habar do.

14. If they have beaten him (as we hear) then give me word quickly.

15. Agar log áen̲ to girjá hogá.

15. If people come, there will be church.

16. Agar log áen̲ge to girjá hogá.

16. If people will come, there will be church service.

17. Agar tum us ke nazdík jáoge, to tum gunagár hoge.

17. If you go near him (it), you will be blameworthy (sinners).

18. Agar yih kám us se ho saká, aur ba-k̲húbí anjám diyá, to main̲ qaul o qarár kartá hún̲ ki main̲ bádsháh se ziyáda salúk karún̲gá.

18 If this work can be done by him, and he brings it to a (good) end, then I promise you that I will treat him better than (could) any king.

19. Agar wuh játá hai, to main̲ bhí chaltá hún̲.

19. If he is going (as you say), then I, too, will go along.

20. Agar main̲ apne qaul par átá hún̲, to uskí

20. If I come according to my promise, then I'll

saltanat k̲h̲ák men̲ milá detá hún̲.	mingle his kingdom in the dust.
21. Agar ham se ho saktá, to ham manzúr karte.	21. If we could we would.
22. Agar us waqt pahun̲che hon̲, tab yih bát kah sakte the.	22. If they had (were) arrived at that time, then they could have said this.
23. Agar bachche ke marne se pahle chaloge, to kuchh fáida hogá.	23. If you will go ere the child die, then it will be of some avail.
24. Agar koí us ke Masíh hone ká iqrár kare, to k̲h̲árij ho.	24. If any one confesses him to be the Messiah, let him be expelled.
25. Agar tum ne mujhe jáná hotá, to mere báp ko bhí jánte.	25. If ye had known me, ye would have known my father also.

LESSON LXXIV.

Chalná and jáná.

1. Hawá jidhar ko cháhtí hai, chaltí hai.	1. The wind goeth whither it wishes.
2. Merí ghaṛí nahín̲ chaltí.	2. My watch won't go.
3. Merá ádmí sáth nahín̲ játá.	3. My man won't go along.
4. Yih rúpaya bázár men̲ nahín̲ chaltá.	4. This rupee won't pass in the bazars.
5. Yih bandúq nahín̲ chaltí.	5. This gun won't go off.
6. Chaukíán̲ le jáo. Chaukíán̲ le chalo.	6. Take the chairs away. Bring the chairs along.
7. Ghoṛá le chalo.	7. Bring the horse along.
8. Uskí ṭáng men̲ itná dard	8. There is so great a pain

hai ki wuh chal nahíṉ saktá.	in his leg that he is not able to walk.
9. Usko itná kám paṛ gayá hai ki wuh nahíṉ já saktá.	9. So much work has fallen to him that he cannot go.
10. Kab jáoge ? (*or*) Kab chaloge ?	10. When will you go ? (or) When will you go (with me) ?
11. Maiṉ yaháṉ se chha baje chalúṉgá aur waháṉ pahúṉchkar Ḍákṭar ke pás jald jáúṉgá.	11. I shall start from here at six o'clock and having arrived there, will go at once to the Doctor's.
12. Maiṉ shahr chalá húṉ, tum bhí chaloge ?	12. I am started to the city. Will you go too ?
13. Yih ghoṛá k͟húb chaltá hai.	13. This horse goes finely.
14. Yih saṛak kidhar játí hai ?	14. Whither does this road lead ?
15. Yih bát sunkar naukar chal diyá.	15. Hearing this the servant started off.
16. Yih nahr kidhar játí hai ?	16. Where does this canal go to ?
17. Chaltí chakkí dekhke wuh ro paṛá.	17. Seeing the moving mill, he wept (fell a weeping).
18. Shám ke waqt bázár jáná mana' hai.	18. It is forbidden to go to the bazar in the evening.
19. Bhíṛ ke sabab chalná bahut mushkil hai.	19. It is difficult going on account of the crowd.

20. Maiṉ roz shahr játá huṉ. Ab játá húṉ.	20. I go to the city daily. I am going now.
21. Shari'at par chalná bahut mushkil hai.	21. It is hard to keep the law (to move on the law).
22. Wuh gáoṉ ko gayá hai.	22. He has gone to the village.
23. Wuh gáoṉ ko chalá hai.	23. He is starting to the village.
24. Wuh gáoṉ ko chalá gayá hai.	24. He has gone to the village.
25. Sáhib ke sámne merí bát nahíṉ chaltí.	25. My word has no weight with the gentleman (goes not before him).
26. Maiṉ tum ko bádsháh ke pás le chalúṉgá.	26. I'll take you to the king.
27. Maiṉ is ghoṛe ko bádsháh ke pás le chalúṉgá.	27. I'll take this horse to the king.
28. Sáhib qánún par púre púre chalte haiṉ.	28. Sahib goes strictly by rule.
29. Sab log chale gaye haiṉ.	29. All the people have gone.

Ghaṛí .. watch, clock, a little water jar, which when put into a larger jar, sank, as it had a hole in the bottom, in 24 minutes, and this constitutes a "*ghaṛí*" of time, and this, later, was applied to the watch, or clock, as time measurers.

LESSON LXXV.

Exercises in Lagná.

1. Patá nahín̲ lagtá.	1. I cannot find out. (Trace does not touch.)
2. Kyún̲ nahín̲ lagtá? Áj hí lagá lo.	2. Why can't you? Find out this very day.
3. Ghar ghar se lagá hai.	3. House touches house.
4. Mujhe bahut ḍar lagtá hai.	4. I'm very much afraid.
5. Yih bát tumko achchhí nahín̲ lagtí.	5. You do not like this affair.
6. Bachchon̲ kí báten̲ míṭhí lagtí hain̲.	6. Children's sayings please people.
7. Uske sak̲h̲t choṭ lagí. Choṭ lagí tum ko?	7. He was badly hurt. Did you get hurt?
8. Ghoṛá gáṛí men̲ lagá húá hai.	8. The horse is hitched to the carriage.
9. Yih kitáb tumhen̲ kahán̲ se háth lagí?	9. Where did you get this book?
10. Tálá darwáze par lagá húá hai.	10. A padlock is fastened on the door.
11. Báġ men̲ tarah tarah ke búṭe lage hain̲.	11. In the garden all sorts of shrubs are planted (or, various sorts of).
12. Sáhib ke kám men̲ kitne mazdúr lage hain̲?	12. How many labourers are on the gentleman's work?
13. Wuh sawere niklá táki apne báġ men̲ mazdúr lagáwe.	13. He went out early that he might set labourers to work in his orchard.
14. Is koṭhí par kitná rúpaya lagá hai?	14. How much money was spent on this house?

15. Jí se jí lagá hai.	15. Heart answers to heart.
16. Uske kurte men̲ paiwand lagá hai.	16. He has a patch on his shirt.
17. Takh̲te par kyá ishtihár lagá hai?	17. What notice is (fastened) on the board?
18. Wuh apne kám men̲ lagá rahtá hai.	18. He sticks to his work.
19. Sab masáleh lag chuke hain̲.	19. All materials are spent.
20. Sáhib ke áne kí ummed lagí húí hai.	20. We are expecting the gentleman.
21. Use ilzám kyún̲ lagá?	21. Why was he accused?
22. Sab chízen̲ durustí se lag gayí hain̲.	22. All things are set in order.
23. Láhaur jáne men̲ do ghanṭe lagen̲ge.	23. It will take two hours to reach Lahore.
24. Dhúp men̲ án̲khen̲ nahín̲ lagtín̲.	24. I cannot sleep in the sun.
25. Shahr men̲ baṛí ág lag gayí hai.	25. There is a big fire in the city.
26. Koṭ ko kitná kapṛá lagegá?	26. How much cloth will it take for a coat?
27. Dímak darí ko lag gayí hai.	27. The white ants are at the carpet.
28. Munshí sáhib ke mun̲h lagá hai.	28. The munshi has the ear of the sahib.
29. Chár din se mujhe sardí lagtí hai.	29. I have been chilly for four days.
30. Is darakh̲t par baṛe achchhe phúl phal lagte hain̲.	30. This tree bears excellent flowers and fruit.
31. Us ko bímárí lag gayí hai.	31. He has contracted the disease.

32. Tambákú mere mun̲h lag gayá hai.
32. I've acquired a taste for tobacco.

33. Is hisáb men̲ baṛí ġalatí lag gayí hai.
33. There is a big mistake in this account.

34. Is lakṛí par pítal lagá do.
34. Fasten the brass to this wood.

35. K̲húb zor lagáo.
35. Exert yourself. Put to your strength.

36. Málí, sab búṭon̲ ko qatár men̲ lagáo.
36. Gardener, put all these plants in a row.

37. Dawáí uske háth par lagáo
37. Put the medicine on his hand.

38. Dawáí us kí án̲kh men̲ ḍálo.
38. Put the medicine in his eye.

39. Mez lagáo. (Palang, darí, sab chízen̲).
39. Set the table. (Make the bed. Put down the carpet. Put everything in place.)

40. Is lifáfe par do paise ká ṭikaṭ lagáo.
40. Put a two-pice stamp on this envelope.

41. Itní der kyún̲ lagí? Phir mat lagáná.
41. Why have you spent so much time? Don't do it again.

42. Us ne mere bháí se dostí lagáí hai.
42. He has made friends with my brother.

43. Uske chábuk lagáo. (Koṛe lagáo.)
43 Whip him. (Scourge him.)

44. Jí lagákar K̲hudá ka kám karná cháhiye.
44. One ought to do God's work with the whole heart.

45. Ilzám na lagáyá karo.
45. Do not make accusations.

46. Baggí par rang lagáná cháhiye.
46. You ought to paint the buggy.

47. Apná ikká dúsre ke sáth lagáo.	47. Have your ekka follow the other.
48. Merá unke sáth kyá lagáo hai?	48. What have I to do with them?
49. Maiṉ unse alag (a+lag) rahtá húṉ.	49. I stay apart from them.
50. Merá dil yaháṉ nahíṉ lagtá.	50. I don't like this place.
51. Koṭ ko miṭṭí lag gayí hai. Jháṛ do.	51. There's earth on the coat. Dust it off.

Conjugation.

Maiṉ das baje roṭí pakáne lagtá húṉ, lagtí húṉ.	I begin to cook the meal at ten o'clock.
Tú das baje roṭí pakáne lagtá hai, lagtí hai.	Thou beginnest to cook at ten.
Wuh das baje roṭí pakáne lagtá hai, lagtí hai.	He, She, begins to cook at ten.
Ham das baje roṭí pakáne lagte haiṉ, lagti haiṉ.	We begin cooking at ten.
Tum das baje roṭí pakáne lagte, lagtí, ho.	You begin cooking at ten.
Áp das baje roṭí pakáne lagte, lagtí, haiṉ.	You begin baking bread at ten.
Wuh das baje roṭí pakáne lagte, lagtí, haiṉ.	They begin baking bread at ten.
Maiṉ kal subh likhne lagúṉgá lagúṉgí.	I shall begin writing to-morrow morning.
Tú kal subh likhne lagegá, lagegí.	Thou wilt begin writing in the morning.
Wuh kal subh likhne lagegá, lagegí.	He, She, will begin writing to-morrow morning.

Hamkal subh likhne lage<u>n</u>ge, lage<u>n</u>gí.	We will begin writing tomorrow morning.
Tum kal subh likhne lagoge, lagogí.	You'll begin writing tomorrow morning.
Áp kal sawere likhne lage<u>n</u>ge, lage<u>n</u>gí.	You'll begin writing early tomorrow.
Wuh kal fajr likhne lage<u>n</u>ge, lage<u>n</u>gí.	They'll begin writing tomorrow morning.
Mai<u>n</u> kal sawere banáne lagá thá, lagí thí.	I began to make it early yesterday.
Tú kal sawere banáne lagá thá, lagí thí.	Thou didst begin early yesterday to make it.
Wuh kal sawere banáne lagá thá, lagí thí.	He, She, began early yesterday to make it.
Wuh parso<u>n</u> shám banáne lagá thá, lagí thí.	He, She, began to make it day before yesterday evening.
Ham parso<u>n</u> banáne lage the, lagí thí<u>n</u>.	We began to make it day before yesterday.
Tum parso<u>n</u> shám ko banáne lage the, lagí thí<u>n</u>.	You began at even, day before yesterday, to make it.
Áp parso<u>n</u> shám ko banáne lage the, lagí thí<u>n</u>.	You began at even, day before yesterday, to make it.
Wuh parso<u>n</u> shám ko banáne lage the, lagí thí<u>n</u>.	You began at even, day before yesterday, to make it.

LESSON LXXVI.

Passives.

1. Dekhá jáegá. (Usko dekhá jáegá.)	1. I'll see about it. (It'll be seen to.)
2. Mai<u>n</u> áp ke zer sáyá liyá jáú<u>n</u>.	2. May I be taken under your (shadow) care.

3. Wuh shahr ke pás dekhe gaye the.	3. They were seen near the city.
4. Qismat se laṛá nahín̲ játá.	4. One can't fight with fate.
5. Mán̲go to tumhen diyá jáegá. Khaṭkhaṭáo to tumháre wáste kholá jáegá.	5. Ask and it shall be given unto you. Knock and it shall be opened for you.
6 Kyún̲ki jis ke pás hai use diyá jáegá, magar jis ke pás nahín̲ hai us se wuh bhí jo uske pás hai, le liyá jáegá.	6. For whoso has to him shall be given, but whoso has not, from him even that he has shall be taken away.
7. Madrase ká band kiyá jáná unke liye baṛí taklíf kí bát thí	7. The school's being closed was a great vexation to them.
8. Makkhan kal bhejá gayá thá.	8. The butter was sent yesterday.
9. Pachás ádmí laṛáí men̲ máre gaye.	9. Fifty men were killed in the fight.
10. Yih kám roz roz kiyá játá hai.	10. This work is done daily.
11. Yih kám mujh se nahín̲ kyá játá, *or*, Yih kám mujh se nahín̲ hotá.	11. I can't do this work.
12. Kyá wuh roṭián̲ unko dí gayí hain̲.	12. Have those loaves been given them?
13. Tín loṭe láye gaye hain̲.	13. Three jugs have been brought.
14. Áj mujh se roṭí kháí nahín̲ játí.	14. I can't eat to-day.
15. Sab darwáze band kiye gaye hain̲.	15. All the doors have been shut?

16. Agar us taraf le jáo, to ghoṛá márá jáegá.	16. If you take him that direction, the horse will be killed.
17. Agar main̲ wahán̲ gayí, to márí jáún̲gí.	17. If I went there, I'd be killed.
18. Yih merá baṛá laṛká "Qází" kahlátá hai.	18. My elder boy is called "Judge."
19. Wuh is laṛáí men̲ bhejá gayá táki wahán̲ par jákar márá jáe.	19. He was sent into the fight that he might go there and be killed.
20. Zarúr hai ki yih kám áj kiyá jáe.	20. It is imperative that this work be done to-day.
21. Cháhiye ki yih ṭhag áj hí márá jáe.	21. It is fitting that this thug be killed to-day.
22. Lázim thá ki yih bát áp se púchhí jáe.	22. It was proper that this thing be asked of you.

LESSON LXXVII.

Passives and Causals.

1. Kis ne yih bartan toṛá ?	1. Who broke this dish ?
2. Memsáhibá, yih to mujh se ṭúṭá.	2. Madam, I broke it (accidentally).
3. Sáhib Urdú paṛhte hain̲, munshí unko paṛhátá hai, kyún̲ki mishan (sarkár) paṛhwátí hai.	3. Sahib is studying Urdu, the munshi is teaching him for the mission (the Govt.) makes him learn it.
4. Yih shart húí ki jo háre uske kán káṭe jáen̲.	4. This wager (condition) was laid that whoever lose, his ears be cut off.
5. Bábá so rahá hai, kyún̲ki áyá ne sawere sulá	5. The baby is sleeping, for ayah put it to sleep

diyá, is liye ki memsáhiba roz isí waqt áyá se sulwá detí hain̲.	early, because madam has him daily put to sleep by the ayah at this time.
6. Áp kí gáṛí ban rahí hai? Hán̲, mistrí Ibráhím baná rahá hai. Main̲ apná kull lakṛí ká kám usí se banwátá hún̲.	6. Is your carriage making? Yes. master-workman Abraham is making it. I have him do all my wood work.
7. Súji, áṭá, álú, yahán̲ bikte hain̲.	7. Soojee, meal, and potatoes are sold here.
8. Yih bajáz ájkal kapṛá sastá bech rahá hai, is liye ki mausim guzarne par dúsre dukándár apná mál yahín̲ bikwáte hain̲.	8. This shopkeeper is selling cloth cheap these days, for when the season is over (passing), other shopkeepers have their goods sold here.
9. Sipáhion̲ ne usko márá thá (már ḍálá).	9. The soldiers killed him.
10. Logon̲ ne milkar sarkár ke hukm se usko marwáyá thá.	10. The people agreeing together (meeting) had him killed by the governor's order.
11. Jab sáhib darwáze khulwáne lage, to berá kholne gayá, lekin wuh áp se áp khul gaye.	11. When the master began to have the doors opened, the bearer went to open them then, but they came open themselves.
12. Jald uṭhkar yih sandúq uṭhá lo, kyún̲ki main̲	12. Get up quickly and take up this box for I am

is kamare se sab chízen̲ uṭhwá detí hún̲.	having all these things taken out from this room.
13. Ghoṛe ne pání pí liyá hai ?	13. Has the horse been watered (drunk) ?
14. Hán̲, main̲ har subh nau baje pilátá hún̲, kyún̲ki málik safar se pahle pilwáte hain̲.	14. Yes, I water him every morning at nine o'clock, for the master has him watered before a journey.
15. Cháhe tum káṭo cháhe kaṭáo, zarúr hai ki áj kaṭ jáe.	15. Whether you cut it or have it cut, it must be cut to-day.
16. Totá kis tarah tumháre háth se chhúṭá ?	16. How did the parrot get out of your hand ?
17. Main̲ ne to nahín̲ chhoṛá, bábá ne mere háth se chhuṛáyá.	17. I did not let it go, the child took it from my hand.
18. Málik ne gáe mujh se muṛwáí, aur main̲ ne bahuterí moṛí, par wuh na muṛí.	18. Its master had me head off (turn) the cow, and I tried to (turned her a lot) but she did not turn (would not).

Conjugation.

Passive, Present Indicative and Subjunctive.

Pání garm kiyá játá hai.	Water is being warmed.
Pání garm ho rahá hai.	Water is getting warm.
Yih kám abhí kiyá jáe.	Let this work be done at once.
Log pák sáf kiỵe jáen̲.	Let the people be cleansed now.

Yih laṛkián abhí paṛhái jáen.	Let the girls be taught at once.
Yih mere kapṛe áj dhoe jáen.	Let these clothes of mine be washed to-day.
Mere kapṛe dúsre tísre roz dhoe játe hain.	My clothes are washed every second or third day.
Mere kapṛe kúen par dhoe já rahe hain.	My clothes are being washed at the well.

Passive Future.

Main wahán par jákar márá jáúngá (márí jáúngí).	I shall go there and be killed.
Tú wahán par jákar márá jáegá (márí jáegí).	Thou wilt go there and be killed.
Wuh wahán par jákar márá jáegá (márí jáegí).	He, She, will go there and be killed.
Ham wahán par jákar máre jáenge (márí jáengín).	We'll go there and be killed.
Tum wahán par jákar máre jáoge (márí jáogín).	You'll go there and be killed.
Áp wahán par jákar máre jáenge (márí jáengín).	You'll go there and be killed.
Wuh wahán par jákar máre jáenge (márí jáengín).	They'll go there and be killed.

Past Tense Passive.

Main kal márá gáyá (márí gayí).	I was beaten yesterday.
Tú parson márá gáyá (márí gayí).	Thou wast beaten day before yesterday.
Wuh atarson márá gáyá (márí gayí).	He, She was beaten 3 days ago.

Ham áj máre gaye (márí gayíṉ). — We were beaten to-day.

Tum kal máre gaye (márí gayíṉ). — You were beaten yesterday.

Áp parsoṉ máre gaye (márí gayíṉ). — You were beaten day before yesterday.

Wuh pársál máre gaye (márí gayíṉ). — They were beaten last year.

LESSON LXXVIII.

Relative Pronouns. Ism-i-zamír.

1. Jo ghoṛá kal hamko milá thá, wuh bahut hí achchhá hai.
   The horse we got yesterday is a very good one. (What horse yesterday to us met, he is very good).

2. Jis ádmí ne mujh ko márá, wuh merá bháí hai.
   The man that beat me is my brother.

3. Jis ‘aurat se áp ne merí kitáb lí, wuh merí áyá hai.
   The woman from whom you got my book is my ayah.

4. Jis laṛke ko hazúr ne paise diye, wuh mere bháí ká beṭá hai.
   The boy to whom you gave the coppers is my brother's son.

5. Wuh dúkándár jinhoṉ ne áp ke pás kitábeṉ bhejí haiṉ, kutub-farosh haiṉ.
   Those shopkeepers who sent you the books are book-sellers.

6. Jo lafz áp ne abhí isti‘-mál kiyá, uske kyá ma‘ne haiṉ ?
   What is the meaning of that word you used just now ?

7. Jo ho, so ho.	7. Let come what may, or, What will be, will be.
8. Jo kuchh wuh tum se kahe, wuhí karo.	8. Do whatever he tells you.
9. Jaisá kiyá waisá páyá.	9. As he did, so he got. He got tit for tat.
10. Jitná tum ko cháhiye, utná le lo.	10. Take as much as you need.
11. Jab tak sáns tab tak ás.	11. While there is life there is hope.
12. Wuhí Sindbád jise tum múá jánte ho, main hún.	12. That Sindbad that you thought (think) dead, I am he.
13. Jin laṛkon ne mere laṛke ko márá, wuh bázár ke sharír laṛke hain.	13. Those boys who beat my boy are the bad boys of the street.
14. Jidhar ko moṛo, udhar ko játá hai.	14. Whithersoever you turn him thither he goes.
15. Wuh ádmí jis se tum ne roṭí lí, wuh baṛá bad-ma'ásh ádmí hai.	15. The man from whom you got bread is a very bad man (criminal).
16. Áp kaunsá kapṛá cháhte hain?	16. Which sort of cloth do you wish?
17. In men se áp ko kaunsí kursí cháhiye?	17. Which of these chairs do you want?
18. Yih lakṛí kis kám kí hai?	18. What is this wood good for?
19. Is dawáí se kuchh fáidá húá hai?	19. Has this medicine relieved you?
20. Jis ko jitní tankhwáh báqí hai, dí jáegi.	20. Whatever pay is back (owing) to whomsoever, it will be given him.

The relative is usually with its antecedent, as in 1, 2, 3, 4, or it may follow it as in 5, after the English manner. "So" in 7, is not much used in Urdu but a good deal in Hindi.

Diversification.

Take the nouns *roṭí*, *roṭián̲*, *ádmí*, *páni*, *kitáb*, *kitáben̲*, *mez*, *ghoṛián̲*, *laṛke*, *rúpayá*, *rúpae*, and substitute in 1 for "*ghoṛá*," making the necessitated changes in sentence, until you can do so without hesitation. It will be a most valuable exercise in genders, as well as in relatives.

Likewise take sentences 2, 3, 4, 5, and change numbers.

Let the teacher after these relative sentences in one form are mastered, give the other form also.

LESSON LXXIX.

Subjunctive (Present and Past, so called "Aorist" and Past Conditional).

1. Cháhiye ki yih gosht áj pakáyá jáe.	1. This meat ought to be cooked to-day.
2. Jab tak bartan na súkhe, páni na ḍálá jáe.	2. Don't put in the water till the vessel dry (Let it not be put in).
3. Wuh is liye bheje gaye, táki wahán̲ par jákar máre jáen̲.	3. They were sent for this (purpose) that they might go there and be killed.
4. Cháhiye ki yih kám abhí kiyá jae.	4. This work ought to be done at once.
5. Cháhiye thá ki yih kám kal ho játá.	5. This work ought to have been done yesterday.
6. Cháhiye thá ki áp mujh ko k̲h̲att likhte.	6. You should have written me a letter.

7. Zarúr hai ki yih kám pahle kiyá jáe.	7. It is necessary that this work be done first.
8. Zarúr thá ki yih kám pahle kiyá játá.	8. It was necessary that this work be done first (which it was not).
9. Main̲ cháhtá hún̲ ki áp áen̲.	9. I wish you to come.
10. Chalo, tumhen̲ áj bádsháh pás le chalún̲.	10. Come along, I'll take you to the king today.
11. K̲hudá jáne kyá kuchh banegá.	11. God knows what may be the outcome.
12. Sháyad taiyár ho.	12. Perhaps it's ready
13. Main ḍartá hún̲ ki baddu'á na kare.	13. I fear lest he may curse (me).
14. Mumkin̲ hai ki taiyár ho.	14. It is possible that it is ready.
15. Kyá áp cháhte hain̲ ki main̲ isí tarah baṭan lagáún̲.	15. Do you wish me to put the buttons on this way ?
16. Us ne cháhá ki laṛke ko márún̲, par wuh már na saká.	16. He wished to kill the boy ("may I kill the boy"), but was not able to (kill) do it.
17. Uská jí cháhá * ki ghar chhoṛke main̲ aur kahin̲ chalá jáún̲.	17. His heart desired to leave home and go somewhere else.
18. Chor ko chor hí pahcháne.	18. Only a thief recognises a thief. "Set a thief to catch a thief."

* Why they do not say "*jí ne cháhá*," I have not been able to find out.

19. Martá kyá na kartá.	19. What won't a dying man do?
20. Khiyálí piláo pakáe.	20. He cooks imaginary "pilao." He builds castles in the air.
21. Sámp ka káṭá (húá) rassí se ḍare.	21. He whom a snake has bitten fears a rope.

The (present) subjunctive may be called the indefinite future, as it is used to express ideas which *may be* true, things that may come to pass. Consequently, after verbs of hope or fear, doubt, wish, purpose, or obligation we use this indefinite future, or "present subjunctive": while to express ideas that *might* have come true, but did not, we use the past conditional or, as I prefer to call it, past subjunctive.

The present subjunctive is used to set forth axiomatic truth, as in 11, 20, 21.

In 10 we have "*pás*" used with the person, where a place would take "*ko*." Take it to the lady, *Memsahiba ke pás le jao*, but, Take it to the city, *Shahr ko le jáo.*

Diversification.

In 1 substitute *liyá, diyá, kháyá, bhejá, kharídá* (bought), *bike.*

In 4 substitute for "*kám,*" *roṭí, gosht, álú, áṭá,* with "*pakáyá, pakáe.*"

In 6 and 7 substitute in proper form *khatt likhte buláte,* and *láná, dená, lená, rokná, batáná, dikháná, ḍhúnḍhná.*

In 9 put any of these verbs.

LESSON LXXX.

Participles.

1. Wuh roṭí khákar chalá gayá.	1. He, having eaten, went away.
2. Wuh uṭh uṭh kar chalne lagá.	2. Rising with difficulty he (or, After several attempts he arose and) started to go.
3. Unhon ne ján bújhke kiyá.	3. They did it knowingly (having known).
4. Dawáí pilákar jáo.	4. Give the medicine before you go.
5. Dawáí piláte hí jáo.	5. As soon as you have given the medicine, go.
6. Dawáí piláte jáo (*or*, piláte raho).	6. Go on giving the medicine.
7. Dawáí piláte hí laṛkí achchhí ho gayí.	7. The girl recovered as soon as they gave the medicine.
8. Usko márte hí lakṛí ṭúṭ gayí.	8. The stick broke on striking him.
9. Golí ke lagte hí ghoṛá mar gayá.	9. As soon as the ball struck him, the horse died.
10. Wahán chalkar mere liye ṭhahre raho.	10. Go there and wait for me.
11. Pahunchte hí uská ghoṛá gir paṛá.	11. His horse fell on arrival.
12. Wuh khaṛá hokar kahne lagá, ki yih bát sunkar main bhí ġusse húá.	12. Standing up he said, On hearing this I, too, grew angry (in anger I became).

13. Main̲ ne usko beṭá karke pálá. — 13. I brought him up as a son.

14. Ba'z Hindú is patthar ko K̲h̲udá karke mánte hain̲. — 14. Some Hindus honour this stone as God.

15. Main̲ ne us ko mazbút karke bándhá. — 15. I tied it tight (making it strong).

16. Main̲ uske sáth ġulám hoke rahá. — 16. I lived with him as a slave.

17. Gáṛíwán ne ghoṛá már márke chaláyá thá. — 17. The coachman beat and beat the horse to make it go.

18. Main̲ anḍe bechkar murġíán̲ k̲h̲áríd lún̲gá. — 18. I'll sell the eggs and buy hens.

Note.—The time denoted by the participle in "*kar*" or "*ke*" both of which are in good usage, though "*kar*" is ordinarily preferred, is time previous to that of the verb, and so may be used for *past* time, as in 1, 4, 6 &c.; or for *future*, or, as in 18, to denote a course of action; while *karke* and *hoke* are sometimes used as "*as*," 13, 14, 16.

Diversification.—Make a number of sentences on the model of 4.

In 5, 7, 8, 9, 11, "*par*," on, is understood with the participle, so it takes the prepositional form in "*e*."

LESSON LXXXI.

Participles.

1. Main̲ ne usko ghar par baiṭhá dekhá. — 1. I saw him (seated) sitting at home.

2. Ham ne unko shahr se áte dekhá. — 2. I saw them coming from the city.

3. Un laṛkon̲ ne usko shahr kí taraf játe dekhá.	3. Those boys saw him going toward the city.
4. Laṛkíon̲ ne tum ko dauṛte dekhá.	4. The girls saw you running.
5. Log ham ko roṭí kháte dekh rahe the.	5. The people were watching us eat.
6. Main̲ dhobí ko kapṛe dhote dekh rahá hún̲.	6. I am watching the washerman wash clothes.
7. Mán̲ rotí píṭtí beṭí ke ghar gayí.	7. The mother went to her daughter's house, weeping and beating her breast.
8. Laṛkí yih kahtí húí ghar chalí gayí.	8. The girl went home saying this (as she went).
9. Kuttá bhaun̲ktá bhaun̲ktá merí taraf áyá.	9. The dog came barking toward me.
10. Kyá tumne usko múá dekhá ?	10. Did you see him dead ?
11. Yih bháí leṭá húá jágtá thá.	11. This brother was lying awake.
12. Gyára baje se lekar chár baje tak usne mujhe pás biṭháe rakhá.	12. From 11 o'clock to four he kept me seated by him.
13. Din hote hote wuh á pahun̲che.	13. They came as it was getting day.
14. Din hote húe laṛke pahun̲ch gaye.	14. The boys arrived while it was yet day.
15. Main̲ ḍartá ḍartá (ḍarte ḍarte) us pás gayá.	15. I went to him in fear.
16. Sote se uṭhkar wuh Misr ko chalá gaya.	16. Arising from sleep (ing). he went to Egypt.

17. Ham gáte játe hain.	17. We go on singing, or, we go singing.
18. Wuh apní roṭí khátá gayá.	18. He went on eating his bread.
19. K͟har-gosh áj tak kánon̲ ke ḍar ke máre bhágtá phirtá hai.	19. The hare (ass-ears) for fear of his ears goes fleeing about till now.
20. Ketlí phúṭá pání háth men̲ liye átá hai.	20. He is coming with a kettle of boiling water in his hand.
21. Itní rát gayí áp kyún̲ áe hain̲.	21. Why have you come so late at night? (so much night having gone).
22. Memsáhiba kuchh rát rahe se uṭhkar K͟hudá kí ‘ibádat kar rahí hain̲.	22. Madam has been worshiping God since before dawn (arising while yet night).
23. Wuh dauṛtá húá chalá átá hai.	23. He is coming running.
24. Sir níche kiye (húe) khaṛá hai.	24. He is standing with head down.
25. Us ke sámne dáne paṛe húe the.	25. The grains were lying before him.
26. Yih laṛká paṛhá húá hai.	26. This boy is educated.
27. Yih paṛhá húá laṛká hai.	27. This is an educated boy.
28. Darwáze se sir nikále khaṛe the.	28. They were standing wth heads thrust out of the door.
29. Má͟nge baġair tumne kyún̲ liyá?	29. Why did you take it without asking?

30. Bin-mán̲ge unhon̲ ne mujhko diyá.	30. They gave it me unasked.
31. Pás ákar wuh be-púchhe kahne lagá.	31. Coming up he began to say, without being asked.
32. Main̲ battí háth men̲ liye áún̲gá.	32. I'll bring the candle in my hand.
33. Merí kitáb lete áná.	33. Bring my book when you come.
34. Main̲ sab kí kitáben̲ lekar jáún̲gá.	34. I'll get the books of all before I go.
35. Apní naját ke kám kiye jáo.	35. Go on doing works of your salvation.
36. Jahán̲ tak ho sake 'ilm hásil kiye jáo.	36. As far as possible, go on acquiring knowledge.
37. Ápko Panjáb áe kitne baras húe hain̲.	37. How long have you been in the Punjab? (to you, come to the Punjab, how many years have become).
38. Merá phaṭá húá sáya darzí ko dedo, ki wuh us ko sí le.	38. Give my torn skirt to the tailor that he may mend it.
39. Is dúkán men̲ bane banáe júte aur sile siláe kapṛe mil játe hain̲.	39. (You) can get ready-made boots and clothing in this shop, (boots, clothes made, had made, sewn, had sewn).
40. Agar pakí pakái roṭí mil jáe to bihtar.	40. It will be better if (we) can get ready-cooked food (bread).

41. Is dúdh men̲ pání milá húá hai.	41. There is water mixed in this milk.
42. Kyún̲ki ham ímán par chalte hain̲, na ki án̲khon̲ dekhe par.	42. For we walk by faith and not by sight (not on that seen [by] eyes).

Participles are used either in agreement or in the declined form in "*e.*" It is safe, however, to make the participle agree with its noun, or pronoun, if that is a subject; if it, however, is an object, with or without "*ko*," the participle may be in the "*á*" form. When participles are repeated, as in 9, 13, 15, they more commonly are in "*e.*" In 21, "*se*" is understood "*gayí se*," as it is expressed in 22. In 24—28 *húá*, *húe*, may be expressed or understood, as desired.

Diversification.—Interchange the nouns and pronouns of the first ten sentences until you can do it readily. Interchange all the verbs of 11—18, then make all future.

In 37 ask "studying Urdu, writing Urdu, living in this city, reading this book," then use for *baras*, *din*, *mahíne*, *der*; if you have much trouble or hesitation in this, your past work is poorly done.

In 1—10 substitute any participles that may be formed from verbs in these sentences, e.g., in 6 say, *Main̲ dhobí ko kapṛe láte dekh rahá hún̲.*

Have the teacher give sentences showing the usage of these verbs in double and treble roots.

LESSON LXXXII.

Exercises in "wálá," English "er."

1. Yih ádmí k̲h̲úb dauṛne-wálá hai.	1. This man is an excellent runner.
2. Kamiṭṭí in lakṛí, ghás-,	2. The (municipal) commit-

chárewálon̲ ko shahr men̲ bin mahsúl liye jáne nahín̲ detí.	tee does not allow these wood-, grass-, and fodder-men to go into the city without having taken tax (octroi).
3. Yih marnewálá jism baqá ká jáma pahinegá.	3. This dying body shall put on a garment of immortality.
4. Ghoṛewále Kábul se bahut áte hain̲.	4. Many horse-dealers come from Kabul.
5. Yih ádmí baṛá chalnewálá hai.	5. This man is a great walker.
6. Tez dauṛnewálí ghoṛí ham ko cháhiye.	6. We want a swift-running mare.

Never say "*Achchewálá dedo,*" as many do, i.e. "Give a good one," but say "*Koí achchhá sá dedo, Achchhe álú de do, Achchhí roṭí do.*"

7. In Dillí-wálon̲ ke sáth mat rahná.	7. Don't stay with these men of Delhi.
8. Yih laṛká pás ho jáegá. Baṛá honhár hai.	8. This boy will pass. He is a very likely lad.
9. Main̲ apne bhejnewále pás játá hún̲.	9. I go to him who sent me.
10. Jis ká qissa main̲ sunánewálá hún̲.	10. Whose story I am about to relate.
11. Pakánewálí koí nahín̲ hai, is liye shádí kartá hún̲.	11. I've no house-keeper, so I am getting married.
12. Gharwálí kahne lagí ki gharwálá báhar gayá húá hai.	12. The woman of the house began to say, Husband is gone away (out).

13. Sab bátoṉ ko jo honewálí thíṉ jánkar, Masih shahr-i-muqaddas ko chalá.	13. Knowing all things that were about to happen, Christ started to the holy city.
14. Bonewálá aur hai, káṭnewálá aur.	14. One sows (and) another reaps. (Sower other is, reaper other).
15. Jo mere bheje húe ko qabúl kartá hai, mujhe—balki mere bhejnewále ko, qabúl kartá hai.	15. He who receives my sent one, receives me—rather, he receives my sender.

This ending "*wálá, wálí,*" added to a noun or inf. in "*á,*" changes the "*á*" to "*e,*" as *kátná* but *kátnewálá*, *ghoṛá*, *ghoṛewále*. In many instances it has the force of an adjective. Also, "*hár*" and "*hárá.*" This is a common idiom in the Punjabi.

LESSON LXXXIII.

Permissives.

1. Wuh ham ko áne nahíṉ dete.	1. They won't let us come (*lit.* They do not give us to come).
2. Maiṉ tum ko kal áne dúṉgá.	2. I will let you come tomorrow.
3. Bábá mujh ko kám karne nahíṉ detá.	3. The child won't let me do my work.
4. Jáne do, koí bát nahiṉ.	4 Let it go, it's nothing.
5. Rahne díjiye. Kuchh parwá nahiṉ.	5. Let it be. It does not matter.
6 Bímárí usko paṛhne nahíṉ detí.	6. Sickness won't allow him to go to school.

7. Wálid ne mujhko jáne na diyá.	7. Father did not let me go.
8. Tum ne pání kyún na píne diyá?	8. Why did you not let him drink?
9. Bárish ham ko báhar nikalne nahín detí.	9. Rain won't let us go out.

Diversification.—Substitute ten verbs.

Compulsives.

1. Tumko kal Láhaur jáná paṛegá.	1. You'll have to go to Lahore to-morrow. (To you going will fall.)
2. Mujh ko likhná paṛegá.	2. I'll have to write. (To me writing will fall.)
3. Hamen chha baje subh kám par jáná paṛtá hai.	3. We have to go to work at six in the morning.
4. Roz roz do daf'a dúdh nikálná paṛtá hai.	4. We have to milk twice daily.
5. Munshi ko har waqt Urdú bolná cháhiye.	5. The munshi ought to speak Urdu at all times.
6. Shágird ko imtihán men Urdú bolná paṛegá, is liye cháhiye ki abhí bolá kare.	6. The pupil will have to speak Urdu in examination, so he ought to speak it now.
7. Mujhe ghar ká sárá asbáb bechná paṛá.	7. I had to sell all my furniture.
8. Tum ko likhná hogá.	8. You will have to write.
9. Unko apne háth se lakṛí káṭní paṛegí.	9. They'll have to cut wood with their own hands.

10. Agar jáná paṛá, to— khair, jáúngá.	10. If I have to go, then,— Well, I'll go.
11. Use yih bát kahní paṛí aur tumko bhí kahná paṛegá.	11. He had to tell it and so will you.
12. Roz gharwále ko chiṭṭhí likhní paṛtí hai.	12. She has to write to her husband every day.
13. Laṛkon ko baṛe baṛe kám karne paṛe.	13. The boys had to do big jobs.

What we translate as subject is really in the dative case with "*ko*" and *paṛná* may be used in mas., or fem. of present, past, future, but of course only in the third person, as the subject is always an infinitive. "*Cháhiye*" denotes moral obligation, while "*paṛna*" is simple compulsion. "*Hogá*" denotes a still weaker constraint.

Diversification.

Change the pronouns to all other persons and numbers. Instead of nouns and pronouns, substitute boy, boys, girl, girls, man, men, woman, women, in 6. For verbs substitute buy, sell, eat, feed, break, open, or any other familiar verbs, with these or other nouns as objects.

LESSON LXXXIV.

Potentials.

1. Wuh isí waqt bázár játá hogá.	1. He must be going to the bazar just now.
2. Unko baṛí taklíf hotí hogí.	2. They must be enduring great trouble.
3. Main ne wuh ghoṛá dekhá hogá, yád nahín.	3. I must have seen the horse. I don't remember.

4. Diyá hogá. Pata nahín̲ rahá.	4. I suppose I did give it. I don't recollect.
5. Sach hogá. (Sach bát hogí).	5. It may be true.
6. Wuh shahr gaye hon̲ge.	6. They must have gone to the city.
7. Unhon̲ ne áp ko chiṭṭhí likhí hogí	7. They no doubt wrote you a letter.
8. Laṛkí áj tak mar gayí hogí.	8. The girl must have died by to-day.
9. Wuh dhúp men̲ marte hon̲ge.	9. They must be dying in the sun (hyperbole).
10. Kyún̲ ghabráte ho? Wuh átí hogí?	10. Why are you so disturbed? She must be coming.
11. Yih chárpái áp ko cháhiye hogí.	11. You must be needing this bedstead.
12. Áp ne baṛe baṛe safar kiye hon̲ge.	12. You must have taken wonderful journeys.

Continuative with "rahná."

1. Wuh din bhar yihí kám karte rahte hain̲.	1. They keep doing this work all day.
2. Chup raho. Chupke se baiṭhe raho.	2. Be quiet. Sit in silence.
3. Wuh sárá din baiṭhá rahtá hai.	3. He sits all day.
4. Wuh khá rahí hai. Wuh khátí rahtí hai.	4. She is eating. She continues to eat.
5. Go main̲ ne usko mana' kiyá thá, wuh sharáb pítá játá hai.	5. Though I forbade him, he goes on drinking liquor.

6. Wuh sárá din sharáb pítá rahtá hai.	6. He drinks liquor all day.
7. Agarchi máṉ ne buláyá thá, wuh paṛhtá gayá.	7. Although his mother called him, he went on reading.
8. Uská sárá mál játá rahá hai.	8. All his property has been lost.
9. Mere do rúpae játe rahe haiṉ.	9. I've lost two rupees.
10. Laṛkí yaháṉ se dikhái na detí thí.	10. The girl could not be seen from here (was not giving appearance from here).
11. Yih bát sunkar sab ke sab chal diye.	11. Hearing this everybody went off.
12. Wuh sitára kis waqt dikhái diyá thá?	12. When did that star appear?
13. Top kí áwáz áj sunái na dí.	13. The cannon was not heard to-day.
14. Dono shágird uske píchhe ḥo liye.	14. Both disciples followed him.

Note that verbs of 11—14 agree with sub. not with obj.

LESSON LXXXV.

Prepositions.

1. Agar yih K͟hudá kí taraf se hai, to tum se kuchh na banegá.	1. If this is of God, then you can do nothing.
2. Yih chár din kí bát hai. Áp ne nahín suní?	2. This happened four days ago. Have you not heard it?

3. Wuh is liye gayá ki sáhib ká hukm thá.	3. He went because it was the master's order.
4. Is kí mánind tín gaz kapṛá láná.	4. Bring three yards of cloth like this.
5. Yih bát sáhib kí bát ke mutábiq hai.	5. This is in accordance with what the sahib said.
6. Qurán Injíl ke mutábiq nahín̲ hai.	6. The Koran does not agree with the gospel (evangel).
7. Merí taraf se kah dená ki Á jáo.	7. Tell him from me to come.
8. Áp ke chár áne merí taraf hain̲.	8. I owe you four annas.
9. Tumhárí taraf sawá rúpaya hai.	9. There's Rs. 1/4 against you.
10. Is men̲ aur us men̲ zamín ásmán ká farq hai.	10. There is a world of difference between this and that.
11. Mujh men̲ aur tujh men̲ kitná kuchh farq hai.	11. What a difference between you and me.
12. Itne ('arse) men̲ laṛká á gayá.	12. In the meantime the boy came.
13. Áp mujh par ġusse na hon̲.	13. Don't be angry with me.
14. Yih le jáo, *but*, Is ko* le jáo.	14. Take it away, *but* Take him (her) away.
15. Is men̲ se pání pí lo.	15. Drink water out of this.
16. Do míl par áp ko ek pul milegá.	16. Two miles on you will come to a bridge.
17. Main̲ waqt muqarrar par áún̲gá.	17. I'll come at the appointed time.

* *Ko* with person, or with definite thing.

18. K̲h̲udá kí bandagí karní mujh par farz hai.	18. To serve God is an obligation on me.
19. Us ke háth men̲ angúṭhí aur uske páon men̲ jútí pahináo.	19. Put a ring on his hand and shoes on his feet.
20. Samsún ádmíon̲ men̲ zoráwar thá.	20. Samson was the strongest of men.
21. Das baras ká laṛká já rahá thá.	21. A ten-year old boy was going along.
22. Yih kahán̲ kí ráh hai ?	22. Where does this road go to ?
23. Hamárí tarah árám se raho.	23. Be quiet like us.
24. Rasúlon̲ men̲ se do gáon̲ kí taraf gaye.	24. Two of the apostles went toward the village.
25. Sab ke sab kahte the ki yih baniye len den ke khare hain̲.	25. Everybody said that these shopkeepers are honest in dealing.
26. Us ne wa'da kiyá ki jo kuchh main̲ dúngá dúdh ká dúdh dúngá.	26. He promised that Whatever I shall give, I will give pure milk.
27. Unhon̲ ne chár din ká wa'da kiyá thá.	27. They promised (it) in four days.
28. Sab ke sab mun̲h dekhte ke dekhte rah gaye.	28. The whole lot stood looking in each other's faces [in blank astonishment].
29 Main̲ ne apná ghoṛá faqír ke háth bechá.	29. I sold my horse to the faqir.
30. Laṛkí sotí kí sotí rahí.	30. The girl slept right on.
31. Un kí aulád na thí (Un ke hán̲).	31. They had no children. (In their place.)

32*. Yih ghoṛiáṉ kitne kitne meṉ lín ?	32. How much did you pay for each of these mares ?
33. Baṛí to main ne sau ko lí, aur yih do chhoṭíáṉ maiṉ ne sawá sawá sau se líṉ.	33. I got the big one for 100 and the two small ones for 125 each.
34. Yih log ápas meṉ kyá báteṉ kar rahe haiṉ ?	34. What are these people saying among themselves ?
35. Yíh mál háthoṉ háth bik játá hai.	35 These goods sell like hot cakes (from hands to hand, not from shelves).
36. Almárí par se ṭopí utár dená.	36. Give me my hat off the top of the ward-robe.
37. Sab log daryá ke pár utar gaye haiṉ, kyá mujhe bhí na utároge ?	37. Everybody has crossed over the river, will you not put me over too ?
38. Áp ke ghar meṉ kaun utará hai ?	38. Who (guest) is stopping at your house ?
39. Ghoṛe kí ṭáng utar gayí hai.	39. The horse's leg is out of joint.
40. Daryá ká pání áj hí utar gayá hai.	40. The river has just gone down to-day.
41. Buk̲h̲ár subh chaṛhtá aur shám ko utar játá hai.	41. The fever goes up in the morning and goes down in the evening.
42. Maulví ne K̲h̲udá ke	42. The Maulvi (an Arabic

* Note the three prepositions of price.

nám ká ghar banáyá hai.	scholar) has built a house for God (of God's name).
43. Pahlí áyat se lekar daswín tak paṛho.	43. Read from the first verse to the tenth.
44. Kapṛá mez ke úpar (not par) ṭangá hai.	44. The garment is hanging above the table.
45. Kapṛá mez par (*or*, ke úpar) paṛá hai.	45. The garment is lying on the table.
46. Sáhib ghar par haiṉ. Sahib ghar ke upar haiṉ.	46. Sahib is at home. Sahib is on top of the house, or above it [as on a hill side]).
47. Áp ke sáth shahr tak ho áúṉgá.	47. I'll go as far as the city with you.
48. Maiṉ ne barasoṉ tak uskí k͟hidmat kí.	48. I served him for years.
49. Pání kosoṉ tak phailtá gayá.	49. The water went spreading for miles.
50. Sipáhí ján tak farq nahíṉ kartá.	50. A soldier does not regard his life. (Makes no difference up to life.)
51. Áp ne kaháṉ tak paṛhá ?	51. How far did you read ?
52 Jaháṉ tak ho sake hásil kiye jáo.	52. As far as possible go on acquiring.
53. Wuh kal mere pás thá.	53. He was with me yesterday (sitting).
54. Wuh kal mere sáth thá.	54. He was with me yesterday (going).
55. K͟habardár ! Isko baṛí k͟habardárí se le jáná.	55. Look out ! Take this with great care (manner).

56. Main pahle yih bát jántí hún.	56. I have known this before.
57. Yih chauthe roz kí bát hai.	57. (This is a matter of the fourth day.) This happened four days ago.
58. Idhar udhar kí báten hone lagín.	58. All sorts of talk now began.
59. Log ghar ke áge píchhe khare the.	59. People were standing before and behind the house.
60. Sámne se (*or*, Áge se) hat jáo.	60. Get out of the way (from in front).
61. Yih log mere ba'd pahunchenge.	61. These folk will arrive after me.

(" After " is translated by "*ba'd*," when it refers to time, but by "*píchhe*," when it refers to place. "Before" in time, is "*pahle*," but of place it is "*sámne*" or "*áge*," which two are interchangeable.)

62. Yih ádmí mere badle (men) kám karegá.	62. This man will work in my place.
63. Yih ádmí merí jagah (merí 'iwaz) kám karegá.	63. This man will work in my place.
64. Mahsúl kí chaukíán shahr ke ware pare hain.	64. Tax-houses ("Seats of custom") are on this and that side of the city.
65. Das baje ke qaríb main ne bís ek ádmí dekhe.	65. About ten o'clock I saw some 20 men.
66. Dar ke sabab se qaríban sáre bhág gaye.	66. For fear nearly all fled.

67. Báġ ke nazdík koí sau faqír rahte hain, aur mere nazdík wuh achchhe ádmí nahín hain.	67. About a hundred fakeers live near the garden, and in my opinion they are not good men.
68. Merí chiṭṭhián Ḍákṭar sáhib kí ma'rifat pahaunchá kartí haín.	68. I (usually) get my letters in the care of the doctor.
69. Log mere khiláf (barkhiláf) kyún uṭhte hain ?	69. Why do people rise up against me ?
70. Do ádmí mere muqábale men khaṛe húe.	70. Two men stood up against me.
71. Is khiṛkí ke muqábale men darwáza cháhiye.	71. There ought to be a door opposite this window.
72. Siwá uske sab bhág gaye.	72. All but him fled.
73. Áp mere hawále kar den, aur, mere zimme. bajáe iske main áp kí khátir koí achchhá ghoṛá láúngá.	73. Put him in my care, and I, I assure you (in my responsibility), instead of this, will bring you a good horse.
74. Jaisá usne kiyá main ne bhí kiyá.	74. I did as he did.

Be careful to attain speed and readiness in the use of these prepositions, and be accurate with the "*ke*" or "*kí*," always thinking of them as, not that "for" is "*wáste, liye*," but "*ke wáste, ke liye*"; "about" is not "*bábat*," but "*kí babát*."

Diversification.—Learn these sentences very completely, and then take any nouns from the list that seem suitable and substitute.

Remember that repetition of these idioms again and again is necessary to fix them in the memory. Get them so that you can use them freely.

LESSON LXXXVI.

Conjunctions.

1. Agar main̲ pahle chhoṭon̲ se shurú‘ karûn̲, (*or*, Agar main̲ ne pahle chhoṭon̲ se shurú‘ kiyá) to wuḥ jald ráh-i-rást par á jáen̲ge.	1. If I should begin with the little ones first, they will speedily come on the right path.
2. Agar wuh haqq kí ráh par na áen̲, to ghar se nikal jáen̲	2. If they do not come on the right path then let them get out of the house.
3. Agarchi (Go) main̲ ne baṛon̲ se shurú‘ karke baṛí koshish kí, tau bhí (táham) wuh náfarmán rahe the.	3. Although I began with the big ones and worked hard (made a big effort) still they remained disobedient.
4. K̲h̲wáh wuh áe k̲h̲wáh na áe, tumhen̲ áná hogá.	4. Whether he come or not, you must.
5. Cháhe yih lo, cháhe wuh, mujhe parwá nahín̲.	5. Take either this or that, to me it is of no concern.
6. Na chhoṭá áyá na baṛá, dono ke dono be-farmán rahe.	6. Neither the big nor the little one came, both remained disobedient.
7. Is kám ko áhistagí se shurú‘ karná cháhiye, aisá na ho ki yih nayá ḍhang dekhkar, laṛke haṭ jáen̲.	7. This work should be begun slowly, lest the children, seeing this new fashion, draw back.

8. Peshtar is ke ki main̲ já sakún̲, wuh gayá.	8. Before I could go, he went.
9. Jab tak zindagí hai, tab tak ummed bhí hai. Jab tak sán̲s tab tak ás.	9. While there's life, there is hope. While there is breath, till then is hope.
10. Jis waqt yih bát mujhe yád paṛtí, main̲ (us waqt) beik̲h̲tiyár hokar han̲stá hún̲.	10. When I recall this, I cannot keep from laughing. (At what time this falls to mind, I, out of hand, laugh).
11. Mán len̲ ki yih bát sach hai, tumhen̲ kyá ?	11. Granted that this is true, what's that to you ?
12. Admí, tú koí kyún̲ na ho, tere pás koí 'uzr nahín̲.	12. Man, whoever thou art, thou hast no excuse.
13. Main̲ mansúk̲h̲ karne nahín̲ balki púrá karne áyá hún̲.	13. I came not to abolish, but to fulfil.
14. Us se púchho ki Khánà taiyár hai yá nahín̲ ?	14. Ask him, Is dinner ready or not ?
15. Mujhe shakk thá ki áyá main̲ jágtí hún̲, yá k̲h̲wáb dekhtí hún̲.	15. I was in doubt whether I was awake or seeing a dream.
16 Kásh ki yih tamíz jo K̲h̲udá ne tum ko 'atá kí hai, sab men̲ hotí.	16. Would that this discretion, which God has given you, were in all.
17. Kásh ki yih ádmí merá bháí Fazl ho.	17. Oh, may this man be my brother Fazl.

18. Kásh ki log is bát ko samjhen.

18. Oh that people may understand this.

19. Kyá khúb hotá ki áp áte.

19. How well it would have been if you had come.

20. Chhoṭe baṛe áe hain.

20. Small and great have come.

21. Kam o besh bís báís din lagenge.

21. It will take 20 or 22 days, more or less.

22. Main kisí se máng láúngá.

22. I'll get it from somebody (anybody).

23. Wuh to kab ká pahúnchá hogá.

23. He must have arrived a long time ago.

With "sá."

24. Laṛká murda sá paṛá thá.

24. The boy lay as dead.

25. Mujh sá dukhiyá áp ne kabhí na dekhá hogá.

25. You can never have seen one so distressed as I.

26. Merá sá dukh áp ne kabhí nahín dekhá.

26. You have never seen such trouble as mine.

27. Wuh gorá sá laṛká áp ká hai ?

27. Is this fairish boy yours ?

28. Wuh laṛáí men sher sá ádmí hai.

28. He is like a tiger in fight.

29. Yih darakht bahut sá phal látá hai.

29. This tree bears a lot of fruit.

30. Us ká rang o raugan kuchh ká kuchh ho gayá.

30. His colour and complexion quite changed.

31. Sab ádmí ek se nahín hote.

31. All men are not alike.

32. Uskí sher kí sí súrat ḍarauní thí.

32. His tiger-like form was terrible.

33. Bandagí, janáb.	33. Good evening, sir. (Service, sir).
34. Salám alaikum.*	34. Peace to you.
35. Walaikum salám.	35. And to you peace.

* Used by Moslems.

APPENDIX.

URDU GRAMMAR.

The most outstanding feature of Urdu is its distinctions of GENDER. Not only animals but all inanimate objects and abstract nouns are either masculine or feminine. This distinction shows itself most prominently in the verb and adjective forms. Generally speaking *á* is the ending which denotes the masculine, and *í* that which denotes the feminine. This is so for verbs, and usually so for adjectives, and predominantly so for nouns. There are, of course, exceptions, but only eight such words in *í* are masculine, *páni* being the most common. *Dawá*, medicine; *hawá*, air; on the other hand, feminine, though the form *dawái* also occurs. Such words as *laṛká, laṛkí, ghoṛá, ghoṛí, kuttá, kuttí*, show the masculines in *á*, boy, horse, dog, with the corresponding fems. in *í*. Also words in *-ish*, *-t* are ordinarily fem. The genders of other words ending in various consonants must be learned.

PRONOUNS have but one form for both genders. Where we say He came, She came, They came, Urdu would have *Wuh áyá, Wuh áí, Wuh áe, Wuh áin̲*, which convey the same idea, with the added refinement that *Wuh áe* is they (men) came, *Wuh áin̲*. They (women) came. It is a bit puzzling at first to think of genders in all things, but constant practice makes it second nature.

The Urdu noun is very simple in its DECLENSION, as the outline below indicates. All masculine nouns in *á* and *a*, excepting titles, as Rája, Lálá, have two forms in the singular and three in the plural. All other masculine nouns ending in vowels or consonants, have but one form in the singular, and that same form does duty in the plural, save in the vocative, which is in *-o*, and the form that goes with prepositions, which ends in *-oṉ*. Thus we have the absolute form (for the nominative and objective cases), the vocative, and the prepositional form.

	Sing.	*Plur.*	*Sing.*	*Plur.*
Abs.	laṛká	laṛke	parda	parde
Prep.	laṛke	laṛkoṉ	parde	pardoṉ
Voc.	laṛke	laṛko.	parda	pardo
Abs.	ádmí	ádmí	ghar	ghar
Prep.	ádmí	ádmíoṉ	ghar	gharoṉ
Voc.	ádmí	ádmío	ghar	gharo
Abs.	k͟hánsámáṉ	k͟hánsámáṉ		
Prep.	k͟hánsámáṉ	k͟hánsámáṉoṉ		
Voc.	k͟hánsámáṉ	k͟hánsámáṉo		

Feminines have but one form in the singular; the plural absolute of those ending in *-í* is formed by adding *áṉ*, while the prepositional form is made by adding *-oṉ*, and the voc. with *-o*. Fem. nouns ending in other vowels or in consonants have no change in singular and form the plural by adding *-eṉ*, *-oṉ*, *-o*. Thus we have—

	Sing.	*Plur.*	*Sing.*	*Plur.*
Abs.	laṛkí	laṛkíáṉ	dawá	dawáeṉ
Prep.	laṛkí	laṛkíoṉ	dawá	dawáoṉ
Voc.	laṛkí	laṛkío	dawá	dawáo
Abs.	kitáb	kitábeṉ	'aurat	'aurateṉ
Prep.	kitáb	kitáboṉ	'aurat	'auratoṉ
Voc.	kitáb	kitábo	'aurat	'aurato

ADJECTIVES ending in any letter save *a* or *á* have but one form. Those ending in *a* or *á* have two forms in the mas., and one in the fem., that in *í*.

	Sing.	*Plur.*	
Abs.	achchhá	achchhe	Fem. (for all forms in
Prep.	achchhe	achchhe	both nos.), achchhí,
Abs.	táza	táze	tází.
Prep.	táze	táze	

When used as nouns, we would say, *In achchhon ko do*, Give to these good folk; or, Give these good ones.

The VERB is rather full in tense forms, but they are regular, with only six irregular verbs. It has three root forms: the passive, or intransitive, as *kaṭná*, to be cut; *chhúṭná*, to get away; the transitive, or first causative, as *káṭná*. to cut; *chhoṛná*, to let go; and the second causative, *kaṭáná*, to cause to cut; *chhuṛáná*, to cause some one to let something go. Also a compound form *káṭá jáná*, to be cut; for the passive voice. All these forms demand careful study and much repetition before they are fixed in mind.

The Infinitive, Participles, Imperative, Indicative, and Subjunctive, with an old Infinitive make up the verb; as *káṭná*; *káṭtá, káṭá*; *káṭo*; *káṭtá hai*, etc.; *káṭe*; *káṭá*; *jáná*; *játá*; *gayá*; *jáo*; *játá hai*, etc.; *jáe*; *jáyá*.

Drop *-ná* of the inf. and you get the root. To this root add *-át* and *-á* for the present and perfect participles. Add *-o* for the imperative, and for the indicative we have the verb to be, **hai**, **haiṉ**, and **thá**, used with these participles to form the various tenses. The Subjunctive is formed by adding *-úṉ*, *-e*, *-e*, *-eṉ*, *-o*, *-eṉ* to the root; and by further adding *gá*, *ge*, *gí* to this we get the future.

Statements of fact are in the Indicative, while uncertainties are in the Subjunctive.

Participles are like adjectives in their agreement. Possessive pronouns are really adjectives in agreement.

The prepositions usually follow their nouns, and are

mostly used with *ke*, or *kí*, to join the noun and preposition. A few never use *ke, kí*, as *meṉ, se, ko, ke, kí, ká, tak, par*. *Ko* sometimes means "to," and sometimes it is merely the sign of the objective case.

A good deal of diversity is possible in the order of words in the sentence, but the usual order is, the subject with its modifiers, then the object with its modifiers, the adverb, and the predicate last.

Many points of grammar are of course not even hinted at in this brief statement, but if the sentences are thoroughly mastered and the Drill work is faithfully done, there will not be much left that is absolutely new.

Toward the end of the first year, Platt's Hindustani Grammar, Kellogg's Hindi Grammar, and Hooper's Idioms will be useful.

Interrogative.	*Demonstrative.*		*Relative.*
	Near.	*Far.*	
kyá	yih	wuh	jo
kaun	yih	wuh	jo
kaunsá	..	..	jaunsá
kaháṉ	yaháṉ	waháṉ	jaháṉ
kitná	itná	utná	jitná
kaisá	aisá	waisá	jaisá
kidhar	idhar	udhar	jidhar
kyúṉ	yúṉ	tyúṉ	júṉ
kab	ab	tab	jab
kis tarah	is tarah	us tarah	jis tarah
What?	this	that	which
Who? / Which?	this	that	which
Where?	here	there	where
How many?	this many	that many	which many

Interrogative.	*Demonstrative.* *Near.*	*Far.*	*Relative.*
What sort of ?	this sort of	that sort of	which sort of
Whither ?	hither	thither	whither
Why ?	this way	that way	whichever way
When ?	now	then	when
How ?	in this way	in that way	in which way

Interrogatives.

I. WHAT ?	KYÁ.
What is this? This is a ( ). What is that? That is a ( ). Yih kya hai? Yih ( ) hai. Wuh kya hai? Wuh ( ) hai.	Book, table chair, carpet, rug, floor, door, window, room, matting. Kitáb, mez, kursí, ḍarí, ġalicha, farsh, khiṛkí, kamra, chaṭáí.
2. Dish, plate, knife, spoon, fork, cup, saucer, glass, water, tea, coffee.	2. Ḍís, pleṭ, chhurí, káṇṭá, chammach, piyála, pirch, gilás, pání, cháe, káfí.
3. House, verandah, bed-room, dining-room, drawing-room, office, pantry, kitchen, store-room, bath-room, dressing-room.	3. Ghar, barámada, sone ká kamra, kháne ká kamra, gol-kamra, daftar, botal-k͟háná, báwarchí-k͟hána, godám, ġusl-k͟hána, singár-kamra.
4. Bread, butter, meat, rice, fruit, potatoes, peas, vegetables, onions, chicken.	4. Roṭí, makkhan, gosht, cháwal, mewá, álú, maṭar, sabzí, piyáz, murġí.

English	Hindustani
5. Meal, flour, germ meal, sugar, salt, boiled rice, pepper black, red, vinegar, walnuts.	5. Áṭá, maida, súji, misrí, namak, bhát, kálí mirch, lál mirch, sirká, akhroṭ.
6. Paper, ink, pen, post, newspaper, stamp, post-office, postman, letter, pencil.	6. Káġaz, siyáhí, qalam, ḍák, akhbár, ṭikaṭ, ḍák-khána, ḍákwálá, chiṭṭhí, pinsal.
7. Bed, couch, curtain, wall, book-case, cupboard, bedding, box, luggage, bag.	7. Palang or chárpáí, kaunch, parda, díwál, almárí, bistar, sandúq, asbáb, beg or thailí.
8. Broom, duster, shovel, tongs, brush, hat, clothes, dress, shoes, coat, boots.	8. Jháṛú, jháṛan, belcha, chimṭá, bursh, ṭopí, kapṛe, dares, juṭí, koṭ, búṭ or jútá.
9. Train, station, ticket, carriage, fare, railway, porter, guard, engine, luggage-van, booking-clerk, luggage-receipt, class.	9. Gáṛí, isṭeshan, ṭikaṭ, gáṛí, kiráya, rel, qulí, gáḍ, injan, brek, ṭikaṭwálá-bábú, bilṭí, darja.
10. Hand, foot, nose, mouth, eye, ear, head, arm (between shoulder and elbow), face, leg, finger, toe, right, left.	10. Háth, pair, nák, munh, ánkh, kán, sir, bázú, munh, táng unglí, unglí, dahiná, báyán.
11. Hair, beard, elbow, knee, ankle, joint, back, breast, shoulder, stomach, waist, heart, tooth.	11. Bál, ḍáṛhí, kuhni, ghuṭná, joṛ, píṭh, chhátí, kandhá, ṭakhna peṭ, kamar, dil, dánt.

12. Man, woman, child, boy, girl, horse, mare; colt, cow, calf, ox.	12. Ádmí, 'aurat, bachcha, laṛká, laṛkí, ghoṛá, ghoṛí, bachherá, bachherí; gáe, bachcha, bail.
13. Donkey, mule, buffalo, cow, buffalo bull, buffalo calf, camel, sheep, goat, dog, duck.	13. Gadhá, gadhí, khachchar, bhain̲s, bhain̲sé, paṛá, paṛiyá, únṭ, bheṛ, bakrá, bakrí, kuttá, badak̲h̲.
14. Wood, stone, coal, charcoal, fuel, shop, market, rate, grain, wheat.	14. Lakṛí, patthar, patthar ke koele, koelẽ (sing. koelá) índhan, dukán, bázár, nirak̲h̲, anáj, dána, gehún̲.
15. Sheet, handkerchief, towel, blanket, pillow, pillow-case, mattress, shirt, undershirt, drawers, waistcoat, trousers, flannel, night-clothes, table-cloth, napkin, tray-cloth, cuffs, collar, skirt.	15. Chádar, rúmál, tauliya, kambal, takiya, takiya-ġiláf, gadelá, qamíz, banyán, darás, wáskoṭ, patlún, falalain, rát ke kapṛe, mez kí chádar, mez ká tauliya, trel kí chádar, kaf, kálar, sáyá.
16. Diseases: fever, diarrhœa, consumption, pain.	16. Bímáríán̲: buk̲h̲ár, tap, dast, tap-i-diqq, dard.
17. Time, times, season, day, week, month, year hour, Monday, Tuesday, Wednesday, Thursday, Friday,	17. Waqt, auqát, mausim. din, hafta, mahína, sál, ghanṭá, ghaṛí, Pír ká roz, Mangal ká roz, Budhwár.

Saturday, Sunday, Sabbath, rainy season, warm season, Winter, Spring, Spring harvest, Full harvest.	Jum'arát, Jumá', Saníchar, Itwár, Sabt; barsát, garmí, jáṛá, bahár, rabí', k͟haríf.
18. Servant, cook, scullion, waterman, groom, gardener, sweeper, table-servant, coachman, watchman, carpenter, blacksmith, pedlar, cowman, grassman.	18. Naukar, k͟hánsámáṉ, masálchí, bihishtí, sáís, málí, mihtar, mez, k͟hidmatgár, kochwán, chaukídár, baṛhái, (tark͟hán), lohár, bisátí (Eng. bakaswálá) gwálá, ghasiára.
19. Stable, cow-stable, servants' houses, garden, road, thatchroof, keys, any musical instrument, picture, flowers, stone or earth roof, tile roof, flowerpot.	19. Astabal, gausálá, ságarpesha, báġ, saṛak, chhappar, chábíáṉ, bájá, taswír, phúl, chhat, khaprail, gamlá.
20. Tools, hammer, ax, hatchet, plane, saw, file, nail, tack, adze, screw, screw-driver, mattock, trowel, sickle, rope, cooking vessel.	20. Auzár (hathyár), mártaul, kulháṛá, kulháṛí, randa, árí, retí, kíl, biranjí, ṭhesá, pech, pechkash, kahí, ramba, darántí, rassí, degchí.
21. Metal, iron, gold, silver, copper, tin, sheet tin, lead, glass, mirror, eye-glasses, brass, leather.	21. Dhát, lohá, soná, chándí, támbá, qalaí, ṭín, sísá, shísha, áíná, ainak (chashma), pítal, chamṛá.

This lesson is to be taught during the first six or twelve months, and is *not* to be completed before the second is begun.

II. WHERE?	KAHÁN?
Where is the (I)?	(1) Kahán hai?
The (I) is (II_2) the (I).	(I) (I II_2) hai. Kitáb mez par hai.
1. See I (1-20).	
2. On, under, beside, here, there,.	2. par, ke niche, ke pás, yahán, wahán.

Kitáb mez par hai, mez ke níche hai, mez ke pás hai, yahán hai, wahán hai.

These questions must be practised until the pupil gives each answer readily.

III. WHY?	KYÚN?
Why did (the woman) come from the city? go to the well? go to the city? to the house? to this country? to our bungalow? Is (she) coming? going? eating? talking? looking? sending the chair? buying food? the book? the meal? etc.	('Aurat) shahr se kyún ái? wuh? tum? gayí? kúen ko? shahr ko? ghar ko? is mulk ko? hamárí koṭhí ko? Kyún á rahí hai? já, khá, bol, dekh, bhej, mol le, rahí (rahá rahe) hai? kitáb, kháná, áṭá, waġaira.
*Why did you (give) him the (book)? the table, the money, the beds, the waterpots, the watches? take, bring? send?	Áp ne us ko (kitáb) kyún dí? mez, rúpaya, chár-páíán, ghaṛe, ghaṛíán? waġaira, liyá, bhejá? láyá?

---

* This section will be used after a month or two.

Substitutes.—The man, the men, the women, the boys, the girls, you, he, they.

IV. WHO ?	KAUN ?
Who is this boy ? man ? woman ? girl ?	Yih (laṛká) kaun hai ? ádmí ? 'aurat ? laṛkí ?
Hindu, Sikh, Moslem, waterman, our servant, cook, gardener, groom.	Yih Hindú, Sikh, Mussalmán, bihishtí, hamárá naukar, k͟hánsámán̲, málí, sáís, hai.
Who is coming from the city ? going to ? the house, well, tree ?	Shahr se kaun á rahá hai ? já ? ghar, kúen̲, darak͟ht, ko ?
Who drew the water ? gave you the book ? sent the table ? took the money ?	Kis ne pání bhará ? tum ko kitáb dí ? mez bhejá ? rúpaya liyá ?
Who said this ? Who told this ?	Kis ne yih bát kahí ? Kis ne batáyá ?
V. WHOSE ? WHOM ?	KIS KÁ, KIS KO ?
Whose (1) is this ?	Yih kis kí (kin kí) (kitáb) hai ?
That is my book, ours, yours, his, theirs, yours, the boy's, the girl's, the boys', the women's, the girls', the man's, the men's.*	Wuh merí kitáb hai, hamárí, tumhárí, uskí, un kí, áp kí, laṛke, laṛkí kí, laṛkon̲ ká, 'auraton̲ ke, laṛkíon̲ ke, ádmí ka, ádmíon̲ kí.
Whom did he strike ? kill ? ask ?	Us ne kis ko márá ? már ḍálá ? púchhá ?
To whom is he speaking ? giving ?	Wuh kis ko boltá hai ? de rahá hai ?

* Use your most vivid imagination to give life to these exercises.

For whom is he bringing? sending?	Wuh kin ke líe lá rahá hai? bhej?
Ans.—Me, you, him, her them, us, you, the boy, the boys, the girl, the girls.	*Jawáb.*—Mujhe, mere, tumhen̲, tumháre, us ko, ke, unko, ke, ham ko, hamáre, áp ko, áp ke, laṛke ko, ke, laṛkon̲ ko, ke, laṛkíon̲ ko, ke.
VI. WHICH?	KAUNSÁ? KAUN?
Which table do you wish?	Kaunsá mez cháhte ho?
Which book is yours?	Kaunsí kitáb áp kí hai?
Which men are Hindus?	Kaunse ádmí Hindú hain̲?
Books, book-case, carpet, rug, cup, shoes, watch; servant, girls, women, Mohammedans, Sikhs, Christians?	Kitáben̲, almárí, darí, ġalichá, piyála, jútíán̲, ghaṛí; naukar, laṛkíán̲, 'auraten̲, Mussalmán, Sikh, Masíhí or 'Ísáí.
VII. WHAT SORT OF? WHAT KIND OF?	KAISÁ? KIS QISM KÁ?
What sort of a (book) is it?	Wuh kaisí kitáb haí?
Man, woman, boy, girl, table, pen, watch, water-pot, chair, carriage, carpet?	Ádmí, 'aurat, laṛká, laṛkí, mez, qalam, ghaṛí, ghaṛá, kursí, gaṛí, darí?
Ans.—Red, green, white, black, brown, orange, yellow; large, small, round, thin, thick.	*Jawáb.*—Lál, sabz, sufed, kálá, k̲h̲ákí, basantí, pílá; baṛá, chhoṭá, gol, patlá, moṭá.
VIII. WHAT O'CLOCK?	KYÁ BAJÁ?

Interrogative Exercises. Sawáliye Jumle.

1. Kyá bajá hai? or kitne baje hain.	1. What time is it? (What has struck?) or how many have struck?
2. Ek bajá hai. Sawá bajá hai.	2. It is one o'clock. 1/4 more than one.
3. Ḍeṛh bajá hai.	3. It is half past one.
4. Paune do baje hain.	4. 1/4 less than two have struck.
5. Do baje hain. Tín baje hain.	5. It is two o'clock. It is three o'clock.
6. Ḍháí baje hain. Chár baje hain.	6. Two and a half have struck. It is four.
7. Paune tín baje hain. Sawá tín baje.	7. 1/4 less than 3. 1/4 more than 3.
8. Sawá tín, sáṛhe tín, paune chár baje hain.	8. 3:15; 3:30; 3:45, or, 3 1/4, 3 1/2, 3 3/4.
9. Sawá chár, sáṛe chár, paune pánch.	9. 4 1/4, 4 1/2, 4 3/4.
10. Sawá pánch, sáṛhe panch, paune chha.	10. 5 1/4, 5 1/2, 5 3/4.
11. Sawá chha, sáṛhe chha, paune sát.	11. 6 1/4, 6 1/2, 6 3/4.
12. Sawá sát, sáṛhe sát, paune áṭh.	12. 7 1/4, 7 1/2, 7 3/4.
13. Sawá áṭh, sáṛhe áṭh, paune nau.	13. 8 1/4, 8 1/2, 8 3/4.
14. Sawá nau, sáṛhe nau, paune das.	14. 9 1/4, 9 1/2, 9 3/4.
15. Sawá das, sáṛhe das, paune gyára (or, yárá).	15. 10 1/4, 10 1/2, 10 3/4.

16. Sawá gyára, sáṛhe gyára, paune bárah.	16. 11 1/4, 11 1/2, 11 3/4.
17. Sawá bárah, sáṛhe bárah, paun bajá.	17. 12 1/4, 12 : 30, 12 : 45.

Note that in numbers, "*sawá*" is a qr. *more* than, and "*paune*" a qr. *less* than the number it precedes. *Paun* means three-quarters, and is used of one or the unit only ; thus *paun ser. paun sau* = three-quarters of a ser, three-quarters of an hundred ; *paune do, paune das* = $1\frac{3}{4}$, $9\frac{3}{4}$. *Bajá* changes to *baje*, beyond "*ḍeṛh*," one and a half, as it is a participle, and agrees with its noun, "two *have* struck." Avoid saying "*tín bajá*." rather, *tín baje, do baje*. *Sawá* does not change its form, but *paune* is *pauná* with *ek*.

IX. How much? How many?	Kitná? Kitní? Kitne?
How many men have come?	Kitne ádmí áe haiṉ?
How many (chairs) are in this room?	Kitní (kursíáṉ) is kamre meṉ haiṉ?
There is only one chair.	Ek hí kursí is kamare meṉ hai.
Tables, curtains, books, men, women, boys, girls, shoes, hands, eyes, ears?	Mez, parde, kitábeṉ, ádmí, auratеṉ, laṛke laṛkíáṉ, jútíáṉ, háth, aṉkheṉ, kán?
1 to 12;	Ek, do, tín, chár, pánch, chha, sát, áṭh, nau, das, gyárah, bárah;
13 to 100.	terah, chaudah, pandrah, solah, satrah, aṭhárah, unís, bís; ikkís, báís, teís, chaubís, pachís, chhabbís, satáís, aṭháís, untís, tís; iktís, battís, teṉtís, chauṉtís,

	paintís, chhattís, saintís, aṭhattís, untális, chális; iktális, battális, tentális, chauntális, paintális, chhíyális, saintális, aṭhális, unchás, pachás; ikáwán, báwán, tirpan, chauwan, pachpan, chhappan, satáwán, aṭháwán, unsaṭh, sáṭh; iksaṭh, básaṭh, tresaṭh, chausaṭh, painsaṭh, chhiyásaṭh, sarsaṭh, aṭhsath, unhattar, sattar; ikhattar, bahattar, tihattar, chauhattar, pachhattar, chhihattar, sathattar, aṭhattar, unásí, assí; ikásí, beásí, tirásí, chaurásí, pachásí, chhiásí, satásí, aṭhásí, nawásí, nawwe; ikánwe, bánawe, tiránawe, chauránawe, pachánawe, chhiánawe, satánawe, aṭhánawe, ninánawe,
hundred, thousand, lac, karoṛ.	sau; sainkṛá, házár, lákh, karoṛ.

The mastery of these will be distributed over several months.

X. How much?	Kitná? Kitní?
What is the price of this?	Is ké kitné dám hai?
What is the value of this?	Is ki kitní qímat hai?

What is the market rate of this ?	Is ká kyá nirkh hai ?
How much does this sell for ?	Yih kitne meṉ biktá hai ?
Ans.—This sells for ten pice.	*Jawáb.*—Yih das paise ko biktá hai.
The price of this is eight rupees.	Is ké dám áṭh rúpae haiṉ.
The value of this is nine and a half rupees.	Is kí qímat sáṛhe nau rúpae hai.
1-100 pai, annas, pice, Rs.	1-100 pai, áne, paise ru'pae.
How much shall I give ?	Maiṉ kitné dúṉ ? (of price).
How much will you take ?	Kitné loge ? (of price ; kitná of bulk.)

The pupil should provide a number of coins and learn to give and make change.

How much did you pay for this book ?	Áp ne yih kitáb kitne ko lí ?
How much did this mare cost you ?	Yih ghoṛí kitne meṉ áí ?

XI. When ? How long ? Since when ?	Kab ? Kab ká ? Kab se ?
When did you get the book from him ?	Áp ne us se kitáb kab lí ?
When did he give you the book ?	Us ne áp ko kitáb kab dí ?
When did she say this ?	Us ne yih bát kab kahí ?
When did the gardener do this work ?	Málí ne yih kám kab kiyá ?
When did the boy stay in your house ?	Laṛká áp ke ghar meṉ kab rahá ?
When did the girl get sick ?	Laṛkí kab bímár húí ?
Water poured (filled) in	Pání bhará ? chiṭṭhí bhejí ?

vessels ? letter sent ? chair made ? thing told ? were talking ? were hunting ? did see ? did go ? had come ? did die ?	kursí ban gayí ? bát batá dí ? bol rahe the ? ḍhúnḍhte the ? dekh liyá ? gayá ? áí thí ? mar gaye ?
When did this happen ? To-day.	Yih kab kí bát hai ? Yih to áj kí bát hai.
When did this come ? Yesterday.	Yih kab ká áyá hai ? Yih kal ká áyá haí.
How long has the letter been here ? Two hours.	Chiṭṭhí yahán̲ kab se hai ? Do ghanṭe se.
Since when has the water been here ? Since morning.	Pání kab se bhará hai. Subh se.
How long has he been gone ?	Wúh kab ká gayá hai ?
He has been gone since day before yesterday.	Parson̲ ká gayá hai.

N.B.—Use Drill Table of adverbs for answers also.

XII. Whither ?	Kidhar ?
Whither are you going ?	Áp kidhar játe hain̲ ?
Whither did he go ?	Wuh kidhar gayá ?
We ? you ? she ? they ? the boy-s ? the girl-s ? the men ? the women ?	Ham ? tum ? wuh ? wuh ? laṛká, laṛke ? laṛkí ? laṛkíán̲ ? ádmí ? 'auraten̲ ?
Ans.—To the city, the school, the well, the house, home, the station, the P. O.	*Jawáb.*—Shahr, madarse, kúe ko, ghar ko, ghar, isṭeshan, ḍák-k̲h̲ána.

XIII. Whence ?	Kahán̲ se ?
Whence did you get this book ?	Áp ne yih kitáb kahán̲ se lí thí
I took it off your table.	Main̲ ne áp ke mez par se lí ?

Where did this stone come from?	Yih patthar kahán se áyá?
From where you put it.	Jahán se áp ne rakkhá.
XIV. How? In what manner?	Kyúnkar? Kis tarah? Kis tarah se?
How did this happen?	Yih kyúnkar húá?
How have you come? i.e. for what pupose?	Áp kis tarah (wajah se) áe hain?
How did he earn so many rupees?	Us ne itne rúpae kis tarah se kamáyá?
How did this dish break?	Yah bartan kis tarah se ṭúṭá?
What was he (they) saying to you?	Wuh áp ko kis tarah bolte the?
In what manner (as rudely, politely, etc.) was he speaking to you?	Wuh áp ko kis tarah se bolte the?
How will he give it to us?	Wuh ham ko kyúnkar degá?
How can you say this?	Tum yih bát kyúnkar kahte ho?
How did he send it? For nothing? tell? see? hear?	Us ne kis tarah bhejá? Muft? batá diyá? dekh liyá? sun liyá?
XV. What ... of?	Káhe kí?* kis chíz ká?
What is this made of?	Yih káhe kí baní hai?
It is made of brass.	Yih pítal kí baní hai.
What is this table made of? knife? ring? spoon? kettle? chair? jar? bullet? bottle? hukka? house?	Yih mez kis chíz kí baní hai? *Jawáb.*—Háthí-dánt, soná, chándí, lohá, támbá, lakṛí, miṭṭí, sísá, shíshá, qalaí, dhát, patthar.

* Commonly used, but not elegant.

OTHERS.	DÚSRE.
XVI. WITH ANSWER YES EXPECTED.	NA ?
You have my book, haven't you ?	Merí kitáb áp ke pás hai, na ?
Did he go yesterday ?	Kyá wuh kal gayá ?
He went yesterday, didn't he ?	Wuh kal gayá, na ?
Are you going to-day ?	Áp áj játe hain ?
You are going to-day, aren't you ?	Áp áj játe hain, na ?
Sahib orders this bread, doesn't he ?	Sáhib yihí roṭí mangáte hain, na ?
The boys will come, won't they ?	Laṛke parson áenge, na ?
Shall I go ?	Main jáún ?
Shall we do it or not ?	Ham karen ki nahín ?
We shall go, shan't we ?	Ham jáenge, na ?
She went yesterday, didn't she ?	Wuh kal chalí gayí, na ?
You sent the bread, didn't you ?	Tum ne roṭí bhejí, na ?
Can you do this work to-morrow ?	Tum kal yih kám kar sakoge ?
Can you go now ?	Abhí já sakte ho ?
Have you the girl's books ?	Laṛkí kí kitáben tumháre pás hain ?
Have you sent all the things ?	Tum ne sab chízen bhejí hain ?
Has Mr. Smith my mare ?	Merí ghoṛí Ismiṭ Sáhib ke pás hai ?
I am to go, am I not ?	Mujh ko jáná hai, na ?
He had to come, hadn't he ?	Us ko áná thá, na ?

XVII. How long? how big?	Kitná lambá? kitná baṛá?
How long is this carpet?	Yih darí kitní lambí hai?
How high is this horse?	Yih ghoṛá kitná únchá hai?
How big this coat is!	Yih koṭ kitná baṛá hai!
How long is this cloth?	Yih kapṛá kitná lambá hai?
How far is the city?	Shahr kitní dúr hai?
How excellent a city this is!	Yih kaisá umda shahr hai!
How long did you stay in the city?	Áp shahr men̲ kab tak rahe?
How long till you come back?	Áp kab tak wápas áenge?
How long did you work for him?	Áp sáhib ke pás kab tak kám karte rahe?
How often do you eat daily?	Áp roz kitní daf'a kháte hain̲?
How often in the day does the train come?	Din men̲ gáṛí kitní daf'a átí hai?
How often does the mail go in the day?	Ḍák kitní daf'a din men̲ játí hai?

XVIII. What? whether?	Kyá? áyá?
What are you doing?	Tum kyá karte ho?
What did he say to you?	Us ne tum se kyá kahá?
He asked whether you were going to-morrow or not.	Us ne púchhá áyá Sáhib kal játe hain ki nahin̲.
Of what use is this wood?	Yih lakṛí kis kám kí hai?
It is of no use. It's fit for fuel.	Yih kisí kám kí nahín̲ hai. Índhan ke láiq hai.
What was that man giving the boy?	Wuh ádmí laṛke ko kyá de rahá thá?
He was giving money, but the boy wouldn't take it.	Wuh dám (naqdí) de rahá thá? magar laṛká nahín̲ letá thá.

What did the shopkeeper send you?	Dúkándár ne áp ko kyá bhejá?
What did the gentleman give each of the coolies?	Sáhib ne qulíon ko kyá kyá diyá?
He gave them four annas each.	Unhon ne chár chár áne diye.
He asked whether this was true or a lie.	Unhon ne púchhá, áyá yih bát sach hai yá jhúṭh.
Well! what did you tell him?	Khair! Tum ne kyá batáyá?

Drill Tables.*

Nouns.—Laṛká, laṛkí, ghoṛá, ghoṛí, 'aurat, ádmí, Rájá, Rání, páon, gáon, kitáb, rát, gáe, bhains, bhainsá, bail, gadhá, gadhí, chiṛiyá, bháí, bahin, daryá, balá, hawá, dawá, pankhá, parda, kám, káǵaz, jagah, khánsámán (*sings. and pls.*), wálid, wálidain, káǵazát, waqt, auqát, hukm, ahkám, khabar, akhbár, hál, ahwál, sharíf, ashráf, ta'lím, ta'límát, suwál, suwálát, sabab, asbáb, nar, máda, mádín.

Verbs.—(*a*) Dená, lená, áná, jáná, uṭhná, baiṭhná, honá, karná, chalná, banná, banáná, dekhná, dikháná, sunná, bolná, buláná, kahná, rakhná, kharídná, mol lená, láná, milná, bhejná, dhoná, dhuláná, bachná, cháhná, nikalná, hojáná.

(*b*) Marná, márná, marwáná, ṭúṭná, toṛná, toṛáná, bulwáná, chhúṭná, chhoṛná, chhuṛáná, uṭháná, uṭhwáná, diláná, dilwáná, karná, karáná, samajhná, samjháná, rakhná, rakháná, rakhwáná, sunáná, kahláná, miláná, nikálná, nikalwáná, bacháná, bikná, bechná, bikwáná, kaṭná, káṭná, kaṭwáná, chaṛhná, chaṛháná, utarná, utárná, phirná, pherná and phiráná, likhná, likháná, leṭná, liṭáná, bharná, bharáná.

---

* These are to be used where noted in the lessons, and in connection with the following Exercises as a concrete drill in correct oral composition.

(c) Taiyár honá, karná; jama' h. k.; púrá h. k.; baṛá h. k.; khaṛá h. k.; paidá h. k.; mazbút h. k.; yaqín h. k.; shaqq h. k.; hukm h. k.; piyár karná, shukr k., ummed k., madad k., gunáh k., khidmat k: yád áná, yád dilána, yád karná, karáná.

Pronouns.—(a) Maiṉ, ham, tú, tum, áp, wuh, yih; mujh, mujhe, tujh, tujhe, ham, hameṉ, tum, tumheṉ, áp, us, use, un, unhoṉ, unheṉ.

(b) Merá-e-í, terá-e-í, tumhárá-e-í, áp ká-e-í, us ká-e-í, un ká-e-í, hamárá-e-í, in ká-e-í, apná-e-í.

(c) Kaun, kis, kaun, kin, kinhoṉ: jo, jis, jo, jin, jinheṉ, jinhoṉ.

Prepositions.—Meṉ, se, par, tak. ko, ká, ke, kí, meṉ se, par se, meṉ ká, ke líe, ke wáste, ke pás, ke áge, ke sámne, ke píchhe, ke níche, ke andar, ke báhar, ke bích, ke sáth, ke ba'd, ke pahle, ke úpar, ke siwá, ke barábar, ke bá'is, ke sabab, ke láiq, ke ird gird, ke ás pás, ke badle, ke wasíle (se), ke pár; kí babat, kí khátir, kí taraf, kí taraf se, kí cháron taraf, kí tarah, kí ma'rifat, kí mánind, kí nisbat, kí jagah.

Adverbs.—Áj, kal, parsoṉ, atarsoṉ, narsoṉ, pár sál, ab, abhí, ab kí daf'a; jaise, jaháṉ, kahíṉ, jaháṉ kahíṉ, jab, kabhí, jab kabhí, kabhí kabhí, kabhí nahíṉ, nahíṉ, háṉ, na, mat; yaháṉ, waháṉ, idhar, udhar, jidhar, yúṉ, is tarah, usí tarah, bár bár, hamesha, bahut, to, bhí, sawere, baṛá, masalan, faqat, qaríban, hargiz nahíṉ, zor se, ek dam se, wápas, júṉ, jaldí, jhaṭ paṭ, sháyad, phir.

Adjectives.—Achchhá, burá, ṭhanḍá, garm, bhárí, halká, nazdík, dúr, sakht, ásán, mushkil, narm, chauṛá, tang, sáf, mailá, taiyár, bas, únchá, níchá, sachchá, jhúṭhá, khará, khoṭá, nayá, púráná, búṛhá, ġaríb, daulatmand, baṛá, chhoṭá, lambá, 'ámm, sab, ních, ġol, chauras, moṭá, patlá zarúr, band, khulá, desí, waláyatí, ádhá, aur, pahlá, dúsrá, thoṛá, mihrbán, bahut, aglá, ziyáda, kam, píchhlá, mumkin, shukarguzár.

Interrogatives and Indefinites, and Others.—Yih, wuh, aur, aisá, waisá, dono, ġair, ba'z (ba'ze), kaí, kuchh, kull, chand, báqí, aksar.

Kab? Kidhar? Kaun? Kyúṉ? Kyúṉkar? Kis tarah? Kaisá? Kaunsá? Kyá?

Jo, jo koí, koí, jo jo, jo kuchh, fuláná, ek dúsrá, sab kuchh, jitná, aur kuchh, har, har ek, har koí, sab koí, áp, k͟hud, koí koí, koí na koí.

Numerals.—Ek, do, tín, chár, pánch, chha, sát, áṭh nau, das, bís, pachís, tís, chálís, pachás, sau, sainkṛá, hazár, lákh, karoṛ, koṛí, sadí.

Awwal, pahlá, dúsrá, tísrá, chauthá, pánchwáṉ, chhaṭá, sátwáṉ, áṭhwáṉ, nauwáṉ, daswáṉ, bíswáṉ, pacháswáṉ.

Conjunctions.—Aur, ki, táki, lekin, par, balki, to, magar, pas, phir, phir bhí, jis tarah... us tarah, k͟hwáh... k͟hwáh, na... na, cháhe... cháhe, yá... yá, táham, tau bhí, tab bhí, jab tak, jab tak... na, is líe, is líe ki, kyúṉki, chúṉki, aisá na ho ki, warna, nahíṉ to, háláṉki, agarchi, go, go ki, goyá, liháza, tis par bhí.

Exercises in Declensions.

I. Man, boy, horse, dog, jar, house, water, city, answer, time, word, people, fruit, spring, curtain, month, day, day, field, Rajah, uncle, cook.	I. Ádmí, laṛká, ghoṛá, kuttá, ghaṛá, ghar, pání, shahr, jawáb, waqt, kalám, log, phal, chashma, parda, mahína, roz, din, khet, Rájá, cháchá, mámú, k͟hánsámáṉ.
II. Woman, girl, mare, dog, watch, daughter, will, wages, book, eye, spirit,	II. 'Aurat, laṛkí, ghoṛí, kuttá, kuttí, jebí ghaṛí, beṭí, marzí, mazdúrí,

proverb, place, gift, thing, request, labour, bread, medicine, wind or air, cow, way, smell, post, white-ant, hurt.	kitáb, áṉkh, rúh, masal, jagah, baḵẖshish, chíz, bát, darḵẖwást, mihnat, roṭí, dawá, hawá, gáe, ráh, bú, ḍák, dímak, choṭ.

Nouns of class I, i.e. masculines, in *-á* except titles, change, with a preposition, to *e* in sing. and to *oṉ* in pl.; and *á* becomes *e* in pl.

Other nouns of class I undergo no change, only in the plural with a prep., they add *oṉ* and in the vocative *o*, *ádmíoṉ ko*, *ádmío*.

Feminine nouns suffer no change in sing. In plural they add to nouns in í *-áṉ* for absolute, and *-oṉ* for prepositional form, and *o* for vocative.

There are no absolute rules for gender, but generally nouns *-á*, *-a*, are masculine, and nouns in *-í*, *-isht*, *-t* are feminine. Great care should be taken in learning each noun to train the ear, so that masc. adj. forms be associated with masc. nouns, and fem. with fem.

1. These (I* or II) are mine, his, yours.	1. Yih (I yá II) mere, -í, haiṉ, uske, tumáre.
2. This (I or II) is good, better, best.	2. Yih achchhá hai; us se, sab se, achchhá.
3. Give this (I, II) a book (Rs.).	3. Is (I, II) ko kitáb ( ) do.
4. Put these (I, II) in the room.	4. In (I, II) ko kamre meṉ rakkho.
5. In this (I, II) is great excellence.	5. Is (I, II) meṉ baṛí ḵẖúbí hai.
6. In these (I, II) are great excellencies.	6. In (I, II) meṉ baṛí ḵẖúbíáṉ haiṉ.

* Substitute the above nouns.

7. From these (I, II) learn wisdom.

7. In (I, II) se dánáí síkho.

8. From this (I, II) learn wisdom.

8. Is (I, II) se dánáí síkho.

Exercises in Adjectives.

These (I, II) are (good, better, best) III. 1. *Yih* (I, II) (III) *hain.*

III. (*a*) Declinable. Achchhá, burá, púrá, sachchá, baṛá.

(*b*) Indecl. járí, barí, k͟húb, báqí, ṭhík, umda, bhárí.

This (I, II) is (III).

Exercises in Possessives.

1. This (I, II) is yours, his, hers, mine, ours, yours, thine, theirs, the boy's, the girl's, the boys', the girls', the man's, the men's, the woman's, the women's.

1. Yih (I, II) tumhárá hai, uská, uske, merí, hamárá, áp ke, teri, unká, laṛke ke, laṛkí kí, laṛkon̲ ká, laṛkíon̲ ke, ádmí ká, ádmíon̲ kí, 'aurat ke, 'auraton̲ ká.

2. These (I, II) are yours, his, hers, etc.

2. Yih (I, II), tumháre hain̲, us ké, us ke, wag̀aira.

Verb Synopses.

I, m., we, m., I, f., we, f., you, f., you, m., thou, he, you, p. she, they, m., they, fem., The boy-s, girl-s, man, men, woman, women,

1. $\frac{\text{send}}{\text{bring}}$ them a $\frac{\text{chair}}{\text{table}}$ daily (*-tá hún̲*)

2. am $\frac{\text{sending}}{\text{bringing}}$ $\frac{\text{chairs}}{\text{tables}}$ now (*-rahá hún̲*).

3. was $\frac{\text{sending}}{\text{bringing}}$ them a pen yesterday (*-tá thá*).

4. was $\frac{\text{sending}}{\text{bringing}}$ them the books at that time (*-rahá thá*).

20 subjects, 10 predicates,
Other verbs for substitution,
dená,
pahuncháná,
mol lená,
banáná,
rakhná,
rakháná,
nikálná,
bechná,
bikwáná,

5. shall $\frac{\text{send}}{\text{bring}}$ the women a letter to-morrow (*-úngá*).
6. $\frac{\text{sent}}{\text{brought}}$ him the bread and butter day before yesterday (*bhejá*, *láyá*).
7. did not $\frac{\text{send}}{\text{bring}}$ them the bread (*na bhejí*).
8. have not $\frac{\text{sent}}{\text{brought}}$ them the loaves (*nahín̲ bhejín̲*).
9. have $\frac{\text{sent}}{\text{brought}}$ them the meat, milk, bread, potatoes, vegetables, rice, dal, sugar (*bheja -í -e*).
10. had sent them the (   ) before I came (*-á thá*).

Send the money at once (-o*).
Bring them the tables soon.

Sending is better (*-na bihtar hai*).
Bringing is better than sending (*-ná, -ne se bihtar hai*).

Having $\frac{\text{sent}}{\text{brought}}$ $\frac{\text{come}}{\text{go}}$ (*-kar á jáo*).

This is the sender (*-wálá*).

Come as soon as you send (*-te hí á jáo*).

Is this the $\frac{\text{sent}}{\text{brought}}$ book-s (*-í húi*).

---

* One verb in ten forms with 20 subjects in each form, can be gone through in ten minutes. But keep one finger on the subject, the other on the predicate.

I saw him $\frac{\text{sending}}{\text{bringing}}$ two tables to you.

I saw him seated.

I gave him the money to (that he) bring (*táki wuh láe*).

I went to buy bread (*k͟harídne gayá*).

I went to send loaves (*bhejne ko gayá*).

*Special Idiomatic Verb Forms.**

Subjects.		*Past.*	*Past Perf.*	*Present.*	*Future (Rare).*
All nouns		lagá	lagá hai	lagtá hai	lagegá,
All prons.		lagí	lagí hai	lagtí hai	lagegí,
	karne	lage	lage hain̲	lagte hain̲	lagen̲ge,
		lagín̲	lagí hain̲	lagtí hain̲	lagen̲gí,

began to do, etc.

Chukná, to finish doing something.

		Past.	*Past Perf.*	*Present.*	*Future.*
All nouns		chuká	chuká hai	chuktá hai	chukegá,
All prons.	ho	chukí	chukí hai	chuktí hai	chukegí,
	kar	chuke	chuke hain̲	chukte hain̲	chuken̲ge,
	khá	chukín̲	chukí hain̲	chuktí hain̲	chuken̲gín̲.

Sakná, to be able to do, give, etc.

		Present.	*Past.*	*Future.*
All nouns		saktá hai	saká	sakegá,
All prons.	de, kar,	saktí hai	sakí	sakegí,
		sakte hain̲	sake	saken̲ge,
		saktí hain̲	sakí	saken̲gí.

Cháhná with inf., to wish to do, give, etc.

		Present.	*Past.*
All nouns	áná, dená, karná,	cháhtá hai	cháhá.
All prons.		cháhtí hai	
		cháhte hain̲	
		cháhtí hain̲	

* *N.B.*—Use the verbs of Drill Table with these exercises.

Dená with inflected inf., to permit to do, go, come.

	Past.	Present.	Past Progress.	Future.
All nouns	Us ne hám	He does not	detá thá,	degá,
All prons.	ko áne na	let us go		degí,
	diyá,	(*áne nahín detá*),		denge,
				dengín.

Cf. end of Lesson LV.

Inflected Inf. with *píná*, to get (as permission, opportunity), to do something.

		Present.	Future.
All nouns	Wuh áne	pátá hai	páegá,
All prons.		pátí hai	páegí,
		páte hain	páenge,
		pátí hain	páengí.

Old inf. with *karná*, to be accustomed to do something. *Wuh yihí kám kiyá kartá hai.*

Exercises in Prepositions.

1. It was (I) the little/big table-s chair-s, carpets, tree-s, house-s, room-s, wall-s.	1. Wuh chhotí/barí mez, -on (I) thí/thín
I. In, on, over, under, beside, in the middle of, near, before, outside.	I. men, par, ke úpar, ke pás, ke bích, ke nazdík, ke sámne, ke báhar.

2. I		to	room.
We	went	into	well.
You		toward	market.
He		(II) up to the	city.
They	came	from	shop.
She		near	house.

They			garden-s.
You			tree-s.
2. Main	gayá, gayí	kamre	ko.
Ham	gaye, gayí	kúe	men.
Tum		bázár	kí taraf.
Wuh	gayá	shahr	tak.
Wuh	gaye	dúkán	se.
Wuh	gayí	ghar	ke pás.
Wuh	gayí	báġ, -on	
Áp	gaye, gayín	darakht, -on	

3. I (We, You, He, They, She, They, You) went, (came) to (into, toward, up to, from, near), the room (well, market, city, shop, house, garden, gardens, tree, trees).

3. Main (Ham, Tum, Wuh, Wuh, Wuh, Wuh, Áp) gayá (gaye, gayí) kamre ko (men, kí taraf, tak, se, ke pás) kúé, bázár, shahr, dúkán, ghar, báġ, baġíche, darakht.

II. to, into, toward, up, to, from, near.

II. ko, men, kí taraf, tak, se, ke pás.

4. He put (took) the things in the house, from the house.

4. Us ne sab chízen koṭhí men rakkhín, koṭhí men se, liyá, lí, lín. ḍálá, ḍálí ḍálín.

Things:—meal, flour, cloth, vegetables, meat, water, milk, money, hat, shoes, loaves, tables, chairs, pens, watches, books.

Chízen:—áṭá, maidá, kapṛá sabzí, gosht, pání, dudh, rúpae, ṭopí, júṭián, roṭíán, mez, kursíán, qalam, ghaṛíán, kitáben.

5. Do this work (Eat this bread) for me. With, after, before, for sake

5. Yih kám mere líe karo. Yih roṭí mere wáste kháo. Sáth, ba'd,

of, like; by means of; like, in place of—me, us, him, the boys, the girls, the man, the boy, the girl, the women.	pahle, kí kẖátir, ki mánind; kí ma'rifat, ke wasíle; kí tarah, ke badle-mere, hamáre, us ke, kí, laṛkon̲ ke, kí, laṛkion̲ ke, kí, ádmí ke, kí, laṛke ke, kí, laṛkí ke, kí, 'aurat ke, kí.
6. Take this (*) to Mr. Smith and give it to him.	6. Yih (*) Ismit Sáhib ke pás le jákar un ko de áo.
Go to Mr. Smith and get that ( ) and bring it to me.	Ismiṭ Sáhib se wuh ( ) mángke, mere pás lete áo, le áo.

Exercises in Relatives.

Whatever a man sows that he will reap.	Jo kuchh ádmí botá hai, so hí káṭegá.
Reap as much as you sow.	Jitná bo utná káṭ lo.
As you measure, so will it be measured for you.	Jis tarah nápte ho, usí tarah tumháre lie nápá jáegá.
As you sow, so you reap.	Jaisá bote waisá káṭoge.
Just as you give, you take.	Jis tarah do, usí tarah lo.
Just when you wish, bring it.	Jab hí cháho tab hí láo.
Whichever way you turn him, thither he goes.	Jidhar moṛo, udhar játá hai.
As soon as you request it, it is present.	Jis waqt mán̲go, maujúd hai.
1. This was the (man, woman, women, men,	1. Yih wuh (ádmí) thá jis ne kal ham se báten̲

* Substitute list of nouns.

boy-s, girl-s), who spoke to us yesterday, —who speaks to us every day.	kín, ('aurat-en, ádmí, laṛká, -e, laṛkí, -án), —jo roz roz ham se báten kartá (e, í) hai (hain).
2. This is the ( ) that was in the shop day before yesterday; —that we bought(saw) yesterday, (book-s, table-s, pen-s, hat-s, man, men, woman, women, boy-s, girl-s).	2. Yih wuhí (kitáb-en, mez, qalam, ṭopí-án, ádmí, 'auraten, laṛká -e, laṛkí, -án), hai (n) jo parson dúkán men thá (the, thí, thín); jise (jisko, jinhen, jin ko) ham ne kal kharíd liyá (or jo... liye, lí, lín; dekhá, -e, -í, -in).

The pupil should work at these until he can readily give these under 1, sixteen sentences in a minute, and those under 2, thirty-two sentences, in two and a half minutes. If he can do this, he will have a fair command of the relatives.

Exercises in Conjunctions.

Purpose—ki and *táki*, with Subj.	*Iráda.*
He came that he might buy food.	Wuh áyá táki kháná mol le.
She came that she might draw water.	Wuh áí ki pání bhare.
I went that I might do this for you.	Main áyá táki main áp ke lie yih karún.
We will come to do this work quickly.	Ham áenge táki ham yih kám jald karen.

You have come to talk to me.	Tum áe ho táki mujh se báteṉ karo.
Come to-morrow to write a letter for me.	Áp kal áiye ki mere líe chiṭṭhí likheṉ.

Of purpose is more frequently indicated by the inflected infinitive, *Wuh khána mol lene* ( ) *áyá, wuh páni bharne* (*ko*) *áí*, with or without *ko*.

Concessive and adversative—go, agarchi, halanki with Subj. or Ind.

Though it is not from Moses, but has come from the fathers.	Háláṉki wuh Músá kí taraf se nahiṉ, balki bápdádoṉ se chalá áyá hai.
Though Jesus himself did not give baptism, but his disciples did.	Go Yisu' áp nahíṉ, balki uske shágird baptisma dete the.
Although I bear witness of myself, still my witness is true.	Agarchi maiṉ apní gawáhí áp detá huṉ, tau bhí merí gawáhi sachchí hai.

Adversative—magar, lekin, par; balki; táham, tau bhi, tab bhí.

You will seek me but you will not find me.	Mujhe ḍhúṇḍhoge, magar na páoge.
You have not known him, but I know him.	Tum ne use nahíṉ jáná, lekin maiṉ usko jántá húṉ.
He said it indeed, but I didn't believe it.	Us ne to kahá thá, par mujhe yaqín na áyá.

There seems to be no difference between *magar* and *lekin*, and *par*, in meaning, though *par* is less used in Urdu; *balki* is not so strongly adversative, rather it adds something additional, which may be along the same line, and only in part adversative. Observation and use will give the ability to differentiate. *Tá ham, tab bhí* and *tau bhí* are synonomous.

Alternatives—yá, yá . . . yá, k̲h̲wáh . . k̲h̲wáh, cháho . . . cháho, cháhe . . . cháhe, ki; nahíṉ to, warna.

Shall I come or go?	Maiṉ áúṉ yá jáúṉ?
Shall he go or stay?	Wuh áe ki jáe?
Is this correct or not?	Yih ṭhík hai, ki nahíṉ?
Whether the boy come or go, what's that to me?	K̲h̲wáh laṛká áe k̲h̲wáh jáe, mujhe kyá?
Whether I am to go or stay, I am satisfied.	Cháhe jáná ho, cháhe rahná ho, mujhe manzúr hai.
Is this right or a mistake?	Yih ṭhík hai yá ġalat hai?
You ought to go at once, otherwise there will be great loss.	Abhí jáná cháhiye, nahíṉ to baṛá nuqsán hogá.
You must go, else the boy will die.	Áp zarúr jáeṉ, warna laṛká mar jáegá.

Exceptive—jab tak . . . na, jab tak.

No one can do this work, unless God be with him.	Koí ádmí yih kám nahíṉ kar saktá, jab tak K̲h̲udá us ke sáth na ho.
While the master wishes, wait.	Jab tak málik cháheṉ tum baiṭhe raho.

Conclusive—ís líe, phir, so, pas, chunáṉchi.

These are used as introductory to a sentence or paragraph, summing up the conclusion from what has preceded.

Negative Purpose—aisá na ho ki, that it may not be that, i.e. lest.

aisá na ho ki laṛká mar jáe, aisá na ho ki ghoṛá ḍare, aisá na ho ki wuh ham ko máre.

Conditional—agar, jo, jab, if. See Lesson LXXIV.

Causal—ki, jo, is líe ki, is wáste ki, chúṉki, kyúṉki, of which the exercises have many examples.

So if the Son shall make you free, you shall be free.	Pas, agar Beṭá tum ko ázád karegá to ázád hoge.
Since you are not of the world, the world hates you.	Chúṉki tum dunyá ke nahíṉ, dunyá tum se 'adáwat rakhtí hai.

As.... As.

How long will you stay?	Áp kitní der raheṉge?
As long as you do, or, However long you stay, that long I will stay.	Jitní der áp raheṉge, or. Jitní der áp raheṉge utní der maiṉ rahúṉgá.
I will give as much as you do.	Áp ke muwáfiq duṉgá, or, jitná áp deṉge, utná maiṉ dúṉgá.
How much will you give?	Áp kitná deṉge?

INDEX.

Page

Ability (*sakná*) 49
Address, Correct terms of 91, 94
Adjective—
  Drill tables of **21, 22**
  Exercises in **24**
Adverbs—
  Drill tables of **21**
  List of common .. .. lii–liii
Aorist, Exercises in 132–134
Articulation .. .. xxiv–xxxiv
Aspirates .. .. xxii–xxv, xxxiii
Attainment, Testing .. .. .. xiii, xiv, xvii
Causal, Exercises in 126–128
Chalná and *jáná*, Exercises in 117–119
Charts, Pronunciation .. .. .. xlii–xlvi
Clicks xxxviii
Conditional Sentences 111–117
Conjugation 91, 94, 97, 123, 124
Conjunctions—
  Drill tables of **22**
  Exercises in 153–155, **30–33**
    Adversative **31**
    Alternative **32**
    Causal **32**
    Concessive **31**
    Conclusive **32**
    Conditional **32**
    Exceptive **32**
    Negative purpose **32**
Consonants .. .. .. xxiv xxxv, xxxviii–xl
Continuance 103, 104, 145, 146
Conversation xii
Customary action 47, 48
Declension **1–3**
  Exercises in **22–24**
Difficulties and dangers .. .. xiii, xviii–xx, xxxvii
Directions .. .. .. liv, 1–5, 6, 8, 45, 46
Ear—
  Medium of Language Study .. .. .. xi–xiii
  Training of xxxvii

	Page
Gender	1
Exercises in	**23, 24**
Rules for	**1, 2, 23**
Gestures	xxxviii
Grammatical questions	liv, lv
,, Drill	lvii
Homoinymic Sentences	xlvii–lii
Idiomatic Verb Forms	**26, 27**
Imperatives, List of common	lii–liii
Infinitive, Uses of	104–108
Interrogatives—	
Drill tables of	**22**
Exercises in	**5–20**
Particles	**19**
Pronouns	**4**
Intonation	xxxvii
Jáná, Exercises in	117–119
Lagná, Exercises in	120–123
Language, How to learn	xi–xx; Résumé of, lv, lvi
Laws of, study	xvi–xviii
Material	xi
Method	xi
Letters	
Consonants	xxiv, xxv, xxviii–xli; Table of, xxxiii
Doubled	xxxv xlviii–lii
Names of, positional and by formation	xxii
Nasak	xxii, xxxi–xxxiv
Pronunciation of	xxi–xxxiv
Vowels	xxi–xxiv, xl
Medium of Instruction	xi, xv, xvi
Memorizing	xii, xiv, lv
Memory	xii, xiii, xiv, xv, xvi; Training of, xvii, xviii
Nasals	xxii, xxxi, xxxii
Ne, Exercises in	97–100
Noun—	
Declension of	**1, 2**
Drill tables of	**20**
Numbers—	
Cardinal	**13, 14**
Ordinals	**26**
Fractional	**12, 13**
Numerals, Drill tables of	**22**
Order of words in a sentence	lii, **4**
Participle, Exercises in	135–140
Passive Voice—	
Conjugation of	128–130
Exercises in	124–128

	Page
Permissives, Exercises in	142, 143
Phonetics	xx–xxxiv
Cuts	xxii, xxvi–xxxiv
Possessives	**24**
Potentials, Exercises in	144, 145
Prepositions or postpositions	**3, 4**
Drill tables of	**21**
Exercises in	146–152, **27–29**
Pronoun, Demonstrative	**4,** 5
Drill tables of	**21**
Interrogative	**4-5**
Possessive	**3**; Exercises in **24**
Relative	130-132
Pronounciation	xx–xxxiv
Charts	xlii-xlvi
Exercises in	xlvii-lii, lvi
Guide to	xxii, xxiv
Rahná, Exercises in	103, 104, 145, 146
Reading	xi, xli, lvi, lvii
Relatives, Exercises in	**29, 30**
Repeated words	108–111
Repetition	xii, xvi–xviii, xx, lv
Rhythm	xvi, xxxvi
Romanisation	xxxviii–xli
Sá, Exercises in	155, 156
Sentence—	
Conditional	111–117
Order of words in	xv
The unit	xvi
Speech, Standard of	xv
Study, Method of	xi–lvii
Résumé of	lv, lvi
Syllables, Division of	xxxv
Time-table	lvii
Verb—	
Conjugation of	91, 94, 123, 124
Passive	128–130
Customary action	47, 48
Drill tables of	**20, 21**
Formation of	**3**
List of common	lii–liii
Moods of—	
Indicative	**3**
Subjunctive	132, **3**
Synopses of, Exercises in	**24–26**
Special idiomatic forms of	**26, 27**

	Page
Tenses—	
Active Past, Exercises in	22–23
Intransitive Past, Exercises in	25
With *ne*	97–100
Vowels	xxi–xxiv, xl
Defined	xxi
Level	xxi, xxiv
Wálá, Exercises in	140
Writing	lvii

Printed at the Baptist Mission Press, Calcutta.